T0248041

AYN RAND

Ayn Rand

Writing a Gospel of Success

ALEXANDRA POPOFF

Yale
UNIVERSITY
PRESS

New Haven and London

Yale University Press books may be purchased in quantity for educational, business, or promotional use. For information, please e-mail sales.press@yale.edu (U.S. office) or sales@yaleup.co.uk (U.K. office).

Set in Janson Oldstyle type by Integrated Publishing Solutions.
Printed in the United States of America.

Library of Congress Control Number: 2023952239
ISBN 978-0-300-25321-4 (hardcover : alk. paper)

A catalogue record for this book is available from the British Library.

This paper meets the requirements of ANSI/NISO Z39.48-1992 (Permanence of Paper).

10 9 8 7 6 5 4 3 2 1

Frontispiece: Ayn Rand in Chatsworth, California, working on *Atlas Shrugged.* Photo by Julius Shulman, 1947. © J. Paul Getty Trust, Getty Research Institute, Los Angeles (2004.R.10).

ALSO BY ALEXANDRA POPOFF

Vasily Grossman and the Soviet Century

Tolstoy's False Disciple: The Untold Story of Leo Tolstoy and Vladimir Chertkov

The Wives: The Women Behind Russia's Literary Giants

Sophia Tolstoy: A Biography

All lives are metaphors.
All lives resolve themselves into themes.
—Neal Gabler, *An Empire of Their Own*

CONTENTS

PREFACE

In 1926 Alisa Rosenbaum (the future Ayn Rand) ventured to Hollywood from Soviet Russia hoping to find work as a scriptwriter with the famous director-producer Cecil DeMille. At twenty-one she had enormous expectations from America. Many immigrants do when heading to a land of opportunity, but not all succeed in realizing their talents and dreams.

Rand did not become "the greatest star in Hollywood," as she had dreamed, but her career was launched in the City of Movies. Hollywood was by then an industrial city in which eastern European Jews were foundational, boasting a dozen studios and employing thousands. Rand's first article in America evidences her delight in the implacable competition among the studios and her fascination with Hollywood's power over millions of viewers worldwide. In time she would work for Universal, Metro-Goldwyn-Mayer, and Paramount Pictures, and

Warner Bros. would produce a film based on her best-selling novel *The Fountainhead.*

It was in Hollywood that she learned to build the fast-moving plots her readers would love. When later she turned to politics, she shaped her message with skills acquired in filmmaking, exaggeration being one. To succeed in America during the interwar years, when anti-Semitism was rampant, many Jewish immigrants sought to bury their differences. Rand did not openly identify with Jewish issues, but when she spoke on behalf of American capitalists, defending ability, profit, and wealth, she was also fighting Jewish stereotypes. Her characters received gentile names but remain perceptibly Jewish in their otherness, defiance, and morality.

Unlike the majority of Jews who supported left-wing causes, such as socialism, Rand defended American capitalism, prosperity, creativity, self-interest, and power (on which Hollywood stood); her literary heroes were combative and talented high achievers. The Hollywood moguls were anticommunist and conservative, but Rand would become more radical and defiant: her alliances were with the extreme right.

Having witnessed the onset of totalitarianism under Lenin and Stalin, she made it her mission to fight communism. While Marx had declared war on capitalism and prophesied the triumph of the proletariat, Rand, whose family was dispossessed by the Bolsheviks, glorified the industrialist and held the masses in contempt. In *Atlas Shrugged,* her most controversial novel, she promoted laissez-faire capitalism and the morality of rational self-interest. She augured apocalypse in America if it followed the socialist path. Rand promoted her causes with single-minded persistence and messianic fervor and spoke to the world through the defiant genius of Howard Roark and John Galt, her alter egos. Her need for full acceptance, the forceful promotion of her message, and an unrealistic expectation that it would transform the world explain her disappointment and bitterness in later years—despite her celebrity status.

A gifted outsider with an immense drive to succeed, Rand aspired to break into the majority culture and to influence it. An atheist, she saw the Bible not as a holy writ but as a literary text, and she felt free to revise and dispute it. Rand preached individualism and "the virtue of selfishness" and fought against the precepts of altruism and collectivism—ideals exploited by communists. Her attempt to overturn established values made her the most criticized American writer of her day. As Arthur Hertzberg and Aron Hirt-Manheimer point out, "Society resents anyone who challenges its fundamental beliefs, behavior, and prejudices."[1] Though Rand's books have entered American popular culture, they remain outside the literary and scholarly canons.

Prominent and divisive, Rand has long been admired and attacked for her radical views. But regardless of how we assess her heritage, her books have enjoyed success and longevity. Her novels and nonfiction have sold 36 million copies, influencing three generations of Americans—a considerable achievement for a Russian Jewish immigrant who had arrived in America with little English.

I was commissioned to write this biography—not in the least—because of my ethnic background as a Russian secular Jew and immigrant to North America. Through my work on this book I discovered a writer who is deliberately provocative and contentious, compelling her reader to take sides. I refused to fall into the trap. As her biographer, I saw my task as tracing influences on Rand's work and presenting her ideas without preconception. While it was previously assumed that she did not pursue Jewish themes, this book will argue otherwise by revealing connections between Rand's formative years in a traditional Jewish milieu and the stories she told in her books. I believe that writers cannot hide themselves in a literary text, even when they later go back to revise it, as Rand had done. She had claimed that being Jewish did not matter to her, but her Jewishness was about the text, crammed full of ideas, parables, paradoxes, questions, and arguments. Her fictional stories are moral and legal at the same time.

I researched her papers at the Ayn Rand Archive, plowing through her calendars, lectures, correspondence, and the vast collection of the Rosenbaum family letters. The new material and special focus of my book make it different from previous biographies, including the ones I admire, *Goddess of the Market* by Jennifer Burns and *Ayn Rand and the World She Made* by Anne Heller.

AYN RAND

1

Born Jewish

Ayn Rand had remarked that she was *born* Jewish. Upon immigrating to America, she lived her life as an atheist, using an alias that revealed neither her ethnicity nor her sex. It mystified readers, provoking the recurrent question, *Who Is Ayn Rand?* When asked about her family and beginnings, Rand replied that her life was a postscript to her novels and she should be asked about her ideas. Even her father's name had to remain a mystery: on a City of Los Angeles document Rand entered his first name as "Fronz." From there it traveled to Rand's first biography, produced by Barbara Branden (née Weidman), her friend and associate.

Rand was born Alisa Rosenbaum on February 2, 1905, in Saint Petersburg, Russia.[1] Her birth was registered by the chief rabbi, Abraham Drabkin, in the Grand Choral Synagogue, where, a year earlier, her parents were married. Alisa's father, Zelman-Wolf Zorahovich Rosenbaum, was a pharmacist; her mother,

Khana Berkovna, was a dentist. The fact that Alisa's middle-class professional family lived in Russia's imperial capital was a mark of success. Saint Petersburg was a Western metropolis, the center of Russia's economic and cultural life, and its most modern and cosmopolitan city. It was the city of aristocracy and the address of privileged Jews who in the mid-nineteenth century received permission to settle there: wealthy merchants, bankers, members of the professional and cultural elite, and skilled artisans.

Jews had been forbidden by law to reside in Russia's interior. The few Jews who were able to enter the capital in the early eighteenth century were Christian converts. Individual practicing Jews whose services were essential to the state were also brought to the capital. In 1725–27 Levi Lipman, a Jewish commercial agent from Courland (modern Latvia), served as a financial representative at the Russian court.[2] Toward the end of the eighteenth century, during the Partitions of Poland, Russia acquired a large Jewish community. In 1791 Catherine the Great introduced new restrictions, permitting Jewish residence and trade only in the annexed western regions. The area of permanent Jewish residence became known as the Pale of Settlement. Its territory was expanded in 1804 to include southern Ukraine and Crimea, the latter captured from the Ottoman Empire.

In the 1850s, after the Crimean War, the liberal Tsar Alexander II introduced a policy of selective integration allowing merchants of the First Guild to settle outside the Pale. In November 1861 this policy was extended by a landmark decree that lifted restrictions on place of residence and choice of professions for Jewish university graduates.[3] This allowed secular, educated Jewish professionals and other "useful citizens" to move into the country's interior. Jewish intellectual elites and some of the wealthiest bankers and merchants settled in the imperial capital, which offered sprawling markets and professional opportunities. By 1881, at the end of Alexander II's reign, the Jewish population in Saint Petersburg had risen to almost 17,000, making it the largest Jewish Diaspora in Russia's interior. This number had doubled by 1910, when Rand was five.

The Judicial Reform, introduced by Alexander II in 1864, created an autonomous corps of attorneys and judges. It made no distinction on the basis of nationality and religious faith, thus permitting Jewish students to receive training in law. They lost no time: between 1885 and 1890, 22 percent of those admitted to the bar and 89 percent of apprentice lawyers in the empire were Jews. (Rand's paternal grandfather had benefited from this reform.) In Saint Petersburg's influential Bar Association, Jews represented 21 percent of all lawyers and 30 percent of apprentice lawyers. But in November 1889 a decree issued under Alexander III curtailed admissions to the bar for non-Christian apprentice lawyers.

In 1869, during Alexander II's reign, Saint Petersburg's Jewish merchants had acquired permission to build the Choral Synagogue. Because the government demanded amendments to the design and disputed the site, construction was postponed by two decades. In 1893, when the Choral Synagogue was dedicated, the total cost came to half a million gold rubles. The amount was largely covered by Baron Horace Gintsburg, a prominent banker, philanthropist, and scion of a prominent family. The Gintsburgs and other wealthy families supported aspects of Jewish communal life and learning. The Society for the Spread of Enlightenment, founded in 1863, provided stipends to Jewish university students, making it possible for thousands to benefit from selective integration. (In 1887 the policy of selective integration was replaced with discriminatory anti-Jewish quotas on education, and this affected Rand's immediate family.)

Baron Horace Gintsburg became president of the Saint Petersburg Jewish community, which at the end of the nineteenth century included publishers, lawyers, bankers, industrialists, doctors, engineers, and other business and intellectual elites. By the

1880s the empire's capital became the cultural center of Russian Jewry. Saint Petersburg's intellectuals produced over a dozen periodicals in Hebrew, Russian, and Yiddish for readers across the Pale.

Saint Petersburg's Jews were a small but influential minority. In 1910 they represented only 3 percent of the city's entire population, but their share in banking, law, and journalism was a disproportionate one-third. Having mastered Russian and European languages in the spirit of Haskalah (Jewish enlightenment), they were also more acculturated. As the historian Benjamin Nathans points out, "Petersburg Jewry gave rise in Russia to a new image of the Jew as modern, cosmopolitan, and strikingly successful in urban professions (such as law, banking, and journalism)."[4] And precisely because of their rapid success, the government sustained legal restrictions. Russian Jews received political rights only in 1905 and full legal emancipation in 1917, nearly five decades after German and Austrian Jews. Until then, even the wealthiest among them could be threatened with expulsion from the capital. Such was the world of the future novelist—the realm of talented professionals and intellectual elites, and of the menacing government bureaucracy, which impeded their advance. Both irreconcilable worlds would enter her novels.

Alisa was growing up in the city where Jewish achievement in many spheres—from business to cultural life—was conspicuous. The Saint Petersburg Music Conservatory, Russia's first, was founded by the composer and pianist Anton Rubinstein. The famous Brockhaus and Yefron publishing house had produced the first comprehensive Russian Encyclopedic Dictionary. Ilya Yefron, son of a Jewish merchant from Vilna (now Vilnius), also issued the multivolume Russian Jewish Encyclopedia in 1913, an important event in the lives of Russian Jewry.

Alisa's maternal grandfather, Berko Itskovich Kaplan, was a skillful military tailor and merchant. Originally from the city of

Lida, west of Minsk, he came to Saint Petersburg in 1873 during Alexander II's reign. His wife, Sarah, was a pharmacist and a woman of great intelligence, as her family remembered her. She was her husband's bookkeeper and astute adviser, and, according to family lore, Kaplan did not make decisions without consulting her. Military uniforms were in high demand in Saint Petersburg, where elite troops held regular reviews and parades. The regiments of the Imperial Guard were quartered in and around the capital, so Kaplan, upon establishing his reputation, enjoyed a steady clientele of officers from Russia's richest families. He owned a military uniform store on Bol'shaya Pod'yacheskaya, in one of the city's Jewish neighborhoods. As his wealth increased, he bought an apartment on the central avenue, Nevsky Prospect. In 1907, after three decades in the capital, he finally received official permission to reside permanently in Saint Petersburg, regardless of whether he maintained his trade. The Kaplans' comfortable apartment at Nevsky Prospect, 74, was later passed on to their son Mikhail and remained in the family despite expropriations that followed the Bolshevik Revolution.[5]

The Kaplans had seven children. Several of their sons received a university education: Mikhail and Volodya had law degrees; Yakov became an otolaryngologist. Arkady chose an acting career; his stage name was Arkady Nadezhdov. Two of the daughters obtained professional training: the eldest, Dobrulia, was a pharmacist; Khana became a dentist, and Liza married a gynecologist. Alisa's mother, Khana Berkovna, was born in Saint Petersburg in 1880 and attended Liteinaya, a Russian state-run girls' gymnasium. The school gave her a good knowledge of French and German, helpful to her later on, but she also had to study divine law, a mandatory subject taught by Orthodox priests. In 1903, upon graduating from a private dental school, she was qualified as a dentist, a useful profession that allowed her to stay in Saint Petersburg. Russian dental schools were the least regulated, which helped Jewish students overcome stringent quotas on education. By 1913 the Jewish share of doctors and dentists in Saint Petersburg reached 52 percent.

Russian was a language of a larger, secular world; it opened a path to professional success. Before World War I, half of the Jewish population in the city spoke Russian at home, becoming the most linguistically assimilated in the empire.[6] The Rosenbaums, who chose assimilation, used Russified versions of their names and were commonly known as Zinovy Zakharovich and Anna Borisovna. Zinovy Zakharovich Rosenbaum was born in 1869 in Brest-Litovsk, a formerly Polish city that had fallen under Russian control and was by then predominantly Jewish and within the Pale of Settlement. Zinovy's background is little known: he was a reticent man, and Rand was reluctant to share what she knew. His documents do not survive, but some facts emerge from the couple's letters written to Rand in America. Thus, in her letter of 1933 Anna Borisovna mentioned Zinovy's military service in the Russian army. That summer, she wrote, he spent a month camping near the Finnish border and "this brought back his years in the military; it was as if he has forgotten that so much time has elapsed since he was a brave military man."[7] Jews were excluded from the higher ranks: the majority served as infantry privates.[8] The Military Reform of 1874 introduced a universal draft and reduced military service to six years. The six-year service requirement explains Zinovy's entering the University of Warsaw at twenty-seven. The Polish capital was then under Russian control, and the Jewish quota on education prevented him from enrolling as a regular student: Zinovy audited lectures in pharmaceutical chemistry. In 1899 he received a two-year certificate that allowed him to work as a pharmacist and live outside the Pale.[9]

Rand had never met her paternal grandfather, but she knew his profession from Zinovy's letter of 1934.[10] A year earlier she had sent her family a typescript of her courtroom drama *Night of January 16th.* Upon reading it, Zinovy wrote that her grasp of jurisprudence made him immensely proud since both his father and grandfather had been lawyers. Regrettably, he did not mention their names or specify where they practiced law. Rand's paternal grandfather could have worked as a private attorney. According to Benjamin Nathans, Jews constituted more than a quarter of private attorneys in western provinces, all within the Pale.[11] This vital family information, which she never revealed, would explain Rand's fondness for including courtroom trials in her fiction, most famously in *The Fountainhead.*

In 1902, upon arriving in Saint Petersburg, Zinovy Rosenbaum was hired as manager at Zabalkansky drugstore, which belonged to his future sister-in-law Dobrulia Konheim (née Kaplan) and her husband, Iezekiil. Two years later, on May 3, he married Anna Borisovna. The couple's three daughters were born within the first six years of their marriage, so she could only briefly practice dentistry.

The Rosenbaums' first rented apartment was adjacent to the drugstore where Zinovy worked. Alisa and her sister Natasha, two years her junior, would remember the building on Zabalkansky Avenue that housed the drugstore and the famous bakery Bligken and Robinson. It sold chocolate, candy, and biscuits produced by the same firm. (Iosif Bligken and Max Robinson were American citizens and merchants, both skillful chefs. In 1887 they opened a profitable biscuit factory in Saint Petersburg.) The Rosenbaum girls later recalled buying "something good" at this bakery; the expression remained in the family for decades, even as such treats had long disappeared.

In 1910, when Nora, the couple's youngest daughter, was born, Zinovy became the manager of a larger drugstore at Nevsky Prospect, 120. The pharmacy belonged to the German merchant Alexander Klinge and was called Alexandrovskaya. The family lived in the same building, above the store. The windows of their third-floor apartment faced Znamenskaya Square, dominated by the equestrian monument to Alexander III. Behind it was the white Znamenskaya Church with its green domes; on the other side of the square was Nikolaevsky rail station, which connected Saint Petersburg with Moscow, Warsaw, and other cities. As Rand would write in the novel *We the Living*, the doors of the city opened onto the Znamenskaya Square. Her fascination with railroads and trains may have started then: the family lived next to the station for at least eight years. The monument to Alexander III, "a huge gray man on a huge gray horse,"[12] as Rand describes it in the novel, was a reminder of the government's official policy of anti-Semitism, which made Jews "the first among non-equals" in the Russian Empire.[13] Saint Petersburg, the capital, never experienced the pogroms that rolled through Kyiv, Kishinev, and Odesa. But anti-Semitism was pervasive in Russia, a source of perennial insecurity and humiliation.

The years 1911–13 marked the Beilis Affair, the most infamous reemergence of blood libel in Europe since the Middle Ages. The case against an innocent man, the factory clerk Mendel Beilis, accused of ritual murder, was devised with the help of prominent anti-Semites within the government. Minister of Justice Ivan Shcheglovitov played a dominant role in manipulating the trial in Kyiv's Superior Court in 1913 amid domestic and international coverage. Saint Petersburg's famous lawyer Oscar Grusenberg, who had participated in all the major Jewish trials, was the lead defense counsel. The prosecution invited major anti-Semitic activists. Although Beilis was acquitted, the verdict maintained that the Christian boy's killing had been a ritual murder. Nicholas II stated privately that he was pleased with the verdict because it officially endorsed the existence of blood libel: "It is certain that there was a ritual murder," he remarked. "But I am happy that Beilis has been acquitted, for he is innocent."[14] (Although Rand never mentioned the Beilis Affair and did not discuss her encounters with anti-Semitism in Russia, she would speak of "Russian mysticism," associating it "with everything that was dark and evil" and destructive to human life.)[15] Blood libel accusations provoked pogroms, as happened in 1903 in Kishinev, the capital of Bessarabia in the Russian Empire.

Rampant anti-Semitism and denial of civil rights were among the reasons for the Jewish exodus from Russia: between 1882 and 1914, millions fled the empire; the majority emigrated to the United States. In the words of a Jewish migrant who kept a diary in 1882, when he left for America, "It is impossible . . . that a Jew should regret leaving Russia."[16] In Rand's family, her mother's married aunt emigrated in the late 1890s; like most migrants, she sought economic opportunities and succeeded in building a better life in America.

Alisa was growing up in a large Jewish clan—her mother's sisters and brothers and their families. Aunt Lisa and her husband, the gynecologist Isaak Guzarchik, were genuinely religious and observant. They lived in the same house as the Rosenbaums, and their daughters, Vera and Nina, were Alisa's playmates. Nina, the same age as Alisa, became her close friend in childhood and adolescence. Vera, the older sister, humored Alisa, nicknaming her "baby fox" ("*lisyonok*" in Russian). This was a play on her name: "*lisá*" means fox. The nickname may have also reflected some slyness in Alisa's character. Alisa's Yiddish-speaking grandfather led the family's prayers during the High Holidays, which took place alternately in the Rosenbaums' and the Guzarchiks' apartments. During Passover, the girls' favorite holiday, Zinovy made matzo, and Anna Borisovna's family would all gather for the first Seder.[17] For a while after Rand's arrival in America, the extended family congratulated her on the New Year and New Life. Later the family, especially Zinovy and the girls, became more secular and abandoned dietary prohibitions.

Zinovy worked long hours at the drugstore while Anna Borisovna handled the daughters' upbringing and education. Clever, strong-willed, and adaptable, she was the true head of the family. As her brother Yakov Kaplan remarked, their mother, "a remarkably clever woman," passed on her intelligence to Anna Borisovna, who, in turn, had given it to her eldest daughter.[18] Alisa also inherited her mother's confidence, energy, and fighting spirit, but not her ability to get along with people. During the civil war that followed the Bolshevik Revolution, the family relied on Anna Borisovna's ingenuity and perseverance; the hardships made her only more resilient. It was the opposite with Zinovy: his loss of business after the revolution left him a broken man.

In her youth Anna Borisovna loved theater, music, and literature; her letters reveal she was a gifted storyteller. In 1926 she wrote to Rand that she had always aspired to but never experienced the joy of creative work, so she had given her daughters an opportunity to realize their talents. Expecting them to become high achievers, Anna Borisovna began their music education when they were little. "Remember Dalcroze, sports, piano, and violin lessons," she wrote.[19] (She was referring to Émile Jaques-Dalcroze, a Swiss musician and music educator who early in the twentieth century developed eurhythmics, a method of teaching musical concepts through movement.)

Rand would complain that in childhood her mother nagged her to move around and exercise. But the lessons in Dalcroze's eurhythmics were not wasted. During her happiest moments in America, Rand would dance around a room to early twentieth-century music she called her tiddlywink. She associated the thrill of tiddlywinks, a simple game in which flat disks or "winks" are vaulted into a pot, with her enjoyment of lighthearted music.

Like most middle-class families of the time, the Rosenbaums homeschooled their children in preparation for the gymnasium (secondary school). Alisa and her sisters had a Belgian governess who was expected to teach French and German. Since Anna Borisovna was fluent in both languages, this was dictated by social convention and desire for inclusion rather than necessity. The girls received only the basic religious instruction from their mother; some Yiddish was spoken at home, but Hebrew was not taught. Later, along with her daughters, Anna Borisovna took English lessons from her friend Mrs. Maria Strakhova, or "Misses," as they called her. Strakhova came from the family of the Russian Admiral Nikolay Ottovich von Essen, a descendant of Baltic Germans. Her exposure to English was limited to the single year she spent with her father in England in 1906–7. Although the lessons gave Alisa basic familiarity with English, they were also responsible for her strong accent: taught to mispronounce words, she couldn't relearn later on. For several summers Strakhova stayed with the family in their rented cottages by the Gulf of Finland. Like many families in Saint Petersburg, the Rosenbaums vacationed in the Sestroretsk and Terijoki resorts. They took walks along the seashore, where military bands played marches and light, uplifting music that became memorable to Rand and gave her the thrill of tiddlywinks.

Anna Borisovna had indirectly inspired her eldest daughter's love of Romantic literature. Decades later, in a weekly column Rand wrote for the *Los Angeles Times*, she reminisced about first hearing an excerpt from Victor Hugo's novel *Ninety-Three*, which told of the counterrevolutionary revolts of 1793, during the French Revolution. "I heard this scene when I was seven years old, lying awake in the darkness, listening intently to a voice reading aloud behind the closed door of the nursery. It was my mother reading a French novel to my grandmother in the living room, and all I could hear was a few snatches. But they gave me a sense of some tremendous drama." When at thirteen she herself read Hugo's "magnificent novel" and came across the very scene, she experienced "a shock of recognition."[20] Rand would claim that Hugo was the only writer who had influenced her career and destiny. In her 1962 introduction to a new English translation of *Ninety-Three*, she elucidated her "incalculable debt" to Hugo: "He helped to make it possible for me to be here [in America] and to be a writer."[21] Hugo's literature had affected her sense of the heroic. In *Les Misérables*, her favorite novel, she admired Enjolras, a secondary character and a leader of young revolutionaries. "I fell in love with Enjolras," she said later. He "was heroically dedicated to a one-track mind purpose."[22] Rand's childhood inspirations lasted a lifetime. A French children's magazine, to which Anna Borisovna subscribed for her girls, published illustrated adventure serials. "The Mysterious Valley," written by a children's author, Maurice Champagne, captivated Rand and fueled her imagination for years to come. Like Kipling's fiction, the story is set in India under British control. It tells how an English infantry captain, Cyrus Paltons, and his company are kidnapped by Hindu shamans with the help of their trained tigers—and carried to a hidden valley in the Himalayas. Cyrus—strong, heroic, and intelligent, but also ruthless—escapes sacrificial death at the hands of his abductors and leads his men out of captivity. Thrilling and filled with romantic adventure, the narrative incorporated the basic form of fictional morality—the battle between good and evil. A middle-aged Rand recited the episodes of "The Mysterious Valley" with a childish excitement. (She would create her own mysterious valley in *Atlas Shrugged.*) An illustration by René Giffey of a tall, defiant Cyrus standing with a sword later inspired a heroic archetype in her fiction. His Anglo-Saxon appearance, attractive to the Jewish girl, would influence her character portrayals.

The three Rosenbaum sisters were artistically gifted, each in her own way. The middle sister, Natasha, would become a star student of a prominent concert pianist, Nadezhda Iosifovna Golubovskaya. Natasha specialized in performing Franz Liszt's compositions and was praised for her "virtuoso technical skills . . . brilliance, confidence, and artistic temperament."[23] But she did not pursue a career as a concert pianist, for which she was trained at the music conservatory. Although a great performer, confident onstage, Natasha was known in the family as "a sheep." She lacked her older sister's self-assurance; obstacles frightened her.

Nora, the youngest, had a knack for draftsmanship. She produced hundreds of cartoonish characters and drawings, which Rand loved. Nora would work for fashion magazines, in display design, and as a theatrical artist. In childhood she was Alisa's shadow, sharing her interests and echoing her opinions, a devout loyalty her elder sister had encouraged.

Around 1912 Zinovy became the co-owner of Alexander Klinge's drugstore and was soon able to afford a family vacation abroad. In summer 1913, when Alisa was eight, the Rosenbaums set out on their first European tour. They visited Vienna, then an international metropolis and a center of European intellectual and cultural life, and proceeded to Switzerland, staying in the town of Montreux. In Paris, they enjoyed the carefree atmosphere, open-air cafés, and street musicians; sunshine and the lightness of life made a welcome contrast to a grim Saint Petersburg. The Rosenbaums continued on to the South of France.

In those days travelers needed neither passports nor visas. As Stefan Zweig writes in *The World of Yesterday*, "Before 1914 the earth belonged to the entire human race. Everyone could go where he wanted and stay there as long as he liked."[24] In the summer of 1914, during the last months of peace in Europe, the family journeyed to Spain and Morocco. In a letter to Rand of 1933, Anna Borisovna recalled both their European tours, which became the family's last: "Do you remember our first travel to western Europe, our choice of itineraries, searching for catalogues, brochures, and maps; the surprise of a gentleman in a travel bureau, 'How astonishingly has grown the interest to the sea resorts on the coast of France.' (?!) And finally, perhaps, you remember our route, during the following summer, through Spain to the African coast?"[25] During the fateful summer of 1914, European newspapers were filled with alarming headlines, but vacationers did not change plans. Zweig was in Belgium, at a seaside resort near Ostend when, on June 28, "a shot was fired in Sarajevo, the shot that in a single second was to shatter the world of security and creative reason in which we had been reared." The assassination of Archduke Franz Ferdinand of Austria triggered a European crisis. On July 28 Austro-Hungary declared war on Serbia. Given the nature of European alliances and Russia's support for Serbia, the major powers were soon drawn into the conflict. Finally, diplomatic and military escalations reached a tipping point; as Zweig writes, "All of a sudden a cold wind of fear was blowing over the beach, sweeping it clear. People left their hotels in thousands, there was a rush for the trains."[26] By August 2, Russia and Germany were officially at war. The Rosenbaums, by then in France, scrambled to get home. Their escape route lay through Britain, which was still debating the European crisis. After several days in London, the family boarded a crowded ship that took them along the Northern Sea Route to Saint Petersburg.

The global war marked the end of a rational and predictable world as Alisa knew it. The old Europe with its carefree atmosphere ceased to exist. The war devastated Russia, bringing on revolution. But in 1914 patriotic and anti-German moods prevailed, and nobody expected the war to last. By the end of August Russia's capital was renamed Petrograd, which sounded less German. That year the German proprietor Klinge transferred the drugstore business to Zinovy, making him sole owner. The move marked the height of Zinovy's career.

At the outbreak of war, thousands of the empire's Jews enlisted, many believing this would lead to equal civil rights. But the opposite happened. Although over half a million Jewish soldiers served in the Russian army, the authorities accused the Jews in the Pale of supporting the Germans. Beginning in March 1915, hundreds of thousands of Jewish civilians from the western borderlands, where much of the fighting took place, came under suspicion and were forced to leave their homes with a day's notice. They were driven eastward into the Russian interior, either on foot or in freight trains.[27]

When thousands of these refugees reached Petrograd, Alisa first encountered Jewish masses, strikingly different from Europeanized Jews in the capital. Later she detested all bearded men, possibly a sign of psychological self-distancing from the religion and poverty of the Pale. In August 1915 the historian Simon Dubnow visited the city almshouse sheltering Jewish refugees from the Polish town of Malkin.[28] This almshouse was financed by the Jewish community. The Society for the Relief of Poor Jews, formed in Saint Petersburg in 1907 with Baron Horace Gintsburg as chair, helped out-of-town Jews, paid pensions, and provided kosher food. Jewish pharmacies offered free medicine (Zinovy Rosenbaum may have been part of this activity). With thousands of refugees fleeing western provinces, the importance of philanthropy increased. In midlife Rand would eschew philanthropy and barely recognize charity, prescribed in Judaism as an obligation.

In the fall of 1914 she passed entrance exams at the private Stoyunina gymnasium and was accepted in the second grade. The determining factor for the family was that the gymnasium had no quota for Jews. Maria and Vladimir Stoyunin, innovative pedagogues, had cofounded the gymnasium in 1881. (Maria was a friend of Anna Dostoevsky, the writer's widow.) The Stoyunin couple aspired to give girls—and their own daughters—a solid education. Among the best of Russia's private schools for girls, the gymnasium was known for its liberal, individual approach to teaching. It did not follow the officially ordained curriculum: students were allowed to have electives and received no homework. The goal was to raise a Human Being. Students were given an unheard-of degree of freedom: girls could even dress as boys. Education lasted eight years and, because of high tuition, enrollment was moderate. The Stoyunins had developed a curriculum that included natural and mathematical sciences—in addition to a variety of subjects in the humanities, such as French and German languages, world history, and jurisprudence. University professors were part of the faculty. Professor Nikolai Lossky, the preeminent Russian neo-idealist of his day (Stoyunina's son-in-law) taught philosophy. Vladimir Gippius, a poet and literary scholar, instructed in Russian literature. Gippius also worked at the private Tenishev boys' school, where, at a different time, his students were Osip Mandelstam and Vladimir Nabokov. Russian literature did not appeal to Alisa, however: she would later make an exception for Dostoevsky's novels of ideas. She liked math for its clarity: formulas do not change. Orthodox priests taught divine law, a mandatory subject, although Jewish girls were free to sit in the back row doing their own work.

Many of the students came from families of the intellectual elite and artistic milieus. Distinguished graduates included the writer and poet Nina Berberova; the ethnographer and gulag survivor Nina Gagen-Torn; the concertmaster of the Mariinsky Theater Marianna Gramenitskaya, and the legendary Mother Maria (Elizaveta Kuzmina-Karavaeva)—a poet, nun, and member of the French resistance during World War II, who would perish in Ravensbrück concentration camp. Rimsky-Korsakov's granddaughter Irina Golovkina (a future novelist), Dmitry Shostakovich's sister Maria, and Olga Nabokova, Vladimir Nabokov's sister, studied in this gymnasium. Rand may have met Nina Berberova, an older girl whose plays were staged at the Stoyunina gymnasium. In her autobiography *The Italics Are Mine,* Berberova describes how on a morning in October 1913 she learned from her classmate Lyalya Zeiliger, daughter of a renowned Saint Petersburg lawyer, that Beilis had been acquitted. The girls hugged each other and cried. The majority of her classmates, Berberova writes, deeply sympathized with Beilis and discussed the trial. Berberova, of Russian-Armenian descent, would emigrate to Europe after the revolution, eventually settling in America to teach at Yale and Princeton; like Rand, she would receive an honorary doctorate.

As for Olga Nabokova, two years her senior, Rand befriended

her in her third year in the gymnasium. Olga came from a distinguished family of nobility. Her father, Vladimir Dmitrievich Nabokov, belonged to a minority of hardworking aristocracy. A lawyer and forceful debater in Russia's first Duma, he pressed for abolition of capital punishment. He was a founder of the Kadet (Constitutional Democratic) Party, a criminologist, journalist, and outspoken defender of Jewish rights. In his memorable article "The Blood Bath of Kishinev," published in Saint Petersburg's law gazette, *Pravo,* he condemned the police for inciting the Jewish pogrom of 1903. V. D. Nabokov also covered the Beilis trial in 1913 and was fined one hundred rubles (a trifling sum for a millionaire) for his honest reportage. The family had a long-standing tradition of nondiscrimination. Olga's grandfather Dmitry Nabokov, minister of justice under Alexander II, had opposed government anti-Semitic measures. The Nabokovs lived at Bolshaya Morskaya Street, 47, where Rand may have visited Olga. Their nineteenth-century mansion of pink granite stood on an elegant street lined with the palaces of aristocrats and diplomats. The Italian embassy, adorned with marble atlantes and caryatids, and the German embassy were on the same street. (The marble atlantes would inspire the central image in *Atlas Shrugged.*)

Rand was unpopular in school. Self-centered, wrapped up in her own world, she wrote fiction in class, probably adventure stories. Her early fiction and her youthful diary do not survive, making it impossible to verify what exactly she produced. Shy, proud, and desperate to assert herself, she would launch into intense arguments: "I was bashful, alternating between bashfulness and violence," she later admitted. "I would be too violent. I would get too angry."[29] She was also dismissive: a single remark could disqualify a girl from becoming her friend. But at home she was made to feel important: her parents encouraged her writing and praised her intellect.

During the war Petrograd was boiling with discontent. Russia's casualties in World War I—almost 2 million dead and close to 5 million wounded—were among the highest. Staggering losses, the economic strain of war, growing food shortages, and inflation brought on general unrest. The strikes expanded, culminating in March 1917, when workers at the Putilov factory, the capital's largest, walked out.

This was the time when Rand first became alert to political events around her. From the balcony of her apartment building she watched crowds pouring into Znamenskaya Square "and filling the entire square . . . a complete sea of faces and the first red banners."[30] She heard shooting. The Petrograd garrison, called in to disperse demonstrators, fired at the crowd, which only created more disorder. Days later, the soldiers took the protestors' side. Nicholas II, no longer supported by the army or the Duma, had no choice but to abdicate. On March 15, the centuries-long reign of the Romanov dynasty ended.

The Provisional Government, established by the Duma, consisted of liberal ministers representing different political parties, including the Kadets. Alexander Kerensky, a prominent lawyer, served as minister of justice and would become government head in July. V. D. Nabokov was appointed head of chancellery. Later remembering the abdication of the tsar and the establishment of the Provisional Government, Rand would say, "To me it seemed to be the fight for freedom. . . . And therefore I thought it was wonderful."[31] The Provisional Government gave Russia its first liberal laws, guaranteed freedom of the press, of assembly, and of conscience. On March 22 it abolished all discriminatory legislation based on ethnic origin, class, and religion. All citizens received equal rights. The United States, France, Britain, and Italy immediately recognized the Provisional Government, which aspired to make Russia a modern capitalist country. The Provisional Government, however, could not resolve the country's most pressing issue—ending the war.

Russia's swift political changes interested everyone, and

girls at the Stoyunina gymnasium, many of whom were well informed, argued agendas of different political parties. A classmate of Berberova, identified in her memoir as Lyusya M., joined the Kadets. After seizing power, Lenin outlawed non-Bolshevik parties, including the Kadets; he branded its members "enemies of the people." Lyusya attempted to flee but was shot while crossing the Russian border.[32] Rand had apparently known about the incident: decades later she employed it in the ending of her novel *We the Living*.

The Rosenbaums forbade their eldest daughter to meddle in politics and read newspapers.[33] Nonetheless, she discussed developments with her friend Olga. The two talked about the Provisional Government, of which Olga's father was a part, and about Kerensky. Rand's youthful admiration for this politician bordered on worship; as she later remarked, "Kerensky became my great hero at that time."[34] Her friendship with Olga lasted until November 1917. That month the Nabokovs fled to Crimea, where opposition to the Bolsheviks was assembling.

Upon seizing power on November 7, 1917, the Bolsheviks proclaimed a socialist regime. Lenin moved quickly to shut down the democratically elected Constituent Assembly, which had replaced the Duma. The results of the first democratic vote in Russia's history were suppressed. Much later, when these results were reconstructed by experts, it transpired that the Bolsheviks came in second to the Socialist Revolutionary Party (the Right SRs), favored by peasants. On January 5, 1918, peaceful demonstrations occurred in Petrograd and Moscow to support the Constituent Assembly. The Bolshevik government ordered troops to suppress both marches. In Petrograd the Red Guards fired at the crowd, killing many. On the day of their funeral in the capital, shops and schools were closed; Rand stood on her balcony, watching the funeral procession. Below, open coffins were carried to the sound of drum rolls, a spectacle she would long remember with a shudder.

The nature of the Bolshevik government became clear from its first decree—introduction of censorship. Opposition newspapers were being closed, their presses destroyed. Lenin launched an offensive on non-Bolshevik parties and ordered the arrest of the leading Kadets. On December 11, 1917, the Bolsheviks institutionalized the concept of "enemy of the people." The Cheka, the dreaded secret police, was established in the same month. Before the Red Terror was officially announced, the Cheka conducted secret arrests and executions. At night people living near the Peter and Paul Fortress, the former tsarist prison, heard rifle shots and bursts of machine-gun fire.

Russia's economy lay in shambles, and production ceased. Aristocrats and the professional and business elites, including Jewish bankers, industrialists, engineers, and lawyers, were fleeing the country. In May 1918, faced with severe food shortages, Lenin issued a decree "on the monopoly of food," which deprived peasants of the right to their own produce. Special detachments were sent to the countryside to requisition grain. The Bolsheviks established state control over production and distribution, thus destroying incentive. Accompanied by beatings and public hangings, requisitioning sparked peasant uprisings; these were suppressed by regular troops. Lenin's draconian policies brought on the Russian Civil War, an apocalyptic event: between 1918 and 1922, millions died from fighting, famine, and epidemics.

In 1918 banks, factories, and private businesses were nationalized. The Konheims lost their pharmacy and adjoining apartment. Grandfather Kaplan lost his business and savings, as bank deposits were seized. Like many at the time, he could hide some gold away, which the Cheka tried to confiscate during regular apartment searches. Before the revolution everything could be taken away from a Jew because of his inferior legal status; now the Bolshevik state robbed him of his rights and property. In mid-1918 armed soldiers burst into Zinovy Rosenbaum's drugstore and announced that the store was nationalized. A red seal was stamped on the door of the shop, leaving the family dispossessed. Alisa would forever remember the incident as illustrating the main principle of communism.[35] Zinovy lost more than just property: his political rights were also taken away. The Bolsheviks branded propertied classes "former people." Later, in her discussions with her father, she fully grasped the meaning of what happened at the dawn of the Soviet era. Rand's novels and nonfiction alike would offer passionate, consistent defenses of individual rights and express contempt for mob rule.

The Stoyunina gymnasium was nationalized in June 1918. Its owner and founder became a state employee; her gymnasium was adapted into a labor school, its curriculum revised, and coeducation introduced, as elsewhere. Rand, who attended the gymnasium to the end of the 1917–18 term, witnessed some of the changes. In the new school year her vacated place was taken by Dmitry Shostakovich, the future composer.

Anna Borisovna, being more decisive and practical, urged her husband to emigrate. Zinovy, like many at the time, believed that the Bolsheviks would not last and dreamed of reclaiming his business. But in the fall of 1918 it was no longer possible to remain in Petrograd: there was no food and no fuel, and the Cheka conducted regular arrests. On top of it all, their middle daughter, Natasha, developed incipient tuberculosis. The family headed south. Their initial destination was Odesa. To get there they had to travel through Ukraine, controlled by various military and paramilitary forces in conflict with each other. The anti-Bolshevik White Army (or the Whites) was led by former tsarist commanders, many of them anti-Semitic; Ukrainian nationalists were under Symon Petliura, whose forces perpetrated Jewish pogroms; anarchists had their own leaders, including Nestor Makhno; there were also smaller peasant armies under local warlords. These gangs also committed anti-Jewish violence, which reached unprecedented levels during the civil war.

Although the Bolsheviks had discouraged the violence, they could not control it. As many as 150,000 Jews were killed in the pogroms. According to Laura Engelstein, "It was the work of soldiers—and Cossacks—under both White and Red command, the paramilitaries associated with popular leaders, as well as peasants and townsmen."[36] Adding to the chaos was the ensuing foreign intervention.

There was complete lawlessness in the country, and when crowded trains would slow down or stop in no-man's-land, passengers were terrified. The train on which the Rosenbaums were traveling stopped on approaching Odesa: tracks had been blown up. Passengers had to make their way to the nearest village on foot. The Rosenbaums and a few others hired horse-drawn carts to take them to Odesa. It was getting dark when their caravan was attacked by an armed gang of looters. In Rand's account of events, Zinovy gave up his wallet with a bit of cash but managed to hide the rest. Meantime, she readied herself to meet a heroic death, like Enjolras, who dies fighting at the barricades.[37] By morning they arrived in Odesa.

The Rosenbaums' stay there was brief; they soon headed to Crimea. For the Jewish community in the Crimean peninsula, the years 1918–21 were marked with starvation and constant threat of pogroms. The peninsula was filled with Jewish refugees fleeing violence in Ukraine and en route to Palestine or elsewhere. In December 1918 the Rosenbaums arrived in Yevpatoria, a multiethnic city of 40,000 and a Black Sea resort. Their rented summer cottage was cold and damp during the winter season, and fuel (kerosene and coal) was in short supply, as elsewhere. Zinovy opened a small drugstore, but, having to compete with four established chemists, he could barely make ends meet. Nonetheless, in January 1919 Alisa enrolled in the nearby private Rushchinskaya gymnasium. The majority of her classmates in fifth grade came from the Jewish and Karaite families; some were refugees from Saint Petersburg, Moscow, and Kharkiv.

Slavic girls formed a minority, so Alisa would not experience anti-Semitism.[38] Meanwhile, because there was only one vacancy in the private school, her sisters enrolled in a state-run girls' gymnasium. During this time Anna Borisovna demonstrated her practical sense and resourcefulness. She found a day job as a teacher of foreign languages and in the evenings cooked and managed the household. Food was scarce and—with growing inflation—unaffordable, so she raised chickens in a shed by the house. When there was no meat, the family subsisted on melons, the cheapest food, which she brought from the bazaar by the sack. At the start, having to pay rent and tuition in her daughters' gymnasiums, she may have sold some jewelry. Later, refusing to abandon the girls' education, she paid for private music lessons with the concert pianist Irine Goriainoff (she used the stage name Irine Eneri) and for art lessons as well. In February 1933, reminding Alisa about the hardship they went through, Anna Borisovna described how, even during the civil war, while their family strove to maintain a middle-class life, as "a teacher by day, I would become a cook by night. Meanwhile, the children were growing and studying, losing not a moment of their time."[39] Overcoming adversity would become a major theme in Rand's novels, although her characters struggle and succeed alone.

Alisa's gymnasium had seven grades. The Bolsheviks canceled the old grading system, replacing it with benchmarks: "highly satisfactory," "satisfactory," and "passed." In grade six Alisa received "satisfactory" marks in all major subjects, including math, physics, sciences, and languages.[40] This gymnasium introduced her to American history: it was then, during the bloodshed and lawlessness of the civil war, that she learned about the American Declaration of Independence, which guaranteed unalienable rights "to Life, Liberty and the pursuit of Happiness." The principles of the Declaration and the American Constitution would guide her for the rest of her life.

Foreign literature was not taught in Yevpatoria, but the local public library was well stocked with volumes of Victor Hugo, Walter Scott, Friedrich Schiller, and Edmond Rostand, the writers Rand prized and who forever remained at the top of her list. In *Romantic Manifesto*, written later in her life, Rand extolled Schiller and Rostand as the greatest Romantic playwrights. Rostand's *Cyrano de Bergerac* transported Rand into a world strikingly different from reality; it taught her that literature was a powerful, influential force. In 1962, in a column for the *Los Angeles Times*, she described Rostand's play as the hymn to the grandeur of man. She called Cyrano's "No, thank you" speech "a proud celebration of integrity": the poet and playwright rejects an offer to have his work produced by a cardinal.[41]

Crimea was filled with rumors of looting and executions. These reports would arise with each change of power. Depicting this time in *We the Living*, Rand would mention the "nightly bombardments and fearful mornings when only the red flags or the three-colored banners in the streets announced into whose hands the town had passed."[42] Dominant forces—the Reds and the Whites—committed atrocities and terrorized civilians; the Rosenbaums witnessed the fighting and the horror. They had lived under the Bolsheviks, who held Crimea from April to June 1919, and then under the Whites and their commanders, generals Anton Denikin and Pyotr Wrangel. Although Rand would recount few experiences from this time, the civil war shaped her Manichaean view of the world. On November 13, 1920, the Bolsheviks recaptured Crimea; this marked the final defeat of the White movement. The Whites began an urgent mass evacuation of their military and civilians across the Black Sea to Istanbul. The six ships docked in Yevpatoria could carry 140,000 passengers, a fraction of those who wanted to escape. Thousands of White Army officers and soldiers, including the wounded and medical personnel, were left behind; they would be executed by the Reds. Zinovy, holding on to his dream of reclaiming his business in Petrograd, was reluctant to leave Russia. Years later Rand spoke of her father's decision as his greatest mistake. Remembering their years in Yevpatoria and the defeat of the White movement, she would observe in an article, "The Lessons of Vietnam":

> I lived in a small town that changed hands many times. . . . When it was occupied by the White Army, I almost longed for the return of the Red Army, and vice versa. There was not much difference between them in practice, but there was in theory. The Red Army stood for totalitarian dictatorship and rule by terror. . . . In answer to the monstrous evil they were fighting, the Whites found nothing better to proclaim than the dustiest, smelliest bromides of the time: we must fight, they said, for Holy Mother Russia, for faith and tradition. . . . I knew that the Reds' deepest atrocity was intellectual, that the thing which had to be fought—and *defeated*—was their *ideas*. But no one answered them. . . . The Reds had an incentive, the promise of nationwide looting; they had the leadership and semi-discipline of a criminal gang; they had an allegedly intellectual program and an allegedly moral justification. The Whites had icons. The Reds won.[43]

After retaking Crimea, the Bolsheviks began to purge the peninsula of civilian counterrevolutionaries. Tens of thousands were arrested and executed in what became known as the largest single massacre of the civil war. The Bolsheviks then conducted nationalization. The Rosenbaums were witnessing it again: factories, shops, houses, summer cabins, cinemas, hair salons, and gymnasiums became state property. The state also claimed intellectual property. Professionals—journalists, engineers, teachers, architects, and so on—had to be registered for work. Food rationing was introduced. Former business owners whose property was seized received the status of unemployed, a category unentitled to ration cards.

Again Alisa's gymnasium was renamed a labor school. She

never forgot an incident that took place at the time. The father of one of her classmates, a businessman, was shot, his body remaining on the beach. Meantime, the soldiers searched her classmate's family house and brought some of the loot, girls' dresses, to school. The girls were expected to draw lots—in front of the murdered man's daughter.

On December 18 the city drugstores were nationalized, along with supplies. When everything was taken away from him at gunpoint, Zinovy became unemployed. According to Rand's Crimean biographers, he registered himself as a plumber. It's unknown whether he ever practiced the trade or claimed it to secure a ration card. They were living through the period known as War Communism, introduced by Lenin during the civil war to "legitimize" nationalizations, confiscations, and grain requisitions in villages, the brutal policy that led to widespread famine.

The famine that began in spring 1921 reduced the Crimean population by 20 percent. On top of starvation, the peninsula was struck by cholera and typhus. The Rosenbaums were doing their best to survive. When in January the Bolsheviks announced their literacy campaign (literacy became mandatory), Anna Borisovna obtained a job teaching adults. With hyperinflation, her employment was essential: during the famine it secured a ration card. Alisa, who was graduating that spring, joined her mother as a literacy instructor. It was with trepidation that, at sixteen, she first arrived in her class to teach Red Army soldiers. But they treated the young teacher with awe, and she soon felt safe among them.

In Crimea she kept a diary, which she destroyed before returning to Petrograd. This document alone could reveal when she decided to become an atheist and what turned her against religion. Decades later, Rand told her first biographer that she wrote in her diary at fourteen, "Today, I decided that I am an atheist." In midlife, Rand gave her major reasons for becoming a nonbeliever. One, argued by atheists at all times, was that there's no proof of God's existence. The other was that the concept of God was "degrading to man," for if God is perfect, this implies that "the highest possible" is unattainable to man.[44] But this rational explanation doesn't represent Rand's thoughts as a teenager. In 1919, when she had made the decision, she witnessed a total collapse of morality: during the civil war, murder became commonplace, and the dead were left lying on the streets. The idea of morally "perfect" human beings could not come from life, but could be inspired by Romantic literature, which helped her escape reality. And it was probably the reality of the civil war that turned her into a nonbeliever.

In June 1921, upon completing grade seven, Alisa received her graduation certificate, which allowed her to enter university. The family was now free to return to Petrograd, where the girls would continue their education. By then, Natasha was apparently cured of tuberculosis. Before the civil war, Yevpatoria was renowned for its beaches and sanatoriums. When the family left the peninsula, the only things they missed were the sea and the sun. Anna Borisovna, who described herself as a "sun worshiper," would remind Alisa of how on a sunny day their misfortunes in Yevpatoria would be eclipsed by the joy of living.[45] The idea that life is the highest value is captured in the title of Rand's novel *We the Living* and in Kira's words to the communist Andrei Taganov: "You see, you and I, we believe in life. But you want to fight for it, to kill for it, even to die—for life. I only want to live it."[46] The Jewish theme of choosing life is most perceptible in this novel. The opening chapters are admittedly autobiographical, depicting the return of the Argounov family to Petrograd from Crimea.

It took the Rosenbaums two weeks to make a three-day journey across the war-devastated country. There were no schedules in the crowded stations, so "no one knew when a train would leave or arrive." People waited for days, sleeping on a filthy floor and afraid to leave; when a train would appear, it was besieged by desperate crowds fighting their way in. Trains were filled beyond capacity: travelers "clung to the steps, to the buffers, to the roofs."[47] Compartments and corridors were packed; filth, stench, and lice were everywhere, causing Rand's lifelong pathological fear of microbes and of crowds.

When the train arrived in Moscow, the family's final change before Petrograd, the Rosenbaums had a chance to see the new Soviet capital, bustling with people and activity. Petrograd lost its former status and importance. The station smelled of carbolic acid. A poster on the wall proclaimed the dictatorship of the proletariat; another poster warned that lice spread disease. Alisa returned to her native city, unrecognizable after years of civil war: the city she remembered for grandeur and immense wealth had died. Petrograd's half-starved inhabitants were surviving on government rations. The buildings on Znamenskaya Square where the family used to live stared "with the dead eyes of abandoned shops."[48] The Rosenbaums' apartment was occupied by a family of proletarians.

2

A Second Columbus

THE ROSENBAUMS, now homeless, stayed at first with the Guzarchiks. Aunt Lisa and her husband, Isaak, were still living in the same apartment. Doctors, whose services were valuable, could obtain protective letters from the authorities, so for a while the Guzarchiks were left alone. Later, because of the influx from villages and overcrowding in major cities, the house management forcefully installed tenants in their apartment. The Rosenbaums soon managed to regain a single room in their former flat, where they would remain for two years, until Anna Borisovna found a permanent place to live. Upon returning from Crimea, she reconnected with her brothers, by then well-established in Petrograd: Yakov as an otolaryngologist, Mikhail as the director of the Museum of the Revolution, and Volodya as a lawyer. Volodya did not have to be asked to help: he shared his lawyer's ration with the Rosenbaums, who were jobless and starving, and brought them sacks of potatoes from the market. For years to come, Anna Borisovna remembered his unsolicited help with gratitude.[1] The youngest and the family's favorite, Volodya died of the Spanish flu.

Uncle Mikhail Kaplan, who in October 1919 had been appointed director of the Museum of the Revolution, lived in his parents' apartment on Nevsky Prospect, now renamed the Avenue of October 25th. He worked in the Winter Palace, occupying an impressive office on the second floor, where senior courtiers used to live under the tsars.[2] A graduate of the Law Department of Saint Petersburg University, Mikhail joined the Russian Socialist Democratic Party in 1905, the year Rand was born. His second wife, Alexandra Shakol, was a friend of Vera Figner, the legendary revolutionary who had planned the assassination of Alexander II. Mikhail had important connections and was now head of the family: his father came to consult him. With her brother's backing, Anna Borisovna soon obtained well-paid employment as a tour guide for foreigners: over the coming years she took French and German tourists through the Winter Palace and the Peter and Paul Fortress. An experienced and knowledgeable guide, she also took members of the Soviet government on tours. She would remember fondly her encounters with the People's Commissar Maxim Litvinov (born Wallach-Finkelstein), describing him in a letter to Rand as "a gentlemen to the marrow of his bones."[3] Her other employment, teaching foreign languages at elementary and vocational schools, provided valuable union membership, which came with benefits her entire family relied on.

On August 24, 1921, Rand applied to the College of Social Sciences of the Petrograd University. Before the revolution, university education in Russia was exclusively for men; women attended various "higher courses," and those who could afford it would obtain a university degree in the West. (Horace Gintsburg had sponsored higher education of Jewish women in the largest Bestuzhev Courses in imperial Saint Petersburg.) The

Bolsheviks, however, imposed their own variation of inequality and student quotas. In the 1920s enrollment was conducted on the basis of social origin, not merit: the majority of those accepted were proletarians. Children of former propertied classes and intelligentsia were admitted only if there was a vacancy. Moreover, during the economic collapse that followed the civil war, Soviet universities were unable to educate students for free, and while proletarians were exempt, others had to pay tuition. An exception was made for Rand: her mother's trade union membership allowed her to study free of charge.[4]

In 1921 Petrograd residents were emerging from the caveman-like existence of the first postrevolutionary years, when they would go perennially hungry, sleep in unheated apartments, and watch family members succumb without doctors and medicine. For Rand the abrupt descent into poverty would illustrate the abyss between capitalist and socialist systems. During these years money lost its buying power and was replaced by barter; people were emaciated and walked around in rags. Yet even during this time Petrograd's culture and intellectual life were not extinguished: scholars worked in unheated rooms, professors gave lectures, and there were poetry readings.

In March 1921, faced with widespread famine, peasant uprisings, and a major revolt by sailors at the Kronstadt naval base, Lenin abandoned his disastrous policy of War Communism. It was replaced with the New Economic Policy (NEP), a temporary retreat to private enterprise. In Petrograd new stores were being opened, and goods appeared. In September, in response to Maxim Gorky's appeal for international humanitarian assistance, the American Relief Administration (ARA), headed by the future Republican president Herbert Hoover, sent its first boat with provisions. It docked in Petrograd, where, within days, canteens were opened to feed children. In October the ARA also began distributing food parcels, paid for by relatives living abroad or anyone who wanted to help the starving in Soviet

Russia. Although many in Petrograd benefited at the time, Rand after World War II would oppose America's Marshall Plan and would mock economic assistance to postwar Europe in *Atlas Shrugged.*

At the first signs of economic recovery, the Soviet regime launched an assault on intellectuals and non-Marxist philosophers. In the fall of 1921 ideologically alien teachers were dismissed from universities and replaced by "Red professors." The philosopher Nikolai Lossky, whom Rand had met at the Stoyunina gymnasium, was swept up in this expulsion. Lossky was a representative of Russian idealism and intuitionist epistemology (self-evident knowledge). After the revolution he examined the moral and religious bases of society. Later Rand would tell her biographer of taking a class from Lossky, who had given her an A on an exam. Reportedly, she impressed him with her own interpretation of Plato and promise that her views would one day become a part of the history of philosophy.[5] The story was probably apocryphal: Lossky by then was removed from teaching; his name doesn't appear in Rand's transcript.[6] In August 1922 prominent intellectuals (Lossky among them) were arrested by the Cheka, soon to be deported from Russia on the "philosophers' ships." In November Lossky and his family, which included Maria Stoyunina, the former director of Rand's private gymnasium, boarded the German steamship *Prussia*, which sailed for Stettin, Germany.

Rand would know about the banishment of the brightest minds. Deported to Germany with other religious philosophers and intellectuals, Lossky would become prominent in the West, lecturing in Europe and America. The only professor of philosophy who survived the purge was Alexander Vvedensky, a neo-Kantian and Lossky's teacher. Rand, who minored in philosophy, took logic from Ivan Lapshin (also a neo-Kantian and Vvedensky's student).[7] This was the last course Lapshin taught before his expulsion from Russia in 1922.

Majoring in history, Rand studied a variety of Marxist and non-Marxist subjects, such as historical materialism, ancient and medieval history, history of the Crusades, Russian history, history of socialism, and modern history of the West. The last course was taught by the prominent historian and brilliant orator Evgeny Tarle, who specialized in the history of France. (He was not French, as his name suggests; he was the son of a Jewish merchant from Kyiv.) Although Rand's official transcript doesn't include literature, she could have audited a special course on Dostoevsky, taught by Vasily Komarovich, an authority whose lectures stretched until midnight.[8] Dostoevsky's writings posed vital philosophical and moral questions that, in the twentieth century, sounded as a warning. His absolute rejection of human sacrifice for the sake of building a paradise on Earth made him unacceptable to the Soviet regime. While Dostoevsky's nationalism and preaching of Christianity could not appeal to Rand, she was taken by his literary skill and use of complex plots to illustrate and dramatize his ideas.

Dostoevsky's anti-utopianism influenced Nietzsche, whose works were avidly read by Russian intellectuals and university students in the first quarter of the twentieth century. Nietzsche's opposition to socialism explains why his writings became banned in the USSR, still under Lenin, remaining only in libraries for restricted use. According to Rand, her cousin Vera Guzarchik sparked her interest in Nietzsche, saying that in *Thus Spoke Zarathustra* the German philosopher beat her to all of her ideas.[9] Rand was about nineteen when she read Nietzsche's famous work, which opens with the parable of the death of God. Zarathustra announces the emergence of an exceptional individual, the Superman, who would replace God and reevaluate all moral values. Nietzsche's irreverent critique of religion and tradition, along with his endeavor to establish values that are not based on supernatural sanction, strongly influenced Rand's beliefs.

Rand's interest in Nietzsche was not unusual for a secular

European Jew. The message of cultural renewal and self-realization appealed to early twentieth-century European Zionists, who were aware of a crisis in Jewish tradition. As Steven Aschheim writes, they were not interested "in harmonizing Judaism with Nietzscheanism." What moved them was Nietzsche's "radical antitraditionalism," an affirmation of freedom of individual choice.[10] In 1902 Chaim Weizmann, who would become Israel's first president, advised his beloved, Vera Katzman, to read *Thus Spoke Zarathustra* "regularly and without fail."[11] In 1900 Martin Buber, the Austrian-born Jewish and Israeli philosopher, described Nietzsche as a prophet of renewal who through preaching the Superman "erected before our eyes the statue of the heroic man who creates himself and goes beyond himself."[12] For Rand the idea of the Superman was empowering; reading Nietzsche also helped reject the notion that traditional morality was a given.

Grandfather Kaplan, now staying with his older daughter, Dobrulia Konheim, in the town of Staraya Russa, south of Petrograd, made cautious, mistrustful inquiries about the NEP: he was wondering whether his business could be denationalized. It couldn't. Legalization of private trade and manufacturing was a temporary government measure to revive the Soviet economy. Private traders, many of them Jewish, took advantage of the new policy and quickly became rich. But the Communist Party could never recognize freedom of trade, so the NEP property laws were deliberately entangled. The government remained in control, and in November 1926 Stalin launched his first major assault on the NEP. In *We the Living* Rand portrays the private traders as black marketeers and speculators, which, no doubt, some were. But what she actually detested was a mixed economy: in the early 1920s Soviet state-controlled industries coexisted with private and cooperative enterprises, which the state would squeeze out. In America Rand would forcefully argue against a mixed economy and government interference of any kind; to understand this, one has to know that she had lived through the NEP.

While the NEP brought some relief, daily life remained focused on physical survival. People had to queue for hours to obtain their ration of bread and dried fish—and in these lines one could encounter shabbily dressed famous scholars and writers. Millet, everyone's staple food, was cooked on oil stoves that filled rooms with black soot. Water had to be carried in pails. There was no electricity or heat in the apartments, so in winter people slept in felt boots and coats. The gray monotony of Soviet life was soul-destructive, as Rand describes it in *We the Living*.

The Rosenbaums' luck changed in 1923 when Anna Borisovna succeeded in obtaining a spacious three-bedroom apartment at Dmitrovsky Lane, 16. The flat, registered in her name (a union member paid a lower rent), had a telephone. With widespread overcrowding, few could settle in separate apartments without other tenants, so the family viewed their fortune as a miracle. That same year Zinovy found a job at the State Institute of Medical Knowledge, or GIMZ, as it appears in Petrograd's address books for 1924–26.

In the new apartment Rand alone received a separate room, which was meant to facilitate her writing. By age seventeen she had firmly decided to become a writer, which is known from her 1922 application to the Institute of the Living Word.[13] Founded by a group of prominent writers and scholars in 1918, this research institute studied declamation and provided training for orators, actors, and writers. It existed under the aegis of the People's Commissariat for Education. The main appeal for the Bolsheviks was the institute's oratory division. As Grigory Zinoviev (born Ovsei-Gershon Radomyslsky), then Petrograd's party chief, put it in his report, "The friends of Soviet authority were teaching the art of speech." Education at this institute was free. By the end of 1919 the faculty included the literary scholars and

Russian formalists Boris Eikhenbaum and Victor Shklovsky, the poets Vladimir Piast and Nikolai Gumilev (he would be arrested and shot in 1921), the linguist Lev Shcherba, and Commissar for the Enlightenment Anatoly Lunacharsky.[14] Students in the literary division, where it is most likely Rand had enrolled, could listen to phonographic recordings of readings by Anna Akhmatova, Andrei Bely, Alexander Blok, Sergei Esenin, Osip Mandelstam, Vladimir Mayakovsky, and other distinguished poets and writers. These recordings were made by Professor Sergei Bernshtein at the institute's laboratory where poetic declamation was studied. The institute director, the theater historian Vsevolod Vsevolodsky-Gerngross, impressed the students by telling them that "they would become the luminaries among the next generation of actors and orators."[15] Students had to complete an introductory course on various aspects of the voice, including its capacity to express logical, emotional, and imaginary content. In 1923 the institute attained the status of private institution. That year Leon Trotsky, in his collection *Literature and Revolution*, attacked Russian formalism as incompatible with Marxism. The formalists, Trotsky wrote, "believe that 'In the beginning was the Word.' But we believe that in the beginning was the deed. The word followed, as its phonetic shadow."[16] This was an attack on the Institute of the Living Word and the group of formalists who were its founding members. In 1924 the institute ceased to exist. Rand, who later became a persuasive and effective speaker, did not mention attending it. Like many immigrants, she reinvented herself in America and cut the links to the past. Yet during these formative years she would have met such prominent writers as Evgeny Zamyatin, who was invited to lecture at the institute. A highly influential writer, critic, and literary heretic, he was among the few intellectuals who dared to openly resist the collectivism and conformity of the socialist state. His banned dystopian novel *We* is known to have impressed Rand. In his essays and lectures, which she probably audited, he called on the Russian intelligentsia to defend individual rights and values.[17] Zamyatin's theory of synthetic prose apparently influenced Rand. In his article "The New Russian Prose," he wrote that realistic depiction of daily life "no longer fits the concept of contemporary art."[18] Zamyatin advocated fantastic plots, a blend of romanticism and realism, and wrote, in 1923, that "the adventure novel must be invested with a philosophical synthesis."[19] Rand would inject adventure plots with philosophical ideas and would define her literary method as romantic realism.

Her first literary attempts included an unfinished novel about medieval France, an opera libretto, and a play entitled "Balaganchik." Anna Borisovna gave the play to her acquaintances, the theater directors Alexander Kugel and Nikolai Petrov, who highly praised it.[20] Although the play was never produced, Kugel and Petrov's endorsement opened doors. Rand began receiving phone calls with offers of work, which she rejected. Kugel's commendation of her play was significant. The son of a rabbi from Belarus, Alexander Kugel was a graduate of the Law Department of Saint Petersburg University. In 1897 he started editing a weekly magazine, *Theater and Art*, turning it into an influential Russian theatrical publication. In 1908, together with his wife, the actress Zinaida Kholmskaya, he cofounded the Crooked Mirror satirical theater, inviting Nikolai Evreinov, a famous Russian-French dramatist, theater historian, and philosopher, to serve as its artistic director. Ten years later Kugel was arrested by the Cheka, and his popular theater shut down. He was rescued from prison by Lunacharsky. In 1920 Kugel, Evreinov, and Nikolai Petrov collaboratively staged a mass spectacle, *The Storming of the Winter Palace*, re-creating the pivotal event of the 1917 Bolshevik Revolution. It was performed in the square in front of the Winter Palace, where a wooden amphitheater was built for 100,000 spectators. The mass spectacle created a historical myth about the 1917 event as a popular uprising, which in reality was a Bolshevik coup. In 1922 Kugel reopened his theater, but, because of tightening Party control over the arts, never matched his former success.

Rand was making her first literary attempts at a time when many writers, poets, and artists, finding it impossible to realize themselves in the Soviet state, were leaving the country. When in 1922, during the NEP, Soviet borders temporarily opened, Berberova, twenty-one (the same age as Rand when she emigrated), and her partner, the poet Vladislav Khodasevich, promptly received travel passports. As Berberova tells in her memoir, their goal was to survive, both physically and spiritually. In Vladimir Nabokov's view, there have always been two disparate forces in Russia: its splendid, freedom-loving culture and its brutal police force. Rand, whose family had experienced legal and social discrimination, would completely reject her country of origin, along with everything in it.

As a teenager she developed a passion for operetta, which allowed her to escape the bleakness and monotony of Soviet life. She frequented Carl Millöcker's *The Beggar Student* (she saw it eleven times) and operettas by Emmerich Kálmán and Jacques Offenbach. A while later, she discovered her true calling: melodramatic silent American and German films by D. W. Griffith and Fritz Lang; stylish urban comedies by Ernst Lubitsch became an obsession. She kept meticulous notes on each film she watched, jotting down names of directors and actors, and rating the films on a scale of 0 to 5. In 1924 she watched almost fifty movies, both Russian and foreign (predictably, Russian ones never scored high), and in 1925 over a hundred. Her younger sister Nora and cousin Nina Guzarchik became her closest companions, following her to the centrally located Piccadilly and Parisiana cinemas and smaller houses.

Nina Guzarchik, cheerful and sociable, held dancing parties at her parents' apartment, and Rand joined the group. They called themselves "Uno Momento." It was a circle of brilliant young men and women from Jewish families, many of whom studied at the Technological Institute. Here Rand met Lev Bekkerman, a future engineer who became her first love. Among Lev's friends, whom Rand knew, were the engineers Leonid Rappoport and Alexander Shugal (and his sister Marusya), the electrical engineer Nadezhda Bershtein, and a future architect, Zhenya Rabinovich, who would marry the prominent radio physicist and engineer Alexander Mints. All had nicknames: Rand was Alix, Nina was Nix, Lev was known as Lyolya B., Leonid Rappoport was Lyolya Ra, and so on.

A morose-looking young man with deep-set eyes, Lev Bekkerman held strange fascination for Rand and other girls he dated. Rand fell desperately in love, which she did not care to conceal, and Lev, who was not planning to attach himself to her, stopped inviting her out. She started pursuing him, but her insistence only made things worse: he now pointedly avoided her. Lev was raised in a well-to-do Jewish family of a Saint Petersburg medical doctor. His father, Boris Bekkerman, had been granted personal nobility, which some Jews could attain through state service. As the historian Seymour Becker points out, Alexander II was the first emperor to confer nobility on Jews who had not converted. Those who held an advanced university degree became eligible for civil service appointments. Upon entering the Russian bureaucracy, they began their service in ranks eight through ten. Class nine conferred personal nobility, which, unlike hereditary nobility, could not be passed on to children.[21] In *We the Living* Lev Bekkerman serves as an inspiration for the major character of Leo Kovalensky, a descendant of Russian aristocracy. But rather than portraying a Russian aristocrat, Rand invested her character with recognizably Jewish traits, such as pride and defiance. Her protagonist is an outsider with the proud face "of a god, a face promising a superior, profound, fascinating man."[22]

December 1923 marked a student purge, more pervasive than the previous one in 1922. Universities were being cleared of students who belonged to the former upper classes; upon expulsion they would be blacklisted, losing the right to apply to any Soviet university. In this purge the Soviet secret police, the OGPU, arrested Lev Bekkerman and his closest friends at the Technological Institute, Alexander Shugal (apparently a Trotsky follower) and Leonid Rappoport. All three were accused of belonging to "a counterrevolutionary Menshevik organization." Bekkerman was released within two weeks and reinstated at the institute; Shugal was exiled to Kazakhstan, where he was later rearrested and shot in 1937.[23] Rand was in her third year when her name also appeared on the list of those expelled. As a senior student she was reinstated and passed final university exams in summer 1924.

Rand had lost Lev Bekkerman to a worthy competitor. Lev was in love with Lili-Maria Pal'men, daughter of a Swedish baron and a talented young engineer who was his classmate at the Technological Institute. Lili-Maria and Lev were inventors specializing in motor design. Upon graduating, both worked at a military plant, engineering motors for Soviet tanks. In 1927 Lili-Maria and Lev married, which Rand, by then in America, learned from family letters. News of the couple's divorce, five years later, was also communicated to her. But Rand did not know what happened next. In 1934 Lili-Maria was arrested and charged with counterrevolutionary activity. Arrests of engineers came in waves: scapegoated for failures in Soviet industry, they were falsely accused of sabotage as well as plotting against the regime. Lili-Maria was sentenced to ten years in the gulag, where she would spend decades—first as an inmate and later as a semi-free laborer designing motors for airplanes, tanks, and tractors. Lev remarried, but he continued to correspond with his first wife until 1936, when he also was arrested. Charged with counterrevolutionary activity, Trotskyism, and espionage, he was shot in 1937, at thirty-six. His second wife, Ata Ris Bekkerman, an architect, was deported from Leningrad for being the wife of "an enemy of the people."[24]

Decades later, continuing to think of Lev Bekkerman, Rand described him as "the focus" of her life in Russia. As a young girl she "did not really understand him" and later wanted to know what he "was really like." Lev's rejection truly bothered her, so she fantasized that he had married mediocre women (though she had met them both—a talented engineer and an architect). She regarded herself as by far superior and thus, according to her logic, Lev's choice of partners did not make sense. She would remark that "the whole issue in my mind is still an unfinished story."[25] What matters is that Lev remained a source of inspiration—and not only for *We the Living*. In her final novel, *Atlas Shrugged*, she used his physical portrait for Francisco d'Anconia. Lev may have also served as an inspiration for John Galt, an ingenious engineer who designs a revolutionary motor powered by ambient static electricity. Yet Rand had realized that Lev's rejection was her good fortune. Had he accepted her, she would have married him and stayed in the USSR, where she would have perished. Lev Bekkerman understood her better than she cared to understand him. In 1934 Rand learned from Nina Guzarchik's letter that Lev praised the single-mindedness and dedication with which she moved along her chosen path.[26]

In October 1924 Rand enrolled at the Leningrad State Institute for Screen Arts. She studied acting, biomotion, and screenwriting for one full year. Her portrait in a turban, taken as a school assignment, was displayed in the window of the Alexander Borovikovsky photo studio on Nevsky Prospect. Like a silent-era movie star, Rand was acting out a dramatic moment. The American silent films she had watched at the time were censored for Soviet audiences and mercilessly cut; the action on the screen did not correspond to the Russian subtitles. But there was something that vigilant censors could not destroy—

"a shot of New York at night . . . skyscrapers, floors and floors of lighted windows on the black sky." America, as she wrote in *We the Living*, was then a "distant, miraculous world."[27] Rand subsidized her costly expeditions to the cinema with a part-time job as a tour guide. On weekends she substituted for her mother taking tourists through the Peter and Paul Fortress.

Rand soon proved to herself that she could win a man. Seryozha Sils, with whom she studied at the institute, became her boyfriend. He was accepted in her family, and the two got engaged. (Intermarriages became common in Soviet Russia. Uncle Yakov Kaplan had married a Russian woman, a leading dermatologist and academician, Olga Podvysotskaya.) But in early 1925 a letter that arrived from Anna Borisovna's American cousins changed the course of Rand's life. In the late 1890s her grandfather Kaplan had sponsored his sister's emigration to America. Now Eva Kaplan, her husband, Harry Portnoy, and their married daughters Minna Goldberg, Sarah Lipton, and Anna Stone lived in Chicago. Sarah Lipton owned a movie theater, the New Lyric, on Chicago's South Side. Correspondence ensued between Anna Borisovna and the Portnoys, who, upon learning of Rand's desire to visit America, sent her an affidavit of support, sworn on June 29, 1925. Rand, upon receiving the document, promptly applied for her travel passport. Her application stated that she intended to visit the United States for a duration of six months.

As Rand waited for the response—impatiently, panicking that her trip to America was being postponed or worse—Anna Borisovna asked whether she was sure of herself, whether she wouldn't later regret leaving everything (and her boyfriend) behind. Rand had no hesitations, no regrets.[28] By then Anna Borisovna knew that Rand was not planning to return. She had a good grasp of her daughter's character, having told her that she passionately pursued her goals but, upon achieving them, no longer appreciated what she had gained.[29] Rand was ambitious and quickly bored with achievement; she would go through life setting ever-higher goals in pursuit of success.

During her final year at home, she read literature on American filmmaking. Her essays on Hollywood, some composed in 1926, were later published in Leningrad as a booklet. Written with confidence and verve, they told thrilling stories about American movie stars, directors, and "an amazing city" where films were produced. The booklet opens with an essay on Pola Negri, "a woman with dark, tragic eyes" and "a mysterious contemptuous smile," who was born in Poland as Apollonia Chalupiec and became a leading movie star, first in Germany and then in America. In Leningrad Rand saw two films with Pola Negri, both directed by Lubitsch—*Carmen* and *Montmartre*. Pola Negri was not her favorite actress (that was the Austrian film star Mia May), nor did Rand think much of the films she had seen. This essay, written while she was still at home, illuminates Rand's expectations as a twenty-year-old, soon to venture to America with the goal of going right to the top in Hollywood.

Pola Negri, writes Rand, "did not struggle for her fame . . . did not walk the slow and difficult road of a movie actress establishing her name. She came and she conquered." (This was a myth Rand readily embraced. In fact, the actress's career did not take off swiftly and easily.) The secret of Pola Negri's success, Rand justly remarks, was in establishing her own style that set her apart from other stars. "Her type is the proud woman-conqueror. . . . Her heroines exemplify everything in a woman's character which is strong, insolent, occasionally crafty, and always victorious." Rand admired the actress's ability "to portray any nationality" and her total dedication to her creative work.[30]

The walls in Rand's room were plastered with pictures of movie stars (her favorite male star was the German actor Conrad Veidt). She may have also had a picture of DeMille, whose films *Male and Female* and *Adam's Rib* she had seen. "Who hasn't heard of Griffith or Cecil DeMille?" she wrote in another essay.[31]

She intended to meet the director in Hollywood, and Cecil DeMille became the family's household word. Nora composed doggerel about her sister meeting the famous director, but she never thought this would indeed happen. In Nora's doggerel "Cecil DeMille" rhymes with "pterodactyl," which was Rand's nickname at home. The sisters' nicknames came from Conan Doyle's *The Lost World:* Rand was "Dact I" and Nora "Dact II." Rand shared her ideas for future scripts and her aspiration to become a major Hollywood writer; Nora made sketches of her sister as a prima donna, admirers at her feet. Another drawing shows a movie theater, with multitudes of little figures running to watch Rand's picture. Rand's dream was to see her name lit brightly with electric lights on a marquee. Nora would make a sketch of this in 1926 and send it to her sister in America.

In summer of 1925 the Rosenbaums rented a dacha in Sestroretsk on the shore of the Gulf of Finland. Seryozha visited and Rand took walks with him by the sea. But her heart was no longer in Russia: she was actively preparing for the journey, studying English with her mother's friend Mrs. Strakhova and traveling back to Leningrad to check the mailbox for any news. In late fall she received from the People's Commissariat of Internal Affairs the long-awaited permission to go abroad.

Anna Borisovna, who had dreamt of emigrating, was able to realize her wish through her eldest daughter. Energetic as ever, she developed an itinerary and connected with her Jewish network of family and friends along her daughter's route, which would take Rand through Moscow, Riga, Berlin, Paris, Le Havre, New York, and Chicago. She bought train tickets to Moscow and Riga and paid the whopping 340 rubles for the first-class cabin on the French liner S.S. *De Grasse.* Every detail of Rand's journey was meticulously arranged. Yet the Rosenbaums knew that the major obstacle to Rand's travel was still ahead. The U.S. Immigration Act of 1924 had severely reduced the flow of immigrants from countries outside the Western Hemisphere. The

80 percent reduction from the average before World War I and specific quotas for individual countries had affected eastern European Jews and Slavs especially. Anna Borisovna bought return tickets for the crossing to help Rand persuade the American consul in Riga of her intention to return to the USSR.

On January 17, 1926, the Rosenbaums, a few friends, and cousin Nina arrived at the station to see her off. Rand boarded the train with Seryozha, who accompanied her to Moscow. Just before the train began to move, Rand, in a theatrical moment, shouted from the platform, "I will return famous!" At home, her grandfather, now living with the Rosenbaums, commented in Yiddish: "Tsu zog oys vi an actrise" (she announced this as an actress).[32]

Anna Borisovna wrote anxious letters, advising her daughter not to do anything in her absence that she wouldn't have done at home. She also instructed her not to spare money and eat well. Rand was given a gold pendant with a diamond, a remnant of her mother's jewelry. It was agreed that she would take it to America and keep it for a rainy day. But if the consul in Riga would ask for a pledge of her return Rand could offer the pendant without the precious stone. Anna Borisovna was hoping, however, that Rand would use her skill of *logical* argument, for which she was known at home, and that the story about her fiancé, Seryozha, coupled with the return ticket, would be sufficient for her to receive the visa. Zinovy, in a separate note, wished his daughter success and, playing on her dramatic words of farewell, wrote, "May the news of your glory reach us sooner than you will."[33] Both parents were happy that Rand was leaving Soviet Russia; both believed in her future. Nora, in her letter, drew a six-pointed star. Rand had celebrated her upcoming twenty-first birthday with Seryozha. She was leaving for Latvia and soon made a note, marking the beginning of a new life: "Alisa Rosenbaum's 21st birthday. Alice's 1st birthday."[34] Her interview with the American consul was her first triumph, which she reported to her family. They were thrilled: "Joy, joy, joy!"[35] Zinovy wired 175 rubles to Berlin for Vera Guzarchik. (Rand's older cousin was studying medicine at the Institut Robert Koch in Germany; she was not planning to return to Leningrad.) Nora was urging her sister to speedily complete her itinerary "Moscow—Riga—Berlin—Paris—Le Havre—New York—Chicago—Hollywood—Cecil DeMille and your final destination, the *Screen.*"[36] In Berlin, Rand and Vera went to the stylish Steinmeirer restaurant to celebrate her birthday and her escape to the West. Later Vera sent Rand a card with a picture of that restaurant, a cozy place with a jazz band and smiling, well-dressed customers.[37] Rand dismissed her mother's advice to enjoy her stay in Europe. She left Berlin in a hurry, without visiting her cousin Volodya Konheim, a medical doctor and venereologist. Volodya had emigrated after the revolution, and they had not seen each other since. Earlier, in Moscow, Rand had failed to see her father's family, including relatives who helped arrange her trip. In Paris the Mordukhovich family, who had been the Rosenbaums' close neighbors in Crimea, were left disappointed. The two families had struggled together during the civil war, but the past held no value for Rand. Focused on her goal, she was charging ahead. She bought herself a typewriter.

While in France, she received her mother's letter asking her to keep a diary during the crossing, to send a telegram upon arriving in New York, and to write detailed letters from America. "You may consider yourself a second Columbus opening America, for none of us have ever been there."[38] In another letter Anna Borisovna asked her daughter to remember while "heading to conquer the world" that everyone nearest to her "remained behind in the North-Eastern corner of Europe." Zinovy, in his note, asked, "Don't forget us, hostages."[39]

A new worry for the family was an announcement in a Soviet newspaper of a serious storm in the Atlantic. Rand would not heed her family's advice to wait. On February 10 she sailed for America on the S.S. *De Grasse*. A list of alien passengers included such information as sex, age, occupation (Rand stated none), spoken languages (Russian, French, and English), "race or people" (Hebrew), permanent address, relative or friend (she had given her father's name). It was winter, and the sea was rough. Ten days later the French liner docked in New York Harbor, and U.S. immigration officials boarded the ship to inspect the visas. When it was over and Rand disembarked, there was heavy fog, which obscured the New York skyline and the Statue of Liberty. Rand cried for joy: she had reached America. She sent a telegram home, which was received on February 20: "ARRIVED HAPPY SAFE KISSES ALICE." A separate telegram for her grandfather was in Yiddish: "Ikh khob dir gezogt, ale lakhn" (I told you, everyone laughs). In Leningrad, these telegrams and her card produced "boundless joy." Grandfather Kaplan was proud of Alisa, saying it's not a trifle for a young girl to journey alone to America. Zinovy wrote he was anticipating the news of his daughter's "substantial success."[40] Now that she had crossed the Atlantic, her mother was cheering her on: "Having tackled the ocean, start wrestling with the ocean of life."[41]

3

Apprenticeship in Hollywood

Rand spent four days in New York, staying with relatives at Sutton Place on Manhattan's East Side. She fell in love with skyscrapers, with the lights of the big city: everything appeared cheerful and non-Soviet. In a Broadway theater she watched *The Sea Beast* with John Barrymore, her first silent film in America. Soon she was off to Chicago, walking through Grand Central Terminal, its size and magnificence leaving her spellbound; in *Atlas Shrugged* she would re-create it as Taggart Terminal.

In Chicago she was greeted by the large Harry Portnoy clan, the families of his married daughters Anna Stone and Minna Goldberg. At the start she stayed with Anna and Mandel Stone, who owned a lumberyard and other property in Illinois, and later with Minna and her husband, Sam Goldberg, who ran a grocery store on Chicago's North Side. The Goldbergs lived in a small apartment where Rand disturbed their sleep by typing nights on her noisy typewriter. Rand kept her own schedule, so the two families took turns accommodating her. Grandfather Harry Portnoy, who had invited her to America, learned little about the family in Russia; to his inquiries Rand replied reluctantly and would change the topic. She was eager to talk about her future in America and of getting into the movie business. The Goldbergs' daughter, Fern Brown, then a child, remembers her dancing happily around the room and singing over and over again, "I'm Sitting on Top of the World," the song that had just appeared in an Al Jolson recording.[1]

In May, sitting on the roof of Chicago's Wrigley Building, designed by Graham Anderson, Rand wrote a card to her family, asking them to imagine what it was like to be living on "top of the world." She wrote that streets in Chicago were broader than Nevsky Prospect, and that there were many wonderful buildings.[2] Rand was happier than her family could ever remember her being, and her first letters from America were long. The one with ecstatic descriptions of buildings in New York and Chicago ran forty-two pages and was nicknamed at home "a skyscraper." The Rosenbaums received it at the end of March, days before Passover, and read it aloud during the first Seder. As Anna Borisovna wrote, their family feast was "illuminated with the lights from Broadway."[3] Zinovy knew her letter by heart, and even his drugstore "was filled with news from Chicago."[4] Also in March, Rand wrote to her beloved sister that she had chosen a pseudonym, and Nora replied that "Ayn Rand" had a good, energetic sound; she liked it more than "Lil' Rand," which they had discussed previously.[5] "Ayn Rand" kept her initials. An obvious reason for changing her Jewish name was her desire to succeed through assimilation. Months into her stay in Chicago she boasted in a letter to Lev Bekkerman that she had become "so Americanized" she no longer needed to look up at skyscrapers. She dreamed of becoming "the greatest star in Hollywood."[6]

Rand's letters to her family described American technical achievements. "You must feel you entered another century, another epoch," Nora replied.[7] Anna Borisovna and Natasha had been translating books, so Rand was asked to send the latest fiction and brochures on technology. The proceeds would actually help support Rand during her first years in Hollywood. The Rosenbaums were sending fifty dollars a month, an amount then permitted by Soviet authorities. *Manhattan Transfer* by John Dos Passos, which Rand sent them, was accepted for translation by Lev Utevsky, a Jewish writer and cooperative publisher in Leningrad. Cooperative publishers paid well, but the state was about to establish full control and squeeze them out. In July Rand sent her family Theodore Dreiser's novel *An American Tragedy*, of which the Rosenbaums made an abridged translation.

Rand's English was shaky when she arrived, and she also mispronounced most words. She wrote her scripts in Russian and translated them with her cousins' help. At nights she was typing translations, preparing to submit them to Cecil DeMille's studio; her confidence undiminished, she was expecting "to conquer" Hollywood and become famous within a year. Rand worked doggedly, driving herself to headaches; upon learning this, Anna Borisovna quoted from the Gospel of Mark: "The Sabbath was made for man, not man for the Sabbath."[8] She believed in her daughter's talent and praised her energy but advised against expecting immediate results: "Only in American films things are done quickly, while, perhaps, in American life one has to struggle and struggle for success."[9]

In preparation for Hollywood, Rand watched 134 silent films. She rated highly *The Road to Yesterday*, produced by Cecil DeMille in his newly founded independent studio. The marital drama featured Joseph Schildkraut, whom Rand admired and would meet in Hollywood. Critics described the film as "furnished with beautiful backgrounds and settings" and containing "the greatest train wreck scene ever shot."[10] Rand would create a more impressive train crash in *Atlas Shrugged*. DeMille's films were highly popular and commercially successful, but critical response was mostly unsympathetic. The critics disparaged DeMille for calculated commercial success. Rand would learn many things from the great producer, and her career would follow a similar trend. Another DeMille film she watched in Chicago was *The Volga Boatman*, the newly released romantic drama about the Russian Revolution, to which she gave a top mark on her scale.

The family in Chicago helped extend Rand's visa and bought a train ticket to Los Angeles. Sarah Lipton, whose New Lyric Theater on Chicago's South Side Rand frequented, obtained a letter of introduction from her distributor, who dealt with Cecil DeMille's studio. The distributor Harry Lord was asking Billy Leyser in DeMille's publicity department to give Rand's scenarios a careful reading. At the end of August, Rand boarded the train for Los Angeles with her typewriter, four film scripts, and a hundred dollars, a substantial sum from her Chicago family. She promised, upon getting rich, to send the Goldbergs a Rolls-Royce and a mink coat for Minna but would forget her promises.[11]

Decades later, in the introduction to *The Fountainhead*, Rand would write about "a sense of enormous expectation" in youth.[12] This captures her mood when, after half a year in America, she headed to Hollywood to impress one of the most successful director-producers in the film industry. Her scripts and the letter of introduction submitted to DeMille's publicity department secured only a formal interview. On September 4, determined to meet DeMille, she stood on the parking lot by the main entrance to his studios in Culver City. When an open-topped touring car pulled in, she recognized the middle-aged director. Rand had planned the fateful meeting while still in Russia and had prepared her lines. DeMille launched many careers and respected ambitious people. He sympathized with Rand, a "little Russian immigrant girl" who ventured to Hollywood with a hope of making a career. If she wanted to write scripts, he told her, she had to see how films were made. DeMille, who was shooting the second part of his biblical trilogy, *The King of Kings*, drove her onto the set, and Rand found herself on a street in Jerusalem at the time of Jesus.

Production of *The King of Kings* had begun on August 24. DeMille's intention was to present the New Testament in an unbiased way: as he told his actors, "The Jew is put in the most unfortunate place of any race in the Bible." Although *The King of Kings* was based on the Gospels, DeMille dropped the provocative line from Matthew following the Crucifixion: "His blood be on us, and on our children." In the film the blame for the crucifixion was placed on one man, the High Priest Caiaphas, who was Rome's appointee. But neither DeMille nor the Jewish actors Rudolph and Joseph Schildkraut (father and son), who played Caiaphas and Judas, respectively, avoided accusations of anti-Semitism. The High Priest, shown as corrupt and scapegoated in the film to absolve the Jewish nation, was a greedy Jew stereotype. Artistically *The King of Kings* was DeMille's most accomplished film, and the director himself valued it more than *The Ten Commandments*, which he had previously produced.

Rand began her apprenticeship with a director who was open about his Jewish heritage, but whose faith was unconventional: he was raised in the family of an Episcopalian father and a Jewish mother who converted to Episcopalianism. According to the *Jewish Tribune*, while shooting *The King of Kings*, DeMille praised Jewish actors who were outspoken about their origin and disparaged others who weren't. According to the actress Dame Angela Lansbury (who appeared in DeMille's 1949 biblical drama *Samson and Delilah*), he "ruled the set with an iron hand, and an iron voice." He carried a megaphone and commanded attention, directing "the actors, and the extras, and the animals, all at the same time."[13] After a week as an observer on the set of *The King of Kings*, Rand was hired as an extra receiving $7.50 a day, a small fortune. DeMille kept her occupied for several months, whenever extras were needed in street scenes. At home the news of her first job was met with alarm. Anna Borisovna wrote that with her talent and "exceptional intellect," becoming a movie extra was a mistake. She must develop her literary gift and the family would support her.[14] Rand disregarded the advice.

Meeting DeMille and having him as a mentor was vital for Rand in many ways. He had given her a job and she was no longer an outsider in Hollywood. As she would write to him a decade later, "I was a very inexperienced, very bewildered and frightened little immigrant from Russia."[15] Richard DeMille thought his father was impressed with Rand: "He liked assertive, intelligent women. . . . For her, he was the commanding, romantic figure of a film director."[16] It is likely that DeMille helped her secure affordable accommodation at the highly sought-after Hollywood Studio Club, where his wife, Constance, was on the board of directors. Recently opened in the heart of Hollywood, the building on Lodi Place housed career-seeking young women in every branch of the movie industry—actresses, screenwriters, costume designers, and so on. Famous alumnae over the years included Elvia Allman, Donna Reed, Linda Darnell, Shirley O'Hara, and Kim Novak. The biggest star, Marilyn Monroe, then known as Norma Jean Baker, became a tenant in 1948. The rooms had nameplates on doors identifying some of the donors, such as Douglas Fairbanks, Howard Hughes, and Gloria Swanson, the star discovered by DeMille. Here, among America's most beautiful women, Rand spent two and a half years. Her alluring gentile neighbors later inspired her heroines' portrayals. Rand was short, intense, with strong features, and thought people disliked her at first sight. But she would win them over with her intellect, energy, and perseverance.

Hollywood, founded by eastern European Jewish immigrants, now employed Jewish directors, actors, and other professionals. On the set Rand socialized with Adrian Greenburg, the future famous designer later known simply as Adrian, who worked in the wardrobe department in *The King of Kings*. A descendant of Russian and German Jewry, Adrian would become her close friend. Joseph Schildkraut, "a big star" and "enormously good-looking," took her out for lunch.[17]

And it was also here that Rand met the aspiring actor Frank O'Connor. Handsome and tall, Frank had a bit part as a Roman legionnaire and walked around the set in a short toga and sandals. Rand could not secure his attention—until she ran directly into his path and stuck out her foot to trip him; he stumbled and apologized. Frank later told his brother that he met an interesting Russian girl but couldn't understand a single word she was saying. Their first conversation happened on his last day on the set. When Frank disappeared, Rand spent eight months despairing. The blond, blue-eyed Irishman impressed her as having the perfect face of a romantic hero. The real Frank was the opposite of heroic: meek, sensitive, and accommodating, he would help balance Rand's tempestuous nature. He would become her husband of fifty years as well as her model.

During her apprenticeship with the brilliant and influential filmmaker, Rand was absorbing his themes and narrative skills. When in 1927 *The King of Kings* came out, she watched it four times. The strong composition of the film, an archetypal struggle between good and evil, and the larger-than-life characters impressed her. These features would enter her major novels. Earlier, she saw *The Ten Commandments*, which illustrated the Exodus and "the giving of the law," to use DeMille's words. The modern part of the film was a story of two brothers—John, a carpenter who believes in God, and Dan, an atheist and a successful building contractor who breaks every single commandment to get rich and ends up financially ruined and disgraced. Rand detested the conventional morality of the film and had given it a zero in her journal but later borrowed, for *The Fountainhead*'s ending, the scene of ascension to the top of a construction project.

When Rand reminded DeMille about her scenarios, he

turned the matter over to his story editor. She learned the result from DeMille, who said her stories were "not human enough," an opinion she would hear from editors over the years. Rand later admitted that of the four scenarios, three were juvenile, but one contained a germ of a good story. DeMille recognized promise and gave Rand her first writing job: just ten months after landing in America, she became a junior writer receiving a decent salary of twenty-five dollars a week. As she excitedly reported to her family, she had an office and a nameplate on the door identifying her as a writer.[18] Rand was yet to find that writers in Hollywood were laborers, assigned to do rewrites and work collectively on a project that would never become their own. Meantime, she was learning to make adaptations and was synopsizing fictional works. A short story, "The Skyscraper" by Dudley Murphy, had given her the most trouble. The trite plot involved a love triangle: two friends working on construction of a New York skyscraper fall in love with the same woman. DeMille asked Rand to develop the story so that it would project "the drama and heroism of constructing a skyscraper."[19] Rand was building up the story lines, as she always would, through logical questions and answers. But she soon dropped the assignment and started writing her own script, one involving an ambitious architect, Howard Kane, who overcomes various obstacles on his way to success. She invented dramatic events: a fire in the skyscraper, Kane's arrest for criminal negligence, and the ensuing trial; he comes back from disgrace to fame and has a turbulent love affair with a famous actress. Running ahead of herself, Rand designed a poster: "Cecil B. DeMille presents THE SKYSCRAPER by Ayn Rand from a story by Dudley Murphy."[20] In the event, DeMille's studio rejected her plot and in 1928 produced the film based on Murphy's original story. Rand was disappointed, but her script was not wasted: it contained the germ of *The Fountainhead*, in which Howard Roark overcomes numerous obstacles to build the skyscraper he designed.

Rand wrote to her family sporadically, mainly to surprise them with sensational news. In January 1927, after a long interlude, she sent a forty-page letter describing her friendship with DeMille and her job as a scriptwriter in Hollywood. She was making a fortune and no longer needed her family's support. "Forty pages of your letter took forty years off my shoulders," wrote Anna Borisovna, relieved that her daughter was alive and well. "I pray to God with all my soul that He continues to help you." Nora found it extraordinary that her sister became a friend of "*our* Cecil B. DeMille," who had been at the center of their fantasies. Zinovy had a hard time believing Rand's account, which resembled a "beautiful invention."[21]

In May, while researching "The Skyscraper," Rand walked into the public library in Hollywood, where, at long last, she found Frank O'Connor. Born in 1897, Frank grew up in a large Catholic family of seven children in the steel town of Lorain, Ohio. His father was a steelworker, a meek, uneducated, and hard-drinking man. Frank's mother was strong-willed and domineering. When she died, the family fell apart. Frank dropped out of high school and left Lorain with his brothers. He held a number of odd jobs before becoming a movie extra at the D. W. Griffith Studio. When the studio moved to Hollywood, Frank followed, eventually receiving his first bit part in DeMille's film.

Rand reported the big news to her family: she had a handsome boyfriend. When she described his "gorgeous blue eyes," Anna Borisovna quipped: "Alyonochka, please don't become enamoured with young men who have little to offer except for their beautiful eyes."[22] It was a remark Rand would probably not forgive. That fall she suggested that her sister Nora join her and enroll at an art department of an American university. Age seventeen, Nora had recently been accepted at a vocational art college in Leningrad. So it was agreed that she would apply the following year. And since the family no longer had to support Rand, wrote Anna Borisovna, they could start saving for Nora.

In November Rand sent application forms to her sister, who was so grateful and thrilled that she felt like dancing in the street. Then, suddenly, Rand stopped replying to her family's letters. When in April 1928, after a long, inexplicable silence the family received her letter, they had already decided against Nora's travel to America.

Many things were happening in Rand's life. In October 1927 the very first sound film, *The Jazz Singer*, a Jewish drama, revolutionized the movie industry. Based on a play by Samson Raphaelson, it was produced by Warner Bros. Rand did not see it. The end of the silent film era also ended her career as a junior writer in DeMille's studio. In fact, the studio did not use any of her work, and in spring 1928 she found herself unemployed. Talking pictures required more advanced language skills than Rand had at the time. Jewish writers, many of them from New York, headed to Hollywood, and Rand was swiftly replaced. In August 1928 DeMille closed his studio and joined Metro-Goldwyn-Mayer, the largest and best. It was only reluctantly that Rand reported the truth to her family: she was jobless and unable to pay for her room at the Studio Club.[23] Anna Borisovna immediately organized help. She wired to Anna Stone in Chicago, asking to lend Rand $150 and promising to pay it back. The family was somewhat relieved to find an explanation for Rand's silence. Now they all wrote to admonish her; she should have asked for help long ago. Anna Borisovna attained special permission from the head of Leningrad's main bank to wire a lump sum to her daughter in America. In addition, some relatives and Maria Strakhova, then in Riga, sent small amounts. By fall 1928, Rand stopped writing again, neglecting to congratulate her family on Rosh Hashanah or even to send a card for Nora's birthday.

At some point she fell behind on her rent at the Studio Club, where such things were common: most young women had money problems. But when someone donated $50 for the neediest girl, the club director, Marjorie Williams, chose Rand. A while later a beaming Rand arrived at the director's office with a box containing fabulous black lingerie. The story would become known as the funniest in club history. Rand would re-create her delight in purchasing the silk negligee in the novel *We the Living:* Andrei Taganov makes a present of it to Kira; the heroine gasps, holding "a nightgown of black chiffon," utterly transparent and so light that it "felt like a handful of smoke."[24] Frank, who had no steady employment and lived with his brothers, could not afford such gifts.

After losing her job at DeMille's Studio, Rand worked in Hollywood as a waitress (she lasted one day) and as a department store clerk; she also took classes in stenography but would not pursue this career. Rand did not forget that she had come to America to realize her literary ambition. In 1926 she wrote her first story in English, "The Husband I Bought," which projected her ideal of "man-worship." The story tells of a young woman, Irene Wilmer, and her adoration of a man "whom society admired and who laughed at society."[25] Nietzschean influence is apparent from the author's attempt to portray an extraordinary individual. The protagonist, Henry Stafford, is godlike in his beauty and intellectually superior to the rest. He is a former businessman and engineer—the two professions Rand prized. The heroine idolizes him and kneels before his photograph. Rand's idea of man-worship suggests a search for a new religion—without a supernatural component, but dealing with exaltation and reverence. The story would serve as a blueprint for Kira's adoration of Leo in *We the Living.* Rand's 1928 unfinished novella "The Little Street" is an attempt to present the "psychology of a Superman" for whom "other people do not exist." The story is loosely based on the 1928 criminal trial of William Hickman, who brutally murdered a schoolgirl, Marion Parker, in California. At his trial he shocked the public by saying that he kidnapped the girl for ransom, needing money to enter a Bible college. Rand used Hickman as a model for the character of Danny Renahan, whom she describes in her notes as "a Hickman with a purpose" and "without the degeneracy." Danny Renahan kills a pastor, who is highly respected in the town that is governed by "the little street" conventional morality. In contrast, the murderer is "superior to the mob," an antithesis to mediocrity and conformity. His motive for the murder is not money: he commits an ideological crime. As Rand puts it in her sketch, the "crime takes the aspect of a blow against the church, religion, civilization, humanity."[26] The author's sympathy is on the side of the criminal, whose radical rejection of established values she condones. In the projected denouement, Danny Renahan is lynched by the mob. Although Rand's notes for the story contain references to Nietzsche, her hero is more of a nihilist than a Nietzschean Übermensch. His outlook resembles that of Raskolnikov in Dostoevsky's *Crime and Punishment.* Raskolnikov, who divides humanity into extraordinary personalities and the mob, murders an old moneylender to test himself—whether he can rise above the submissive herd and their morality. In the play *Night of January 16th*, written five years later, Rand would again romanticize a criminal who opposes society and its norms. The character of a defiant pariah reflected her view of herself: she was challenging conventional beliefs and values.

In life, unlike her fiction, she pursued a decent and caring man. She was in love with Frank and determined to marry him. Significantly, Frank and his siblings were not religious and held no ethnic prejudice. His sister Agnes had married a Jewish man, Aaron Moses, whose father, I. J. Papurt, had come from Berdichev, within the Pale. Rand would become close with Frank's niece, Mimi Papurt, but warned her against mentioning Berdichev, describing it as "a Jewish ghetto."[27] She also befriended Frank's brothers, engaging in intellectual discussions with Harry, a freelance newspaper reporter in Los Angeles who used the pen name Nick Carter. Nick later gave her literary advice, suggesting she write a novel based on her Soviet experiences, the future *We the Living*. Frank's brother Joe, an actor, wore a beard, which made him look like Christ; it was the character role he performed over the years at the Hollywood Pilgrimage Play Theater.

In early 1929, her visa again expiring, Rand moved to a furnished room where she and Frank could become lovers. To legalize her stay in the country, she had to marry an American citizen. As Rand told Barbara Branden, her first sexual experience was also Frank's: he was still a virgin at thirty-one. Friends knew that Frank was not in love with Rand and married to save her from deportation. According to Rand, "Ours was a shotgun wedding—with Uncle Sam holding the shotgun."[28] Frank and his older brothers were confirmed bachelors. Joe never married, and Nick Carter was known to be gay.[29] On April 10 Frank and Rand's "intention to marry" was published in the *Los Angeles Times*. The couple registered their marriage at the Los Angeles City Hall on April 15. The family in Lorain learned this from an announcement in a local newspaper. Frank's sister Elizabeth was surprised and wrote from Lorain to congratulate and say that she couldn't imagine him marrying unless he was hit pretty hard. Rand sold her mother's gold necklace with a diamond to pay for the wedding and a short trip to Mexico. Two weeks after the marriage, the couple borrowed a car and drove to Mexicali; they then reentered the United States at Calexico, California. Having recrossed the border as the wife of an American, Rand was now entitled to apply for naturalized citizenship.

Rand failed to impress her family with this news: her sister Natasha had married one month earlier and outshone Rand with her choice of partner. Natasha's husband, Isidor Vaks, was Jewish and a talented electrical engineer. "I will begin with what's most important in our opinion, his profession," wrote Anna Borisovna to Rand. Sida, as they called him, was twenty-five, had scholarly publications and secure employment. He had served in the navy for two years, which meant he was in excellent physical health. One couldn't have made a better choice, she wrote.[30] Another letter described preparations for Natasha's wedding, celebrated in grand style in mid-March. Anna Borisovna remodeled the apartment so that the young couple could have separate quarters and their own dining room. She reupholstered the furniture (it was impossible to buy new) and gave the best pieces to the newlyweds. When guests arrived, everyone praised the apartment, which had an "aristocratic look." There were crystal glasses and silver cutlery on the table. The feast included roasted turkeys and geese, Olivier salad, traditional fish with yellow sauce, dessert with oranges, ice cream, and tortes—Aunt Liza's specialty. There was a torte with nuts; custard with pistachios, a torte with whipped cream, liqueur, and spiced wine (Glüchwein). Nora was joking that the event "marked a new era. We will begin our chronology . . . from Natasha's wedding." Aunt Doba and Rand's cousin Evgeniya congratulated her on a new brother and wrote that Anna Borisovna "made miracles," creating a chef d'oeuvre out of thin air. (The feast was truly a miracle: it was the second year of Stalin's forced collectivization, and food shortages were severe.) Rand's photo was prominently displayed in the dining room, so she was there in spirit.[31] As tradition required, Sida wrote to Rand to introduce himself. But Rand, jealous of her sister, did not reply.

When in late April the family received Rand's letter informing them of her marriage to Frank, Anna Borisovna alone congratulated Mrs. and Mr. O'Connor: "I'm happy, very happy for you, my girl."[32] She was kind and diplomatic, but her lack of enthusiasm was apparent. Rand's choice fell short of her parents' expectations, mainly because Frank was an aspiring actor. The fact that his family was Catholic mattered less: Rand's family was liberal.

Anna Borisovna wondered whether Rand's marriage upset their American relatives. In the play *Abie's Irish Rose* by Anne

Nichols, she reminded Rand, a Jewish man secretly marries an Irish Catholic girl because a union out of faith is a blow to those who are Orthodox. Anna Borisovna asked Rand to write to their Chicago family "that you did not change your religion, that your marriage was registered in a civil ceremony."[33] In fact, the relationship with the American relatives was not broken, but the matter did not interest Rand and she never replied to reassure her mother.

When Zinovy finally wrote to congratulate Rand, he began by saying she should remember how much he disliked writing. He proceeded with a formal wish for Frank's happiness and future success.[34] Zinovy's letter disappointed Rand, so she remained stubbornly silent for three months. With no news from her, Anna Borisovna worried herself into a frenzy. "Send us a word," she implored.[35] Having secured her family's undivided attention, Rand broke her silence in September to say she had a new job.

In July, Ivan Lebedeff, a handsome former officer of the Russian Imperial Army turned actor (he received supporting roles as a villainous officer, an aristocrat, and even a gigolo), helped Rand obtain a clerical job in the women's wardrobe department of the Hollywood RKO Radio Pictures studio. The job at RKO was "a godsend," in Rand's words.[36] Initially it paid twenty dollars a week, but within half a year her salary was raised to twenty-five dollars. This could not have come at a better time: Rand had found stable employment shortly before the stock market crash.

As an office clerk at the wardrobe department, Rand scheduled appointments for Hollywood actresses and occasionally helped with fittings, consequently meeting Ginger Rogers, Katherine Hepburn, June Clyde, Bette Davis, Irene Dunn, and Thelma Todd, among others. Her first boss, Walter Plunkett, was a brilliant costume designer who would later work in scores of Hollywood films that would become classics, including *Gone with the Wind* and *Singin' in the Rain.* Rand looked strikingly different from the glamorous people who walked past her desk: Marcella

Rabwin (née Bannett) would remember her as "the worst-dressed woman" in the department, who did not use makeup and had "a terrible figure."[37] Rand seemed to fit the stereotype of a mannish and homely Jewish woman. Nobody then knew that this unappealing office clerk would become famous in her own right.

Rand hated her job and complained that she had to work overtime. But she and Frank, who would get only occasional employment as a movie extra, depended on her salary. In a day when a loaf of bread cost ten cents, she was making twenty-five dollars a week, more than an average secretary. By 1932, her last year at RKO, she was promoted to department head, receiving forty-five dollars a week, a dream salary during the Depression. But the job took her away from writing: by evening, when she would settle down to work on her stories, she felt drained. Occasionally she would snatch a few hours from her morning sleep and write before work. Although time was precious, Rand also aspired to run the household and to cook. In her birth family these chores were performed by a maid and later by Rand's father. But Rand had her own idea of being a proper wife. She surprised her mother by asking her to send recipes.

The couple lived in a small one-bedroom apartment on Gower Street, across from the RKO studio. The area around Gower was residential, inhabited by the lower middle class. Their next-door neighbor, Elena Epps, was a Jewish immigrant from Russia. She lived with her daughter, Marcella Rabwin, an executive assistant to David Selznick, a second-generation filmmaker and head of production at RKO (he would produce *Gone with the Wind*). Rand sensed correctly that Elena Epps, with whom she discussed her writing plans, would put in a word for her. In 1930 she began outlining *We the Living* but soon interrupted her work to write a film script about Soviet Russia, *Red Pawn*. As she would tell Elena Epps, she "loathed the Communist system" and "was dying to expose it."[38] According to Marcella Rabwin, she agreed to help her ambitious young neighbor and approached her friend, a Hollywood agent working for Myron Selznick (David Selznick's brother). The agent offered Rand's scenario to Universal. Around this time, Rand sent a copy of her script to Gouverneur Morris, the author of pulp novels and magazine stories and a staff writer at Universal. Morris thought her scenario "showed positive genius," praise Rand instantly reported to her family. Having become her advocate, Morris helped push *Red Pawn* at Universal. In early 1932 Universal Pictures made an offer for *Red Pawn:* Rand would receive seven hundred dollars for her story and another eight hundred dollars to adapt it for the screen. Her contract, one of Hollywood's "rags-to-riches" stories, made headlines. Chicago's *Daily Times* described Rand as a "Cinderella of the Typewriter."[39] The *Los Angeles Evening Herald* reported that a former employee of a wardrobe department "peddled a film story to Universal."[40] Even the *New York Times* carried a notice mentioning her sale, but, disappointingly, the newspaper misspelled the title of Rand's scenario as "The Red Pan." In Hollywood there was a rumor that the stage and screen actress Tala Birell considered the role in *Red Pawn* of a Russian princess who fights to save her husband from prison. Although *Red Pawn* was never filmed, this first sale marked a new stage in Rand's life and career. From September 2 to December 15, 1932, she worked as a writer for Universal adapting her own story for the screen. In September she quit her job at RKO and moved away from her pedestrian neighborhood to the impressive Trianon Apartments, to live among Hollywood celebrities in the romantic, French château–style building at 1750 North Serrano Avenue.

Red Pawn was her first professional work, as she would say, but her story was not exactly original. As often happened in Hollywood, writers and directors lifted each other's plots. Rand's scenario borrowed from DeMille's silent film *The Volga Boatman*, a romantic drama about the Russian Revolution and civil war. The film, as the prologue describes it, was a story of a princess, a prince, and the Volga boatman. Princess Vera, engaged to the

White Army officer Prince Dmitry Orloff, becomes infatuated with Fyodor, a handsome barge hauler. When the Whites are defeated, Princess Vera and Prince Orloff stand before a Bolshevik tribunal with Fyodor acting as their advocate. Fyodor asks to spare the life of the woman he loves—"and the life of this man [Prince Orloff] because he loves her." The lenient tribunal suggests the two choose between exile and service to the Bolsheviks. Vera chooses to remain with Fyodor in the new Russia; Prince Orloff chooses exile.

Rand employed the love triangle, involving two aristocrats and a Bolshevik, and the idea from the film's denouement. Initially in her scenario the heroine's name was Princess Tanya. She later transformed the Russian princess into an American named Joan. The setting was interesting and original: Rand had undoubtedly known about the Solovki special political prison, set up in 1923 in a former Russian Orthodox monastery on the Solovetsky Islands in the White Sea. (She would also know about dramatic escapes from the islands, organized by the former White Army officers Sozerko Malsagov and Yuri Bezsonov, whose accounts were published in London.)[41] In *Red Pawn* she renamed them the Strastnoy Islands. Commandant Karaev, the loneliest man on the island, needs a concubine and sends to the mainland for a woman. Joan, on a mission to rescue her imprisoned husband, a former engineer and Russian aristocrat, Michael Volkontzev, volunteers. The commandant falls in love with Joan and arranges an escape from the island for all three—himself, his mistress, and Volkontzev. As in DeMille's film, the Bolshevik saves an aristocrat, who is also his bitter rival, for the only reason that they both love the same woman. *Red Pawn*'s denouement also includes a crucial choice made by a woman. When the escapees are captured, the choices for Joan involve staying in Russia, which means certain death, or escaping abroad. Joan betrays Commandant Karaev and deceives the soldiers: she and her aristocrat husband are driven to a place from where they will be able to emigrate. Rand reverses the ending to project an anticommunist message.

Although *Red Pawn* was entirely fictional, the scene in the monastery's former chapel was written with factual detail. While the Bolsheviks were transforming the chapel into a library, they replaced icons with Lenin's portrait; the hammer and sickle were painted over Moses's tablets. (When in 1930 a synagogue in Kazan was converted into a club, portraits of Lenin, Marx, and Engels were posted over the Torah ark.) But the murals depicting biblical scenes were not fully covered by paint; in insufficiently painted spots one could still glimpse the procession following Jesus to Golgotha. The scene suggests that Bolshevik ideology is but another religion; their leaders have become the new saints.

Though never filmed, this first sale continued to produce revenue and employment for the author. In 1934 Paramount secured the rights to her story by trading it with Universal for another property. Rand was hired by Paramount to work on the screenplay: there was a rumor that Marlene Dietrich was considering a role in *Red Pawn.* The rumor was false, but since it was picked up by a Hollywood paper, Rand received additional publicity. That year she sent the ten-page synopsis of *Red Pawn* to DeMille, asking him to read it. She wanted him to know that she justified his interest in her by achieving success. "I am very anxious to show you what I have accomplished," she wrote, "particularly since it is accomplished in accordance with your ideas as to story construction and situations." Rand did not give up her dream of working with DeMille and would send him her published novels. She signed the letter with a pet name DeMille had given her: "Caviar."[42] DeMille had taught her to construct a thrilling plot and fast-moving narrative, skills that would help her achieve popular success.

4

Red Decade

With confidence and money from her first sale, Rand worked on *We the Living*, her most autobiographical and realistic novel. The events take place in Petrograd (later Leningrad) during the years of the NEP, beginning in 1922. The novel shares *Red Pawn*'s anticommunist theme and has a recognizable love triangle. It focuses on three individuals—Kira Argounova, the communist Andrei Taganov, and the aristocrat Leo Kovalensky. Kira studies at the Technological Institute, aspiring to be an engineer, the most respected profession in Rand's birth family.

Engineers were in high demand in the first decades after the revolution, when the entire country became a vast construction site. In August 1931 Nora (following Natasha) married a young Russian engineer named Fyodor Drobyshev. The Rosenbaums now shared their flat with two young couples. Nora had saved Fyodor from tuberculosis by sending him to a sanatorium, with her family's help. Rand recast the outcome into Kira's struggle to save Leo Kovalensky from incipient tuberculosis. Leo's apartment resembles the Rosenbaums': at Rand's request, Nora photographed one of the rooms and sent her a picture. Anna Borisovna was sending postcards with views of their native city to help revive Rand's memory. She reported on the Soviet apartment crisis and the difficulty in obtaining a spot in a sanatorium for a non–union member. All such trivia went into the novel. Nina Gouzarchik's words of the need "to live fully and consciously, to enjoy life, to feel alive" provided additional inspiration for the main theme.[1] Although Rand's characters have Russian surnames, most were based on her Jewish friends and family. Leo's physical portrait was inspired by Lev Bekkerman. Kira is a combination of Nina Gouzarchik and Rand herself. The Rosenbaums, recognizable in Kira's family, are dwarfed by their portrayal. (In Rand's fiction families are a burden: they are either not mentioned at all or abandoned. Mothers represent traditional values, which Rand renounced, and for this reason are portrayed as narrow-minded.)

With this novel Rand attempted to get Russia out of her system. She never entirely succeeded because the revolution, civil war, and Bolshevik dictatorship determined her worldview, the black and white colors of her art. The world in her fiction is split between freedom and tyranny; the good and evil in her characters do not mix. But *We the Living* is an exception: her characters are not abstractions.

As a university student Rand met a number of civil war veterans, distinguishable by their leather jackets. In Andrei Taganov she portrayed a communist idealist who fought in the Red Army under Trotsky's command. Taganov gradually becomes disillusioned by pervasive corruption in the OGPU and Soviet life. He is employed by the political sector of the OGPU, where his job involves conducting apartment searches, beatings, and arrests. (This character is the literary descendant of Commandant Karaev in *Red Pawn.*) As Trotsky's follower, Taganov has no future in the Party. During a meeting of his communist cell he makes an honest report about grain requisitioning in villages and mentions suppression of peasant uprisings by the army. Demoted and expecting to be expelled from the Party, Taganov, like his friend, also a Trotskyist, commits suicide. In her notes for the novel Rand wrote that Taganov was "a born individualist," a self-made man of proletarian background, possessing "unquestionable honesty." His sensuality was "unawakened" until he met Kira, "a woman of the upper classes."[2] Taganov treats Kira with reverence, only to learn that she lives with another man, his class enemy. This discovery is made during Taganov's raid of Leo Kovalensky's apartment, where the three main characters meet.

Kira's sexual attraction to Leo introduces an ever-present theme in Rand's prose, that of man-worship. The heroine surrenders herself to her lover, whose treatment of her is that of "a slave owner." This is justified, in Rand's terms, by Kira's adoration of the man in whom she alone discerns unrealized potential. Rand had intended to show Leo as an exceptional individual, "brilliantly witty . . . distinguished, aristocratic."[3] But in the novel he comes through as someone ill-mannered, lacking principles and ambition. The son of Admiral Kovalensky, who was executed for an alleged counterrevolutionary plot, Leo is doomed because of his social background. In 1924, during a massive student purge, he is expelled from the university, where (unlike Lev Bekkerman but like the author herself) he studied philosophy: Leo is well-steeped in Nietzsche and Spinoza. Upon losing his job at the state publishing house, Leo forms a partnership with a corrupt NEP man and sells stolen goods supplied to his shop by an OGPU employee, Pavel Suerov. Corruption goes unpunished in the communist state, where compliant bureaucrats and mediocrities thrive—unlike talented individuals who find themselves superfluous. The latter have two options: to escape abroad or to kill themselves by bullet or by drink. Filled with self-contempt and drinking heavily, Leo completes his own destruction by becoming a gigolo. Kira, who remains unbroken, plans to escape abroad: "She had to get out." Attempting to cross the Latvian border, she is shot by a guard and is dying in the snow at dawn. The novel's romantic denouement leaves the impression that the state destroyed her physically, but not spiritually: "Life, undefeated, existed and could exist."[4] Here again Rand reaffirms her belief in choosing life.

In the novel's oft-quoted dialogue, Andrei Taganov tells Kira that she, "like so many of our enemies," admires communist ideals, but not "our methods." Kira responds, "I loathe your ideals."[5] Ideals and practices, of course, go hand in hand. In practice Soviet ideology amounted to sacrificing individuals for the common good. Kira broadcasts the author's message, declaring: "What *are* your masses but millions of dull, shrivelled, stagnant souls that have no thoughts of their own, no dreams of their own . . . . ?"[6] The drudgery of Soviet life, its deadening effect on the mind and soul, was memorable to Rand from queuing for hours to receive her meager rations. These realities in the novel are cast against Soviet slogans, such as, "We are the builders of a new humanity."[7]

The Soviets claimed to have a superior morality. They denounced the bourgeoisie and enshrined the poor, the proletarian masses. The Soviet state called itself a true democracy, the freest country in the world. Permeated with humanitarian language, its propaganda was a big lie hiding the edifice of a dictatorship. For Rand, who could read between the lines, all humanitarian rhetoric became forever compromised.

The theme of *We the Living* is the role of the individual in a collectivist state: "individual against the masses."[8] Whereas the purpose of the state is to serve individuals, under socialism they are enslaved. Later, when pitching the book to her agent, Jean Wick, Rand argued that the time was ripe for an anti-Red novel. American audiences heard much about Soviet projects and "slogans on red banners," but her book told of what goes on "behind the red banners." Her novel was "a book for Americans."[9]

Rand wrote *We the Living* during the Great Depression, when the Soviet Union came to represent the land of opportunity for an unprecedented 15 million unemployed Americans. After the stock market crash in October 1929, America plunged into a deep, decadelong economic crisis. Soviet propaganda was effective, and in the early 1930s thousands of Americans headed to "the workers' paradise." The "gold rush to Moscow" was prompted, in part, by Walter Duranty, the Moscow correspondent for the *New York Times* who trumpeted the achievements of the Five-Year Plan. In 1931 the New York–based Soviet trade agency received 100,000 applications from skilled American workers; one-tenth were hired that year alone. The majority were ordinary people, lured by the promise of jobs at "the Soviet Detroit," a giant auto factory built by Henry Ford in the city of Nizhny Novgorod (and of which Duranty had written), and his tractor factory at Stalingrad. In 1934, when the U.S. embassy opened in Moscow, it was besieged by Americans, desperate to return. Because their passports were confiscated upon their arrival, most became trapped and would perish during Stalin's terror campaigns.[10] Yet Western left-wing intellectuals were reluctant to part with the myth of Soviet achievements even when the facts became available.

Eugene Lyons, the Moscow correspondent for United Press International, was in a unique position to know both sides. Born to a family of Russian Jews and brought to America as a child, he grew up among the liberals in New York's Lower East Side. In 1928, a committed leftist, he set out for the Soviet Union, an experience he describes in his first book, *Assignment in Utopia*. Lyons became the first Western journalist to interview the reclusive Stalin. During his six years in Moscow, he witnessed the influx of blurry-eyed American and other Western intellectuals who took guided tours through Soviet Russia. Among them were famous travelers, such as George Bernard Shaw, who were ready to "shout hallelujahs" to Stalin's Five-Year Plans. In August 1931, Lyons writes, Shaw "swept down on Moscow" to praise everything Soviet and disparage "the decaying bourgeois world." Lyons, who by then had parted with his illusions, portrays Shaw as willingly "collaborating in the deception."[11] In October 1931 Shaw's lecture "A Little Talk on America" was broadcast on U.S. national radio and later published in full by the *New York Times* under the title "Shaw Twits America on Red's 'Prosperity.'" Rand read the *New York Times* and might have seen it. Shaw described the USSR as the land of freedom and opportunity and urged Americans crying SOS during "the great financial storm" to jump aboard Stalin's ship, the only one that could carry the unemployed multitudes. His ludicrous lecture, delivered at a time when Stalin's forced collectivization was killing millions of peasants, contributed to the myth of a prosperous socialist Russia. Although Shaw's case was extreme, for he never recanted, he was just one of the many Western intellectuals who became apologists for Stalin's totalitarian regime. Anatole France, Romain Rolland, and the British socialists Beatrice and Sidney Webb all contributed to the myth. The Webbs wrote to admire everything Soviet—from economic achievements to the secret police—and forcefully defended Stalin, describing him as a "duly elected" politician whose power was more limited than President Roosevelt's.[12] The American journalist Anna Louise Strong praised Stalin in her book *The Soviets Expected It;* the journalist Ella Winter published her 1933 absurdly titled account, *Red Virtue: Human Relations in the New Russia.* As Lyons remarked, "The liberals had invented a Utopia and were finding it good."[13]

In *Red Decade,* which has given the name to the phenomenon, Lyons captures the Stalinist penetration of America. During the period, "the United States lived through a grotesque and incredible revolution."[14] In 1931 alone more books appeared on the "Soviet experiment" than in the previous thirteen years.

The American liberal press published unverified information about Soviet achievements, articles that read like "comic supplements to the somber Soviet reality."[15] Rand, familiar with Lyons's books, viewed his anticommunist stand as "uncompromising."[16] Publications by Soviet apologists made her furious.

In Hollywood, where at the time she lived in relative isolation, many professionals—screenwriters, directors, actors, and musicians—were procommunist. Jewish writers who arrived in the city of movies from the east were predominantly leftists. Struck with Hollywood's prosperity in the midst of widespread unemployment and suffering, they formed leftist associations and popular fronts and supported various Soviet causes. The do-gooders believed in moral duty to others, but they remained naive about communist economic structure and political oppression. The novelist Waldo Frank, first chair of the pro-Stalinist League of American Writers, sang praises to the Soviet Union. The Hollywood Anti-Nazi League, which claimed four thousand members, and the Motion Pictures Artists Committee held fund-raising events for Stalinist causes. Lillian Hellman, a successful playwright, screenwriter, and activist for the Screen Writers' Guild, defended Stalin's Show Trials against critics in an open letter also signed by the activist Jerome Davis and the novelists Granville Hicks and Dashiell Hammett, among other prominent Americans. In Hollywood communism became a political religion for some and opportunity for social climbing to others.[17] Rand and Hellman stood at the opposite sides of the political divide, but, curiously, Hellman was lionized long after the end of the Red Decade.

In 1932, the year she sold *Red Pawn* to Universal, Rand made news by jeering at the American Depression. In a brief interview for the *Oakland Tribune*, she said that "the high-priced executive in Russia does not have the physical comforts of the laborer in America."[18] Living in Hollywood, Rand had seen little of the country and mistrusted accounts of desperation, but she justly feared the masses' revolt. A beginner in American politics, she voted that year for Roosevelt on account of his promise to end Prohibition, which she regarded as a violation of human rights. Roosevelt's inaugural address of 1933, broadcast to an audience of 60 million, disappointed her, however. At a time when business and political leaders feared revolution and anarchy, Roosevelt promised that his government would assume responsibility for the economy. The institutions of the federal government created during Roosevelt's presidency, such as Social Security, the Federal Deposit Insurance Corporation, and the National Labor Board, were designed to protect the livelihood of impoverished Americans. Jewish masses supported Roosevelt's New Deal because the program appealed to their sense of justice and they felt a moral obligation to help the needy. Rand, like most conservatives, including the Jewish executives of the Hollywood studios who were Republican, saw the growth of federal administration and social programs established by Roosevelt as a troubling sign. She feared that America was moving toward a government-controlled economy.

From her mother's letter of 1933 Rand knew about Maxim Litvinov's visit to America, which brought about closer ties between the two countries. Anna Borisovna wondered whether Rand would now succeed in publishing her novel. "If I understand the content of it correctly, wouldn't the demand arise on alternative novels [in America]?"[19] It was a perceptive remark: by then the American publishing world was dominated by the liberal left. Rand reached out to her main supporter, Gouverneur Morris. After reading a draft of her novel, he called it "the Uncle Tom's Cabin of Soviet Russia."[20] Morris sent extracts from *We the Living* to the editor of *American Mercury* magazine, Henry Louis Mencken. (Mencken and Albert Jay Nock, another influential writer and editor, were the first to identify themselves as "libertarian." Both stood for individualism and against statism, and they strongly opposed the New Deal.) Having read Mencken's columns, Rand regarded him as "the greatest representative of a philosophy of individualism to which I want to dedicate my whole life." In a letter to Mencken she vowed that she was joining the battle against the Red-minded collectivists, "in defense of man against men."[21] Mencken thought her novel was "an excellent piece of work," but that its anticommunist message could hamper publication. He offered to send the book out to a publishing house of Rand's choosing.[22] She chose Dutton, in a belief it was not pro-Soviet, but the publisher turned down the manuscript without commenting.

The support of Morris and Mencken did not help place the novel. Rand's agent, Jean Wick, approached major publishers—Houghton Mifflin, Knopf, Viking, Scribner, Simon & Schuster, and Harcourt Brace, among others. Not all rejections were motivated by politics. Knopf had recently produced *And Quiet Flows the Don*, a powerful novel about the Russian Civil War, attributed to Stalin's scribe Mikhail Sholokhov. Their Russian list was full, they wrote. Other publishers complained that Rand's novel was too gloomy, too graphic, and not up-to-date, an indication of their Soviet sympathies. Rand wrote to her agent that she refused to believe "America has nothing but Communist-minded publishers."[23] In November 1934 Wick, still unable to sell her book, advised Rand against relying on political backers and suggested obtaining a quote from Upton Sinclair. Of course, Sinclair was an outspoken socialist, while Rand yearned to become involved in American politics on the right.

Rand saw the adverse political climate as impeding her aspirations. Yet the Red Decade was a time when her career was launched with the sale of her first screenplay, first novel, and first stage play. During this productive decade she plotted *The Fountainhead* and wrote *Anthem*, her second novel. For her first stage play, *Night of January 16th*, written in 1933, she received two simultaneous offers. One came from Al Woods, a well-known New York producer of melodramas, and the other from

E. E. Cleve, a British actor who staged plays at a small theater in Hollywood. Because Woods wanted to make changes to the play, Rand refused his profitable offer. Determined to succeed on her terms, she signed with Cleve, who promised to present a faithful production. Rand's play premiered at the Hollywood Playhouse in October 1934. On the eve of the first performance, she sent an excited letter to her family in Leningrad; she was living in the moment and was completely happy.[24] On the big day, she paused in front of the theater to see her name and the title of her play brilliantly lit on the marquee; the sight gave her "a real thrill."[25] Cleve had a good reputation as a producer, and a number of celebrities, including Marlene Dietrich, attended the premiere.

Night of January 16th was a courtroom drama inspired by *The Trial of Mary Dugan*, the popular 1927 play about a showgirl accused of killing her millionaire lover. Written by the American playwright Bayard Veiller and produced by Al Woods, it was performed widely in America and in Europe and also twice made into a film. Rand's other source was the recent case of Ivar Krueger, "the Swedish Match King" who transformed a family-owned business into a global empire. Krueger's companies lent millions of dollars to governments in Europe, Latin America, and Asia in exchange for a monopoly. In 1932 he committed suicide, at which time it was revealed that his financial empire was based on a gigantic pyramid scheme. The deficits of his match business exceeded the Swedish national debt. But for Rand, who idealized exceptional individuals, Krueger represented "a lone wolf" and a "man of genius" who stood above the crowd of mediocrities. (In 1968, introducing a revised edition of her play, she maintained that Krueger was denounced for his ambition and ability, rather than "shady methods.")[26] The play's protagonist, Bjorn Faulkner, is a financial colossus whose gigantic network, a type of Ponzi scheme, collapses when he fails to pay millions in dividends he owes. Faulkner never appears onstage. The action takes place in the courtroom, where Karen Andre, Faulkner's longtime secretary, lover, and partner in crime, is tried for his murder. Whether Faulkner was killed, committed suicide, or escaped to Buenos Aires is never determined. The play is a psychological mystery: contradictory evidence, presented in the courtroom, helps maintain suspense.

Although Rand's play was widely perceived as a version of *The Trial of Mary Dugan*, reviews were mostly positive. The main theatrical innovation of *Night of January 16th* was that the jurors who determined the fate of the woman on trial were drawn from the audience—and this trick became the focus of critical attention. Reviewers also noticed that Rand had written effective dialogues and that the show never became static or monotonous, even as the entire action took place in a courtroom. Nonetheless, Rand was disappointed with the reception because critics failed to recognize her work as "a play of ideas."[27] The theme, as she saw it, was "the conflict of independence versus conformity."[28] Her rebellion against tradition, rejection of community values, and need for personal distinction and power are apparent from her philosophical diary, which opens in April 1934 with an argument that a good life is lived intensely in pursuit of one's selfish goals. "Isn't it as Nietzsche said, 'Not freedom *from* what, but freedom *for* what?'"[29] The major Nietzschean concept, of the will to power, is interpreted in the play as ruthless self-assertion. The protagonist, Faulkner, who illustrates the idea, is described as "young, tall, with an arrogant smile, with kingdoms and nations in the palm of one hand—and a whip in the other." Karen Andre, his secretary, admires Faulkner's arrogance and strength: "He seemed to take a delight in giving me orders. He acted as if he were cracking a whip over an animal he wanted to break." Entirely in Faulkner's power, she satisfies his whims (during their lovemaking she wears a heated platinum nightgown) and partakes in his schemes. Despicably, Faulkner raped Karen Andre on her first day in his office. Even so, she defends him in her testimony: "He was not afraid of the world. He had defied its every law."[30] Defiance is a virtue in the play: Faulkner and his secretary-lover rebel against societal norms and have the author's endorsement. In the play, the defense attorney argues that Faulkner, who has defrauded thousands of investors, is "a scoundrel, a criminal . . . but still a conqueror."[31]

Conventional morality is presented through Faulkner's wife, Nancy Lee, and her father, John Graham Whitfield, a banker and philanthropist. Nancy Lee has bought her husband with her father's money; their marriage was a business deal. When in the courtroom she speaks of "unselfish devotion to the . . . welfare of others," her words are meant to sound hypocritical.[32] The philanthropist John Whitfield, as implied through additional evidence, may have actually killed Faulkner to prevent him from escaping with his millions.

Because the evidence in the case is inconclusive, equally implicating Karen Andre and Whitfield, the jurors, chosen from the audience, have to base their verdict on their own "sense of life." There are "two different types of humanity," they are instructed, those who pursue "egoistic ambition" and those who live for others.[33] The jurors' verdict of guilt or innocence for Karen Andre would determine which side they are on. Because each time it would be a different jury, the heroine might be found guilty one night and innocent the next. The ending was a test of the audience: Rand expected the public to concur with her message and endorse egoistic ambition.

For the producer Al Woods the jury gimmick was a salable idea, so after a short run of the play in Hollywood he renewed his offer for staging *Night of January 16th*. Having produced *The Trial of Mary Dugan* and made a fortune from it, he saw another possibility in Rand's courtroom drama. The new contract allowed Rand a bit more control of the text, and she accepted the terms. Woods planned an immediate production and asked Rand to come to New York. In late fall of 1934 she journeyed with Frank across the continent in their secondhand convertible. The trip took ten days. Along the way Rand was sending postcards to her family in Leningrad, and the fact that she and Frank were driving to New York, "the American Rome," impressed them deeply.[34] In Virginia the car went out of control and nearly overturned. The damage was too expensive to repair, so the couple continued by bus. When they arrived in New York, it turned out that Woods was unable to secure the funding for an immediate production. The couple's savings were depleted by travel, and Rand described their situation as "desperate, not to say a catastrophe."[35] In 1935 she and Frank lived on borrowed sums for half a year while expecting her play to be produced. Through her agent Rand was able to secure a job as a reader at RKO, earning a mere ten dollars a week.

Her collaboration with Woods on the play became exasperating for both: he wanted an entertaining show while Rand was bent on keeping her ideas intact. Woods argued it was her first show whereas he had been in the theater for four decades. But for Rand success involved more than recognition and money: it was the moral message that concerned her most. As an unknown author she could not win the battle for creative control: the result was a painful compromise. Finally, in September, she sent a telegram to her family in Leningrad announcing the first performance in New York. The Rosenbaums responded in a radiogram on September 11: "Extremely happy proud kisses cheerio."[36] On the opening night at the Ambassador Theater, Rand sat in the back row, yawning "out of genuine boredom."[37] In her view, the play was a "disgraceful burlesque."[38] The show was reviewed in major newspapers and described as a "stunt play." On Broadway it had a moderately successful run of half a year; it was also performed in summer theaters across the country. The play yielded substantial royalties: on occasional weeks Rand received $1,200, allowing her to forget about money problems and move to a comfortable apartment on Park Avenue.

Nine years after she arrived in America, Rand had a play on Broadway, attended by celebrities who submitted their names ahead of time to sit as jurors on stage. She had achieved success, but her bigger agenda prevented her from enjoying it.

When in a letter to her family Rand expressed frustration with the Broadway production, Anna Borisovna advised her to think back. Could she have expected, when first stepping ashore in America, that "her work would be performed in one of New York's theaters?"[39] In December 1935 the family received a stack of reviews, which Nora was now collecting in her scrapbook. The Rosenbaums had first read the play in fall 1933 and given Rand "the raves" she wanted. In Stalin's Russia, where the first public trials were launched in 1928, Rand's courtroom drama had a different meaning. In her play an individual stood defiantly against the People's State. An individual had a chance to respond and to prevail, and this thought alone would strike them as sensational. Anna Borisovna translated the play for Zinovy and the extended family. After the first reading at home she wrote to Rand: "Yesterday we had a great, festive, and memorable day. . . . We've always known that Alyonochka was gifted, talented, but I was still astounded with her work. I was impressed with its depth and seriousness." Nora was moved to tears by the "marvelous" play and called her sister "a genius" and "a great woman."[40] Zinovy, whose opinion mattered most to Rand, wrote of his impressions in detail. His father and grandfather had been lawyers, and his daughter's "deep knowledge of jurisprudence" made him "immensely proud." Rand's play struck him as "a classic example of a criminal trial." The opening remarks of the district attorney and the speech of the defense counsel delighted him. (Rand had attended a criminal trial and later studied the transcript, using it to describe court proceedings.) Zinovy read the play several times, admiring its dramatic effects, originality, and suspense. In September 1934 he wrote: "I continue to think of your play with delight. . . . In my opinion it should have tremendous success." Zinovy concluded with a prophecy: "You will live a long, long time, and I'm confident that I'll witness the day when your name will resonate around the world and will be spoken with deep respect."[41] Anna Borisovna urged her daughter to keep fighting for her rightful place with the same "unshakable faith in yourself and your calling."[42] A path to greatness "is hard and uneven," her mother reminded.[43] Like many eastern European Jews, the Rosenbaums valued cultural achievement. They expected Rand to describe the production, but she fell silent, often a sign of depression. Anna Borisovna observed that her daughter's mood changed quickly "from rapture to sadness."[44]

When her play was about to premiere on Broadway, Rand had signed up with a leading literary agent, Ann Watkins. The agent who represented Sinclair Lewis and William Saroyan began a new round of submissions of *We the Living*. Watkins eventually succeeded in placing the manuscript with Macmillan; the news reached Rand in late September, weeks after her play had launched on Broadway. Publication of her novel, she wrote to Morris in 1935, became "the greatest thing in my life so far."[45]

But to her birth family Rand reported the news in two casual sentences, making them think that she "has become spoiled" by success.[46] Their exchange was about to end: in 1935 Stalin launched mass arrests, and maintaining correspondence with the West was becoming dangerous. Anna Borisovna's advice to her daughter was to enjoy life, and when success comes, to take it calmly: "Happiness is found neither in money nor in fame, but in your own heart, in your deep sense of fulfilment. And you have everything to be happy."[47]

Rand was attached to her family: on one occasion she wrote that with no letters from home she could not sleep at night. In January 1934 she surprised her parents by asking them to "relocate to California where old people often retire for their health." Since they were not free to "relocate" abroad, let alone to California, Anna Borisovna replied politely but firmly that they had no such plans. But Rand decided otherwise. In March she wrote to the commissioner general of immigration inquiring about the immigrant quota for Russian citizens. The Broadway production made her financially secure, allowing her to take the first of the many steps to bring her parents to America. In December 1935 the Rosenbaums received her cable requesting their dates and places of birth. They responded in a telegram that they were happy with the possibility of a reunion.[48] The Rosenbaums were moved by her invitation to visit (and they discussed only a visit, since they had two married daughters in Leningrad), but explained this could not happen soon. By then foreign travel was all but impossible for regular Soviet citizens. In 1935 Stalin stepped up the terror to avenge the murder of Sergei Kirov, the Leningrad Party boss and member of the Politburo. Throughout that year hundreds of innocent people were arrested in Leningrad alone. The Rosenbaums, who had owned a business before the revolution, needed to avoid attracting the authorities' attention. Most of their doubts and anxieties could not be reported to Rand, for all foreign correspondence was opened and read. In February 1936 they were "stunned" by Rand's telegram saying that she had paid for their Soviet exit passports through the Intourist representatives in New York and purchased two tickets for the crossing. Permission for foreign travel and Soviet exit passports were formally issued by the Intourist office in Moscow but in reality were decided by the NKVD, the dreaded secret police agency that conducted the purges. The Rosenbaums would want to stay out of sight, but they had no choice now. So they started dealing with formalities and filed an application for permission to travel abroad. Rand sent telegrams urging them to hurry; one communication contained her words "don't lose a single minute of your time."[49] The Rosenbaums, hoping to receive an official response within months, were shaking their heads. It also troubled them that

Rand stopped writing letters: if she was so busy, their visit would only burden her. In April 1936 *We the Living* was published in America and Rand, occupied with promotion, could not spare time to write a letter.

Although *We the Living* fetched 125 reviews, Rand was dissatisfied with the coverage. Almost uniquely during the Red Decade the newspapers did not attack the novel they identified as anticommunist. Ida Zeitlin of the *New York Herald Tribune* praised the book as "passionate and powerful" and written in defense of an individual.[50] On May 9, 1936, the *Toronto Globe* ran a review, "Days of the Red Terror." The reviewer, identified as J.P.C., mildly complained that Rand's picture of Soviet Russia was dated and inconsistent with current depictions by "competent observers like Anna Louise Strong and Walter Duranty." The press described Rand as a native of Petrograd and Leningrad who found Soviet conditions intolerable. It wouldn't be hard for the NKVD to take notice and investigate. Rand might not have realized that her book's publicity jeopardized her family's safety.

When in late spring Rand fell silent, the Rosenbaums pleaded: "Send us at least a card."[51] In mid-June she informed them, in a telegram, that she was "feeling fine" and was "very busy."[52] This telegram offended her family: if she was so terribly busy, it was not too late to reconsider their travel plans. Rand continued to communicate through telegrams: she wanted to know whether her family received official permission for the trip. And since they hadn't heard back from the authorities, she stopped writing altogether. That summer, living in New York, she conducted architectural research for *The Fountainhead* and was also working on a new play, having signed a contract to produce a stage version of *We the Living*. In August she corresponded with Frank, who was away in Connecticut: he got a part in the summer-stock production of *Night of January 16th*.

On November 16 the Rosenbaums received an official response to their application: they were refused permission to travel. "Perhaps, this was only for the best," commented Anna Borisovna in a letter to Rand, in January 1937. "You obviously have no time for us."[53] At the end of May 1937 Rand sent a telegram inquiring whether her parents wanted to reapply for their travel passports independently. The Rosenbaums responded: "Cannot get permission."[54] The year 1937 marked the height of Stalin's Great Purge, and the Rosenbaums, who received letters from America, were extraordinarily lucky to escape arrest. Anna Borisovna, not easily cowed, wrote to Rand in July that her last telegram, which she had sent after months of silence, had surprised them; nonetheless, she encouraged her daughter to stay in touch. That year the American government issued a warning that communicating with Soviet citizens could endanger their lives. In January 1939, months before the global war, Rand would receive one more card from her mother.

In 1936 Rand sent a signed copy of *We the Living* to Ivan Lebedeff, to whom she owed her employment at the RKO wardrobe department. During her work on the novel she held long telephone discussions with the fellow anticommunist. Lebedeff's main contribution to Rand, as he saw it, was his faith in her; he reassured her during moments of doubts and apathy. He believed that she possessed both the talent and character to succeed.

In the United States *We the Living* sold its print run of 3,000 copies, far fewer than Rand had expected. (In comparison, by 1939 George Orwell's early novels had sold on average 2,000 copies.) Rand was tirelessly promoting her book by giving talks and sending copies to influential people, including Alexander Kerensky, Russia's former prime minister whom she had admired as a girl and who was now an exile. In the fall of 1937, attempting to order additional promotional copies, she discovered that her novel was out of print. This was in violation of the contract: Macmillan was supposed to keep the book in print for two years, but moderate sales were expected, and the plates were destroyed upon publication. Shocked by this, Rand met with James Putnam, then an editor at Macmillan, who agreed to issue a new edition if she signed a contract for what would become *The Fountainhead;* however, he offered only a small advance. When Rand requested a promotional budget of $1,200, the editor refused. The rights to *We the Living* were reverted to Rand, and it would be another twenty-three years before this novel would reappear in the United States. Rand's first novel continued to sell in Britain, where her publisher Cassell & Company kept it in print for years.

5

I versus We

RAND SPENT THE SUMMER of 1937 in the coastal village of Stony Creek, Connecticut. Frank had another engagement in the local summer-stock theater and she worked on a new novel, *Anthem*. Stony Creek was "an ideal place for a writer," she told a friend; in its peace and quiet she was doing her best work.[1] Rand completed this short novel in several weeks. In the summary, written decades later, she explained that *Anthem* "projects a society of the future, which has accepted total collectivism with all of its ultimate consequences: men have relapsed into primitive savagery and stagnation; the word 'I' has vanished from the human language, there are no singular pronouns, a man refers to himself as 'we' and to another as 'they.' The novel presents the gradual rediscovery of the word 'I.'"[2] The idea of projecting such a society was not new: it had been explored by the prominent Russian writer Evgeny Zamyatin, whose name would be familiar to Rand from her youth in Petrograd.

The central idea of Zamyatin's satirical dystopian novel *We* was the "relationship of the individual and collective, the individual and the state."[3] Written in 1921, it was promptly banned by Soviet censors. The author passed the manuscript to the West, where during the same decade it came out in English, Czech, and French translations. The English translation was issued in 1924 by the New York publisher E. P. Dutton. Rand, who admitted watching carefully "all the literature on new Russia"[4] that appeared in English, could not have missed Zamyatin's novel of ideas.

An early prophesy of totalitarianism, *We* was artistically brilliant and philosophically complex. It has inspired a number of twentieth-century works, including George Orwell's *Nineteen Eighty-Four*. Orwell, who in 1946 reviewed the French translation of *We*, later acknowledged that he modeled his novel on Zamyatin's. Although Rand did not mention his intellectual contribution (or influences of other writers, except Victor Hugo), she probably attended Zamyatin's courses in Petrograd on contemporary literature and the craft of writing. In his essays and talks the writer promoted the idea that influential books are created not by conformists, but "by madmen, hermits, heretics, dreamers, rebels and sceptics."[5] He believed that literature has the power to affect politics and compared good books to dynamite: while a stick of dynamite explodes once, a "book explodes a thousand times." Zamyatin's banned fiction and essays, written in defense of the individual, circulated widely. As he wrote in one of the essays, "We are living in an epoch of suppression of the individual in the name of the masses; tomorrow will bring the liberation of the individual in the name of man."[6] Curiously, Zamyatin aspired to work for DeMille, whom he met in Moscow in August 1931. That year, with the help of Maxim Gorky, who personally interceded on his behalf with Stalin, the Soviet heretic was released abroad. In Europe he worked as a scriptwriter. DeMille welcomed their collaboration, but Zamyatin never succeeded in coming to Hollywood. He died in Paris in March 1937.

The action in *We* takes place a thousand years after the planet Earth becomes subjugated to the power of the United State, which has replaced freedom with a "mathematically faultless happiness."[7] At the end of the Two Hundred Years' War, which has wiped out most of the planet's population, the state has solidified its magnificent "victory of *all* over *one*, of the *sum* over the *individual!*" The inhabitants of the state have become numbers. *We* is shaped as a diary of D-503, a state mathematician and builder of the *Integral*, a spaceship whose mission is to bring the creed of happiness to inhabitants of other planets. As the official newspaper announces, "Our duty will be to force them to be happy." (This recalls the Bolsheviks' theory of world revolution and their 1918 posters, which may also have been memorable to Rand: "We shall drive mankind to happiness with an iron hand.") D-503 begins his diary when the newspaper calls on all Numbers to praise the greatness of the United State. He faithfully describes their life and activities, supervised by the Bureau of Guardians. During "personal hour," the inhabitants march in their gray-blue uniforms while the state anthem is played through loudspeakers; they eat in unison, making the fifty chewing movements required by law. On "sexual days" the "Living Numbers" receive a pink ticket along with permission to lower curtains in their transparent houses. The state practices eugenics, and there are precise physical characteristics for permitting the "production of children," who will be taken away and raised in herds. Singular personal pronouns, such as "I," are banned, so the inhabitants refer to themselves as "we." They are told that "to be original means to violate the law of equality." But centuries of eugenics have failed to erase all differences. Despite surveillance and public executions of rebels, presided over by the Well-Doer, there are still dissidents. I-330, a femme fatale, is a rebel leader. When D-503 falls in love with her, he develops a soul, an "incurable" illness, and discovers the self. During the Day of Unanimity the dissidents oppose the annual reelection of the Well-Doer. The state cracks down: D-503 is subjected to an operation, which removes the organ responsible for imagination. He becomes an informer on the "enemies of happiness" and betrays his lover, I-330. She is repeatedly subjected to torture in "the famous Gas Chamber," in which oxygen is sucked out, but betrays no one. In Zamyatin's words, *We* was "a warning against the twofold danger which threatens humanity: the hypertrophic power of the machines and the hypertrophic power of the State."[8]

Rand used elements of Zamyatin's plot, shaping it to express her ideas and themes. Unlike Zamyatin, she believed a collectivist state was incapable of technological progress and scientific achievement. Whereas in Zamyatin's novel the state annihilates dissidents by using advanced technology, in the primitive world of *Anthem* heretics are still burned at the stake. *Anthem* shows a collectivist world that has evolved on the ruins of civilization, centuries after the Great Rebirth (or the revolution). Technology and science are forgotten; inhabitants engage in manual labor and use candles to light their dwellings. The idea of civilizational collapse after the Bolshevik Revolution could have been inspired by Zamyatin's essay "Tomorrow" and his famous 1922 story "The Cave," which depicts the postrevolutionary years in Petrograd, its famished inhabitants freezing in unheated apartments and leading a primitive, caveman-like existence.

In *Anthem* the collectivist state similarly turns individuals into numbers and practices eugenics. The narrator is Equality 7-2521 (Rand used telephone numbers and socialist slogans for characters' names). Like D-503, he is an inventor and is keeping a diary. The notable difference is that Rand's protagonist is not a state employee: he is occupied with his own research. His invention is primitive: he rediscovers electricity and builds a lightbulb. Because all individual activity is banned, Equality conducts experiments in a secret tunnel. (The secret tunnel also appears in *We*.) The symbol of lost civilization in both novels is a rail track overgrown by grass. The collectivist state in *Anthem* is more controlling and mean. It is run by powerful bureaucracies that have ruled that "everything which is not permitted by law is forbidden." (This implies Soviet tyranny as well as the treatment of Jews under the law in imperial Russia: everything that was not explicitly permitted to them was illegal.) These bureaucracies are also more restrictive when it comes to sex: males and females are sent to the Palace of Mating solely for procreation. Being different is a transgression, so the narrator, an aspiring scholar, is assigned to work as a street sweeper. In both novels love for a woman leads to overcoming collectivism and discovering the self. In *Anthem* the narrator's independent scientific pursuits also help develop an ego.

Unlike Zamyatin's *We*, Rand's novel is a work of a moralist: collectivism is presented as total evil and individualism as absolute good. In *We* characters are psychologically complex, but in *Anthem* they are mere abstractions, signifying two poles of a moral universe and the basic theme of striving for freedom. Rand's positive characters—the narrator and his beloved, Liberty 5-3000—are physically and intellectually superior to the rest; the negative ones are less than human. When Equality brings his invention to the Council of Scholars, they reject it because it was not made collectively and rule that the lightbulb be destroyed and the inventor annihilated. Rand alludes to the myth of Prometheus, the demigod punished by Zeus for bringing the fire of the gods to Earth. (In Western and Russian radical thought, Prometheus symbolized the romantic image of a man who liberated humanity from religion.)

Like Zamyatin's novel, *Anthem* employs themes from the book of Genesis. The objectivist scholar Shoshana Milgram, upon examining an early draft of *Anthem*, found direct biblical references.[9] Although most formulations were later deleted from the novel, references to the book of Genesis and the book of Ruth remain in the final 1946 edition. When the protagonist escapes into the Uncharted Forest, his beloved Liberty, upon finding him, says, "We have followed you . . . and we shall follow you wherever you go. . . . Do as you please with us, but do not send us away from you."[10] This recalls the lines in the book of Ruth. When Naomi, who has lost her sons, asks her Moabite daughters-in-law to return to their native lands, Ruth alone chooses to follow her to the Land of Israel: "Entreat me not to leave thee, or to return from following after thee: for whither thou goest, I will go."[11] Like Ruth, Rand's heroine determines her destiny. Although she submits herself to male authority, she is a willing partner. When alone in the forest, Prometheus and Gaea, as the protagonists rename each other, learn "the one ecstasy granted to the race of men."[12] Rand alludes to the parable of Adam and Eve to remind the reader of biblical women's strong sexual presence and to reject the doctrine of original sin; a recurrent theme in her prose is that sex is meant to be enjoyed.

Anthem's final part is saturated with Nietzsche's themes and language from *Thus Spoke Zarathustra;* it tells a story of overcoming collectivism in one's soul. Zarathustra, upon descending from the mountain, announces that the basis of all moral judgment is removed. The Superman, as the inheritor of God, will give meaning to the Earth. He will shatter old tablets and will revitalize traditional morality. In Rand's novel Prometheus and Gaea arrive at the mountain summit. Looking down, Prometheus observes "a world ready to be born," awaiting "a spark, a first commandment." He utters the word *I*, banned in the collectivist world, and proclaims, "I am the warrant and the sanction."[13] Prometheus renounces all that has enslaved him—his birth, his kin, and his race. (The statements also suggest the author's own rebirth in America as an individualist.) The protagonist banishes the word "we" and proclaims that "to be free, a man must be free of his brothers." (Rand is referring to Cain's arrogant question to God in the book of Genesis, "Am I my brother's keeper?" In 1943, formulating individualist ethics in her journal, she coined a maxim: "Man is *not* his brother's keeper.")[14] Prometheus becomes a destroyer and creator of new values: "I shall rebuild the achievements of the past."[15] His rebellious monologues are meant to clear the ground for a new rational faith—without mysticism and self-abasement.

In this novel Rand expounds on the tenets of her new faith. As she explained in her journal, "That faith is *Individualism* in all its deepest meaning and implications, such as has never been preached before: individualism of the spirit, of ethics, of philosophy. . . . Individualism as a religion and a code, not merely as an economic practice."[16] Religion, she wrote elsewhere, has monopolized the field of ethics and turned "morality *against* man." The old language of ethics, along with the words *reverence*, *worship*, and *sacred*, must be "redirected at its proper object: man."[17]

Rand's protagonist, after rejecting the established principle of living for others, formulates a code of individualism: "I ask none to live for me, nor do I live for any others."[18] In *Atlas Shrugged* a similar message, carved in granite, becomes an oath for members of a utopian community of individualists. Such a community of free-spirited men was first projected in *Anthem:* Prometheus dreams of building a new land with like-minded friends. Thus, the ending in *Anthem* incorporates elements of a utopian novel: the hero dreams of reforming the world.

A concise work, *Anthem* contains many of Rand's essential ideas, along with her aspiration of remaking the world on individualistic principles. In a 1938 letter to Newman Flower, the British publisher of *Anthem*, she wrote that the novel expresses "my manifesto, my profession of faith, the essence of my entire philosophy."[19] She never stopped emphasizing this novel's importance to her personally. She wrote it while planning *The Foun-*

tainhead and revised it a decade later, when working on *Atlas Shrugged.* Ideas from *Anthem* traveled to both novels.

Focused on her new novel, *The Fountainhead,* Rand did not attempt to speed up *Anthem*'s publication in America. In 1937 her agent Watkins submitted *Anthem* to three American publishers, who chose to pass. Rand decided not to persist because *Anthem* shared the theme of individualism with *The Fountainhead,* becoming, in her words, "one of those preliminary sketches that artists draw for their future large canvases."[20] In Britain *Anthem* was issued in 1938. Reviews were positive. Thus, the *Montrose Review* wrote on May 27, 1938, that *Anthem* was "the parable against the submergence of the individual in the State." *Reynolds News* also picked up political implications in the novel, writing on May 22 that "if the totalitarian State developed without check, a time might come when individuality would be altogether crushed."[21] In America this novel was published in 1946, at the start of the Second Red Scare, by the Pamphleteers, a small publishing company that printed libertarian monographs.

In 1946 Rand sent copies of *Anthem* to DeMille and Walt Disney, writing to both that she would like her story to be developed for the screen. In a letter to DeMille she wrote, "I think you and I are destined to make a picture together." She envisioned a movie "on grand scale," like "the magnificent spectacles" of DeMille's silent era, such as *The Ten Commandments.*[22] Rand may have expected the director to radically change his moral message, to shatter old tablets on the big screen. Six months later, the response came from DeMille's assistant, who conveyed the director's praise for her book. DeMille suggested that Rand approach his niece Agnes de Mille about the possibility of producing a ballet based on the story. Rand did not follow up.

6

The Fountainhead

THE FOUNTAINHEAD begins with a Nietzschean theme and a link to *Anthem:* Howard Roark stands on the edge of a cliff, laughing. He was expelled from a prestigious architectural school, Stanton Institute of Technology, as it's designated in the novel, because he rejected the curriculum. He wanted to design modernistic buildings—not Renaissance villas. Upon expulsion, Roark feels liberated, much like the hero of *Anthem*, who, after escaping the slavery of the collectivist world, laughs at the thought that he has been "damned." Roark is a born individualist and rebel: "I inherit nothing. I stand at the end of no tradition."[1] He doesn't care if he still has a family. When asked why he chose architecture, he replies: "I've never believed in God. . . . I don't like the shape of things on this earth. I want to change them."[2] Roark is on a mission to destroy old values and create new ones. There is a trace of Nietzschean blasphemy in Roark's contempt for the world, in making people feel they do not exist. When drafting the novel, Rand used direct quotations from Nietzsche to set the theme and describe her characters' motivations. She chose the book's main epigraph from *Beyond Good and Evil:* "The noble soul has reverence for itself." Each of the novel's four parts, dedicated to major characters, opened with a defining epigraph from Nietzsche. For the final part, "Howard Roark," Rand selected a quotation from the *Genealogy of Morals* that contains the words "a glimpse of man that justifies the existence of man."[3] Although she later removed these epigraphs, Nietzschean language and themes remain perceptible. Roark is invested with traits of an Übermensch, or "overman," the term Nietzsche explained in *Ecce Homo* as the designation of supreme achievement.[4] Rand's protagonist is a creator-artist, dedicated to his own talent and artistic vision; through this character Rand established the theme of individualism.

Rand read Nietzsche in her late teens, and his philosophy, particularly its ideas of personal empowerment and self-realization, strongly impressed her. The first books she bought in America were English translations of *Thus Spoke Zarathustra*, *Beyond Good and Evil*, and *Anti-Christ*—and these volumes bear her copious markings.[5] In the 1960s, having distanced herself from Nietzsche's philosophy, Rand praised him only as a poet whose works inspire "a magnificent feeling for man's greatness." This sentiment is at the heart of her novel, becoming responsible for its lasting appeal. *The Fountainhead*, in Rand's words, shows that "one's life is important, that great achievements are within one's capacity."[6]

The novel is built "in tiers," the method Rand explains in a letter of 1934: "A plot [is meant] for everyone and an idea for 'the highbrows.'"[7] Ideas were always more important to her than a plot, which served chiefly as a vehicle for her message. Rand defined the theme of *The Fountainhead* as "individualism versus collectivism, not in politics, but in man's soul."[8] Roark is an embodiment of the author's moral ideal. Single-minded and uncompromising in pursuit of his goal, he is among the few creative individuals who move the world with novel ideas. Rand invested her central character with her own psychological characteristics, remarking, "My research material for the psychology of Roark was myself, and how I feel about my profession."[9] Roark invites challenge by pursuing an architectural career without a diploma and prevails because of his self-belief and fierce ambition.

Rand had been planning *The Fountainhead* since 1935, working assiduously on her outline. She chose architecture as Roark's profession "because one cannot find a more eloquent symbol of man as creator than a man who is a builder."[10] In the fall of 1937 she began researching architectural history at the New York Public Library. She was particularly interested in early skyscraper design and modernist styling, and this led her to discover Frank Lloyd Wright and his book *An Autobiography*. Wright's account allowed her to penetrate the mind, character, and philosophy of a self-made architectural genius. She used Wright's concepts, his innovative ideas of "organic architecture," organic simplicity and plasticity, to convey Roark's style and philosophy of building. The story of Roark's first employment in the architectural firm of Henry Cameron mirrors that of Wright's beginnings at Dankmar Adler and Louis H. Sullivan's firm in Chicago. Some of Wright's projects, his "temple to man"—the famous Unity Temple in Oak Park, Illinois—served as a model for Roark's Stoddard Temple in New York, built as a Temple of the Human Spirit.

Later that year she found employment as an office clerk at the New York architectural firm of Ely Jacques Kahn, who alone knew that she was actually researching her novel. She studied drafting techniques, attended professional seminars for architects, and went to their house parties. Rand would dedicate *The Fountainhead* to "the great profession of architecture and its heroes who have given us some of the highest expressions of man's genius." Yet the theme of architecture was secondary to her novel;

as she explains in her journal, it was subordinate to her philosophy. She viewed an architect as an individualist, guided by his vision alone. Her research at the Ely Jacques Kahn firm suggested otherwise: the majority of architects worked for clients, but this did not change her mind. She wrote about things as they should be, not as they were, with a goal of establishing a moral ideal.

The Fountainhead was drawn from a variety of sources. Upon arriving in America, Rand was fascinated with New York's skyscrapers, which she perceived as the finest examples of human achievement in the free world. It was roughly the idea she formulated during her work on "The Skyscraper" script in DeMille's studio, an assignment she soon abandoned to pursue her own plot. Her correspondence with her birth family was another source of inspiration: it provided a glimpse of art and architecture in the collectivist world. Interestingly, in the early 1930s her sister Nora studied at the Leningrad Institute of Civil Engineering, Department of Architecture. Her cousin Nina Gouzarchik apprenticed as a draftsman under the prominent Soviet architect Noah Trotsky, who in the 1930s designed some of the best-known buildings in Leningrad, in the neoclassical style. For obvious reasons the name of this "other Trotsky" could not be mentioned in the Soviet press. Nina was becoming a social climber, she wrote, like Eleanor Stoddard in Dos Passos's novel *The 42nd Parallel.*[11] (The name of the businessman in Rand's novel, Hopton Stoddard, may have come from this letter and Dos Passos's novel.)

Rand's exchange with her father was a major source of inspiration. Back in 1934, she had solicited his ideas on human motivation. Zinovy, who had to overcome the Jewish quota on education, wrote that "masses of mediocrities" create impediments to genuine talent: "They instinctively struggle against everyone who is exceptional and hold him back as not to let him rise above the crowd. . . . But despite this and much more, the talent will achieve recognition. . . . The talent will find a way!" In Zinovy's view, "exceptionally gifted individuals," a select few, become "prime movers in science, art, and progress in general; also in spheres of philosophy and morality."[12] When Rand mentioned "inner integrity" as a source of motivation, Zinovy replied that she aptly expressed what mattered most to him personally. Understandably, he wrote, this trait is rare because "inner integrity" becomes an impediment in life's struggle, so people do not develop it. The majority is motivated by personal benefit and material success. If most people possessed "inner integrity," there would be paradise on Earth, he concluded.[13] The idea of creative integrity is pivotal in her novel. In 1937, asking Frank Lloyd Wright for an appointment (not granted until later), Rand wrote that her book was the story of an architect who remains true to his artistic vision: "His story is the story of human integrity."[14]

Roark's antagonist in the novel is Peter Keating. A mediocre "second-hander," he is motivated by vanity to become an architect and later lives off the work of others—mainly Roark's. Keating represents everything the author despises: his sense of fulfillment depends on what others think of him. In Nietzschean terms, "strong consideration for the opinions of men" is a sign of conformism.[15] Rand's initial inspiration for this character was, curiously, Marcella Rabwin, the executive secretary at Universal who had helped place *Red Pawn*. (Rand occasionally modeled her male characters on women and vice versa.) When Rand asked Marcella what she wanted out of life, her reply suggested that she wanted to live a notch above others. Thinking it over, Rand used her words to describe Keating's motto in life: "If anyone has a car, I want two cars. If anyone has two cars, I want three cars. And I want to be sure they know it."[16] The idea led her to develop a concept of "second-hand lives," initially the novel's title.

In her journal she described Roark as the prime mover, and

Keating as a "mob man at heart."[17] A social climber, he graduates from Stanton with honors because Roark helps him with assignments. There is no rational justification for Roark to assist the man, who envies his talent and who is described in the novel as a "parasite." (The dynamics of the relationship and division between higher and lower men appear in *Thus Spoke Zarathustra:* "O my brothers, see to it that no *parasite* climbs with you! . . . The parasite is the lowest type; but he who is the highest type nourishes the most parasites.")[18]

Upon graduation, Keating begins his climb, while still relying on Roark to help him on major projects. He joins the prosperous Francon & Heyer firm, achieving promotions through a combination of social skills and scheming. In contrast, Roark apprentices with an ingenious and near-destitute Henry Cameron, formerly a leading architect. Cameron, whose character is partly based on Louis H. Sullivan, Frank Lloyd Wright's mentor, has designed some of the first and most original skyscrapers. Sullivan's career declined partly because of the classical revivalism in architecture. In the novel Cameron works to realize his vision—unlike architects at most firms that work for clients. Likewise, Roark believes that clients are only the means, not the end. His attitude challenges the architectural establishment and creates additional obstacles to success.

When Cosmo-Slotnik Pictures of Hollywood decides to build a home office in New York, Keating enters the competition for the best skyscraper design. Roark doesn't participate, knowing that his original ideas will be rejected by a mediocre jury. (As Wright quips in his autobiography, "Any architectural competition will be an average upon an average by averages in behalf of the average.")[19] Roark improves Keating's design, accomplishing in a matter of hours what the talentless man could not do in a week. When Keating wins the competition and comes to share the prize money, Roark refuses to take the check. The design for the Cosmo-Slotnik building is below his standard and he forbids Keating to disclose that he had anything to do with it. Roark's sense of superiority fuels Keating's hatred. At the height of his worldly success as a partner in Guy Francon's firm, he lives in fear of failure and is tormented by envy of Roark's talent and confidence.

Rand used Nietzsche's major concept of the will to power, which he saw as the basic force underlying all human activities, to establish her characters' motivations. In Roark the will-to-power principle is sublimated in his creativity. His motivation in life is his need for self-realization or, as he puts it, "my work done my way."[20] He refuses a major commission from the Manhattan Bank Company because of proposed changes to his design. His revolutionary ideas frighten the board. When asked to compromise, to allow at least "a stylized Greek ornament," which would give the building a more traditional look, Roark argues, in a way Wright would, that buildings must have integrity. He chooses to withdraw his bid. Called "fanatical and selfless," Roark replies, "That was the most selfish thing you've ever seen a man do."[21] In fact, Roark is driven by the "self," his ego, which the author considers to be the best of all motivations.

Rand's archetype of an American hero would be embraced by Americans as capturing their distinct traits and values. Roark is an American in his struggle to beat the odds, his defiance of authority, his heroic individualism, and his will to prevail. He stands alone against the crowd, "knows what he wants and . . . needs no other reasons, standards or considerations."[22] Intensely ambitious and uncompromising, Roark presents an idealized version of Rand herself. Curiously, this character also resembles the type of the "new Jew" imagined by Zionists, who replaced Jewish powerlessness in the Diaspora with traits necessary to succeed in Palestine. Likewise, Rand imagined the type of man who could succeed in America. In a life-imitating-art scheme, Rand would reinvent herself in Roark's image and quote his pronouncements.

Untypically for a novel, and one written by a woman, all four central characters in *The Fountainhead* are men. In addition to Roark and Keating, there is Ellsworth Toohey, an influential architectural critic and Marxist as well as the novel's chief villain. He is most resourceful in undermining Roark, whom he instinctively perceives as a threat. Toohey is a foe of individualism and creativity. His regular column, combining architectural criticism with collectivist propaganda, appears in the popular *New York Banner*, the leading newspaper of Gail Wynand's chain. The last of the quartet, Wynand is a successful publisher of the yellow press; he established a newspaper empire and placed his intellect in service of the masses. The publisher's story is partly based on that of America's first media mogul, William Randolph Hearst. Unlike Hearst, Wynand begins his rise from being dirt poor. Dominique, the architect Guy Francon's daughter, works at the *New York Banner*, where, like Toohey, she writes an architectural column. Although a lesser character, she is responsible for much controversy in the novel. Dominique becomes Roark's secret lover, his apostate, and in the end, after two marriages, his wife. Her relationship with Roark begins with antagonism.

Roark meets Dominique in Connecticut. After refusing a major commission, which leaves him penniless, he shuts his office and heads out to work as a laborer in a quarry that belongs to Dominique's family. Their first meeting is depicted with sexual symbolism. From the edge of the quarry Dominique watches Roark working in the sun, his drill, sinking slowly into the granite, is "trembling in a long convulsive shudder." Rand brings the theme of creation into the scene through the primeval world of the quarry, where "sparks of fire" are shooting through granite. As Dominique watches Roark break the stone, future sexual violence between them is implied: "She thought of being broken—not by a man she admired, but by a man she loathed."[23] The heroine, Rand wrote in her journal, "is a masochist and she wishes for the happiness of suffering at Roark's hands."[24] There is also a sadistic streak in Roark, who enjoys breaking Dominique's will and defiance. The "rape" scene, which Rand argued was not to be interpreted as a rape, was unprecedented in literature of the time. In 1965, explaining the scene to a reader, Rand described it as "a symbolic action which Dominique all but invited. . . . Needless to say, an actual rape of an unwilling victim would be a vicious action."[25] But in the novel Dominique tells Wynand that Roark raped her, so the episode will continue to create confusion.

The quarry scene is artistically brilliant and employs Nietzschean themes from *Beyond Good and Evil.* Roark's insulting glance that strikes Dominique as "an act of ownership" is an indirect reference to Nietzsche, who writes that a man "must conceive of woman as a possession, as property that can be locked."[26] In *Thus Spoke Zarathustra* Nietzsche describes sexual love as an expression of man's power, his domination of a woman. Nietzsche's misogyny is well established, but Rand always denied her bias. Yet her views on the woman question were behind the times.

Dominique's impulsivity, fickleness, and irrational behavior are unusual in Rand's mature fiction. When Roark returns to New York, where his career picks up, Dominique works to hurt his reputation by engaging in "journalistic hooliganism" and publishing wicked articles about his buildings. Joining forces with Toohey, she conspires to take commissions from Roark and divert them to Keating, who is a partner in her father's firm. Her malicious campaign against Roark, whom she loves possessively, is not depicted in terms of revenge. Dominique is vying for power, but she succeeds only in harming Roark's prospects for a major commission. Although she carries on her secret affair with Roark and admires him (predictably, his face strikes her as "the face of a god"),[27] she marries first Keating, whom she despises, and later the publisher Wynand. Rand's intention was to show her heroine's progress from the collectivist world of

Toohey to Roark's individualism. Actually, Dominique's contradictions and self-destructiveness resemble Nastasya Filippovna's from Dostoevsky's novel *The Idiot*. But unlike Dostoevsky's heroine, whose volatility is precipitated by sexual abuse in her teens, Dominique's desire to hurt herself and the man she loves appears psychologically unjustified.

Ellsworth Toohey, the proponent of collectivism, bears the full brunt of Rand's sarcasm. He is the author of a popular architectural book, *Sermons in Stone*, and a major ideologist of the left whose lectures draw vast crowds. The character is based on Harold Laski, a prominent English political theorist and economist, who was also an influential spokesman for Marxism. Having attended Laski's lecture in New York, Rand has given Toohey his physical portrait and hypnotizing voice. Laski struck her as "a cheap little snide Pink."[28] Toohey, who has made a transition from Christianity to Marxism, preaches equality and humanitarianism while yearning for worldly power: he uses socialist ideology to rise as a leader of the masses. Because Toohey regards genius as "a disease," Roark becomes a thorn in his side. To permanently ruin Roark's reputation, Toohey persuades Hopton Stoddard, who wants to build the Temple of the Human Spirit, to hire Roark as his architect. Because Stoddard is deeply religious and Roark is an atheist, the project is doomed to fail. Roark builds the temple to man, a joyful meeting place, full of light, its horizontal lines not reaching to heaven. (Here Rand employed Wright's philosophy and design for Unity Temple, meant to be a "forum and good-time place—beautiful and inspiring," not a religious edifice.)[29] As Toohey anticipated, Roark's design contains something outright irreverent. The centerpiece of the temple is a nude female statue. Sculpted by Steven Mallory, with Dominique posing as model, the statue radiates the ecstasy of living; liberating joy replaces the notion of suffering.

When the temple is completed, Toohey strikes back with the article "Sacrilege." Although Roark's building is secular and thus the statue is justified, he is attacked by "the Bible brigade," the union of architects, and Wynand's newspaper chain. Roark is also facing a lawsuit, which he will lose. At Roark's trial Toohey testifies on behalf of the plaintiff and argues that the temple should be destroyed and rebuilt. Dominique's testimony is predictably inconsistent: she at once defends Roark's temple as a masterpiece and wants it destroyed, but for a reason different from Toohey's. She tells the judge that Roark was casting pearls before swine, and the public is not worthy of his creation. When Dominique attempts to publish her testimony in the *New York Banner*, Wynand fires her. The judge orders the temple rebuilt at Roark's expense. Initially designed to celebrate "the heroic in man," the temple is remodeled by a team of architects and given to Toohey's charity: it will serve as "a home for subnormal children."[30] Rand follows Nietzsche in his critique of weakness and celebration of strength.

Rand, of course, knew that Frank Lloyd Wright's Unity Temple was a success: he was congratulated upon completing his "temple to man." But in the novel Roark faces an angry mob and stands alone against the herd. The ancient theme of the destruction and desecration of the Holy Temple serves to amplify the vandalism of the collectivists. Rand depicts Roark as a truly religious man—in terms of dedication to his work. The idea is first suggested in her journal: "Scene of Roark on steps of Temple, at night, in the snow, his hat off."[31] The theme is further developed through the words of the sculptor Steve Mallory, who tells Dominique that Roark has "achieved immortality" through his buildings. Creativity substitutes for the Christian promise of eternal life.

Roark's reputation grows through his projects until he becomes "unstoppable" in his achievement: by the end of the novel he receives commissions from across the country. Then comes the famous climax: at Keating's request, he designs Cortlandt Homes, working anonymously and without pay on the condition that his design of the low-cost government housing project will remain intact. As was the case for the author herself, Roark's impulse to exercise full creative control matters more than money.

Roark is absent during the construction of Cortlandt Homes: he sails away with Wynand. As the two friends are relaxing on Wynand's yacht, they discuss ethical issues, such as altruism and egoism, and determine that selflessness is a feature of secondhand lives, originating in "the absence of a self."[32] (The play on words comes from *Beyond Good and Evil:* "a man without substance and content, a 'selfless' man.")[33] Wynand, who founded a newspaper and real estate empire using his energy and intellect, is a complex character. As a publisher of tabloids, he lacks integrity: he despises the crowd but knows that appealing to their tastes has made him rich. Upon marrying Dominique, he falls "desperately in love" with her, and she becomes his most precious possession (the theme of ownership in love is repeated intentionally). Unlike other characters, whom Rand refuses to humanize, Wynand is a tragic figure: Dominique will leave him, and he will lose his business empire. When Roark returns to New York, the first of several Cortlandt buildings has been completed, and its integrity is compromised. Keating tried but failed to prevail over government commissions and boards that demanded additions to the design. With Dominique now acting as his accomplice, Roark dynamites the housing for the poor, is arrested, and faces collective anger during a second trial.

This climax also tests Wynand's sense of power: he backs Roark in his papers and challenges public opinion for the first time. He soon discovers that he does not shape public perceptions, that the masses hold the keys to his business empire. As he publishes articles defending Roark, his readers and advertisers abandon him. Toohey, who has been plotting to take over the *New York Banner* and prepared the ground by recommending socialists to the staff, organizes a strike of unionized employees.

When reporters and staff walk out, Wynand has no choice but to yield and reverse his stand on the Cortlandt case. By the time his papers begin to attack Roark, Wynand's reputation and empire lie in shambles. Defeated by the collective, the publisher shuts down his remaining newspaper, the *New York Banner*, in time to save it from Toohey's takeover.

During the trial Roark refuses a lawyer and delivers a defiant speech—an opportunity for Rand to recapture her moral philosophy. As in the play *Night of January 16th*, where the verdict is based on the jury's "sense of life," it's not Roark's violent action, but the principle behind it, that is on trial. The main charge against Roark is moral. Rather than accusing him of destroying government property, the prosecutor delivers a critique of selfishness, referring to Roark as an "arrogant egotist." Destroying the home of the destitute is an aggravating factor, as it would be during the Red Decade, when the novel was written.

Roark begins his courtroom speech by pitting collectivist morality against individualist values and ethics: "The first right on earth is the right of the ego. Man's first duty is to himself." Roark argues that all creation and innovation belong to an individual sphere, that "a symphony, a book, an engine, a philosophy" are products of individual genius. (This disregards the fact that the Bible was a collective creation.) Creators are naturally selfish: they work for themselves, but their achievements become "the glory of mankind." He juxtaposes the moral code of prime movers, who prize independence, initiative, and freedom with that of parasites. "The creator originates. The parasite borrows. . . . He preaches altruism . . . the doctrine which demands that men live for others." A major point in Roark's speech is that, throughout history, innovative ideas were met with resistance. An outsider fighting the establishment, he expresses his loyalty to "every creator who lived, struggled and perished unrecognized before he could achieve."[34] This passage acknowledges centuries of Jewish discrimination in the Diaspora, Jews' striving to succeed in an alien majority culture by the means available to them, their own intellect and perseverance. Through Roark, Rand tells the story of the marginalized beating the odds, and of her own trial and triumph as an immigrant.

Roark bolsters his arguments by pointing out that America was built on "the principle of individualism," not altruism. This principle—each man's right to the pursuit of his own happiness—became responsible for the country's achievements. The reference to a natural rights theory derived from the Declaration of Independence appears unexpectedly in the novel. It marks Rand's transition from a Nietzschean version of individualism to the conceptions of the Founding Fathers.

The issue of individual responsibility is not addressed. Roark declares: "I designed Cortlandt. I gave it to you. I destroyed it."[35] This logic has no chance to succeed in an actual courtroom: destruction of property is a crime—even if intellectual property is involved. Roark's actions are defended from the perspective of individualism, which recognizes a man's right to his life and work. In the novel the jury becomes persuaded by Roark's arguments and finds him not guilty.

When in 1948 Warner Bros. was shooting *The Fountainhead*, the episode of dynamiting Cortlandt Homes and the trial speech created a major problem for the studio and the author. The Production Code Administration insisted on a proper explanation, and Rand had to revise Roark's speech, weighing every word. After six revisions and eight conferences involving the author, the Production Code Administration, and two attorneys, the original eight-page speech was expanded, becoming the longest ever in Hollywood history.[36] For Gary Cooper, who played Roark, the six-and-a-half-minute speech was hard to memorize, so the trial scene had to be shot in sections. According to Robert Douglas, cast as Toohey, Rand did not allow any improvisation and was highly possessive of her text: "She felt she had written the Bible."[37]

The novel ends with Wynand commissioning Roark to build a skyscraper, the Wynand Building. Erected on a lot in Hell's Kitchen, where Wynand started working as a boy, it would become a monument to his life. Roark designs the most original and tallest skyscraper in New York, this time working without interference: Wynand has given him carte blanche to implement his vision. Then comes the cinematic part: Dominique rides on a hoist to the top of Roark's construction site, rising above the city banks, courthouses, and church spires. "Then there was only the ocean and the sky and the figure of Howard Roark." Inspired by DeMille's *The Ten Commandments* and the heroine's remark in the film, "that's the nearest to heaven I'll ever get," the scene reaffirms Roark as an original creator of everlasting works.

Rand wrote this novel sporadically, suspending her work for as long as nineteen months; it took her seven years to complete. In 1938, with one-third of the book drafted, her agent secured a contract with Knopf. When Rand missed the deadline of June 1939, the publisher gave her a one-year extension. She also missed this second deadline, so the contract was terminated. As the family's breadwinner (Frank's casual employments in a cigar store and shoe store were insufficient to live on), Rand worked as a reader at Paramount and accepted other opportunities to make money. Back in 1936, at the suggestion of the theatrical producer Jerome Mayer, she wrote a stage play based on *We the Living*. This play, *The Unconquered*, failed to raise interest until August 1939, when the Broadway producer George Abbott bought the rights. The play opened at the Biltmore Theatre on February 14, 1940, days after Rand's thirty-fifth birthday. The premiere was attended by celebrities, including Mary Pickford, but the audience was disappointed. Reviews were overwhelmingly negative, and the play closed after six performances. Rand would never produce another work for the theater. The play's failure may have hurt her literary reputation: when Ann Watkins resumed circulating chapters of *The Fountainhead*, she received eight refusals from the leading New York publishers. At this point the agent suggested there might be something wrong with the novel: perhaps her characters were not human enough. Rand responded with a long letter and severed relations with her agent. In fact, the early chapters, written in 1938, were later cut and Rand ended up softening Roark's character.

The 1940 presidential campaign was another major distraction. Roosevelt was running for an unprecedented third term. Rand threw her support behind the Republican nominee, Wendell Willkie. She viewed Willkie as a crusader for individualism and capitalism, and thought, mistakenly, that he was a popular candidate. Both she and Frank signed up to volunteer full-time at the Willkie campaign's headquarters in Manhattan. The couple's savings were depleted by then, but money was never the determining factor for Rand. She worked on the campaign in the National Headquarters of the Willkie Clubs, seeking and distributing literature in support of capitalism and speaking on street corners to anyone prepared to listen. "I was at my best among hecklers. . . . I suppose that's my fighting instinct," she remarked later.[38]

During the Willkie campaign she joined a circle of anti–New Deal libertarian conservatives and was introduced to Albert Jay Nock, the author of *Our Enemy, the State.* Nock was a follower of the English philosopher Herbert Spencer, a defining figure of nineteenth-century conservatism, who applied the biological pattern of evolution to society and coined the term "survival of the fittest." Spencer's book *The Man versus the State* rejected all forms of government interference with the natural mechanisms of society. In 1940, during Roosevelt's presidential campaign, Nock revived interest in Spencer by helping reissue *The Man versus the State.* As he wrote in the introduction, Spencer's views involving "the reduction of State power over the individual to an absolute minimum" were valuable to the contemporary American reader.[39] Rand owned a well-read copy of this edition of Spencer's work and was obviously influenced by his theories. In *The Fountainhead*, the publisher Wynand's rise from rags to riches begins with his reading a volume by Spencer.

As Jennifer Burns points out, the libertarians Rand met during the Willkie campaign, such as Channing Pollock, a playwright and theater critic, and Ruth Alexander, an economist and public lecturer, "replicated the arguments of nineteenth-century laissez-faire" while remaining "circumspect about evolutionary theory."[40] Pollock became the leader of a newly formed organization of conservative intellectuals in which Rand took an active part. Following the November election, which awarded Roosevelt a third term, Rand produced her first nonfiction work, "The Individualist Manifesto." Written in April 1941, the thirty-three-page essay argues for the primacy of the individual over the collective, thus upholding a central idea of *The Fountainhead.* It provides a strong moral defense of capitalism. Rand begins the essay by referring to the Declaration of Independence and its principle of natural rights. She follows with her interpretation of the document, arguing that "these rights are granted to Man not by the Collective nor *for* the Collective, but *against* the Collective," to protect him against other men and the State.

Her definition of totalitarianism is effective: she views it as "the greatest threat to mankind and civilization." Totalitarianism rests on the notion that "the state is superior to the individual." Rand divides all human activity into "the Creative" and "the Political" spheres. (This concept was inspired by Nock's *Our Enemy, the State*, which proposed dividing society into "economic man" and "political man.") Reiterating the thought expressed in *The Fountainhead*, she maintains that all creativity responsible for progress is individualistic. In contrast, the political sphere is unproductive and should be kept to a minimum: "States and Governments have never contributed anything to civilization."

The development of capitalism throughout its history rested on a single source, an individual. Capitalism is the best social system because it employs "a man's natural, healthy egoism." Given the freedom to create, human nature can perform miracles: "Selfishness is a magnificent force. A system which can make use of it . . . is a noble system."[41]

The concluding part discusses false ideals of collectivism, such as "the common good," used as a cover by totalitarian regimes. Capitalism needs moral defense from erosion by collectivist slogans. While collectivism found its defense in Marx's *Communist Manifesto*, capitalism, Rand argues, "has never found its 'ideology.'" The time has come for capitalism to formulate its creed and ideals. Rand finishes with a battle cry: "Individualists of the World, Unite!"[42]

As Isaiah Berlin writes, Marx had identified himself with "the great international class of disinherited workers in whose name he could thunder his anathemas."[43] Rand directed her fire against communism while associating herself with a class of industrialists. In a letter to Pollock, she called her treatise "a basic document, such as the *Communist Manifesto* was on the other side." She was hoping that it would be published and signed by members of their political group: "Let us be the signers of a new Declaration of Independence."[44] Rand was carried away in her enthusiasm: the essay remained unpublished.

Around this time she reached out to Isabel Paterson, a libertarian intellectual, who had a book column in the *New York Herald Tribune*. Paterson, a novelist two decades Rand's senior, was working on her first nonfiction book, *The God of the Machine*. In it she argued that a free-market economy releases the utmost creative energy, turning an individual into "the dynamo." This human energy culminates when the economy is freest of government interference. The book contained a reference to Spencer's views on minimal government. Paterson became a friend and mentor whose discussions of American history, politics, philosophy, and economics influenced Rand. In the early 1940s, when Rand was completing *The Fountainhead*, the two women spent hours in conversation. She was so receptive to Paterson's ideas that the older woman referred to her as a "sister." When in 1943 their books appeared almost simultaneously, Rand's novel became by far more popular, putting her in a position to recommend her mentor's work. Rand regarded *The God of the Machine* as "a basic document of capitalism," while also consistently expressing the credo of individualism.[45] In 1948, in a letter to Paterson, Rand acknowledged her influence: "I learned from you the historical and economic aspects of Capitalism, which I knew before only in a general way."[46]

Absorbed by domestic politics, Rand paid less attention to the global threat: by 1941 Hitler had conquered much of Europe and was about to invade the USSR. Leningrad fell under siege on September 8; more than a million people would die there of starvation and disease. Rand did not write about the war and the Holocaust or anything that dealt with pain and suffering, experiences imprinted on the Jewish psyche. She promoted the notions of power and success. Although she could not entirely shut out thoughts about her family in Leningrad, she was able to withdraw into a habitual sphere of abstract ideas. European events interested her in a theoretical way, in terms of similarities between the Soviet and the Nazi totalitarian systems.

In summer 1941 Rand started working as a freelance reader for Richard Mealand, head of the New York office of Paramount Pictures. After hiring Rand, Mealand became her friend and advocate. He had contacts in the publishing world and recommended *The Fountainhead* to Little, Brown and Company, which had a reputation for producing serious books. The manuscript was evaluated in the house as "high grade literature," although "too intellectual and controversial" to sell. Still, the editor, Angus Cameron, made a dinner appointment with Rand. But when she launched into politics, he misjudged her comments, assuming she was an anarchist.[47] The new refusal put her in a despondent mood: Rand would never forget the night when she was about to give up on her book altogether. Frank, talking to her for hours, managed to reassure her. So she decided to dedicate the novel to him "because he had saved it." Much later, in the introduction to the twenty-fifth-anniversary edition of *The Fountainhead*, she wrote that "Frank was the fuel" helping her carry on with her work during the years when "there was nothing around us but a gray desert of people and events that evoked nothing but contempt and revulsion."[48] These comments, made in 1968 by the author of two bestsellers, reveal her despondent state of mind. Rand was prone to depression and lived entirely for her work. Early on she decided not to have children and to dedicate her life to the pursuit of her goal. At the time she had no hobbies and spent most of her waking hours at her desk. Her husband's moral support was essential: he balanced her moods and gave her a sense of reality. Frank and his brother Nick Carter, the journalist, were Rand's first readers. She discussed her ideas with Nick, who also proofread her typescript.[49] Frank contributed authentic American expressions for her novel.

The fate of *The Fountainhead* was decided with Mealand's next phone call to Bobbs-Merrill, the publishing house that had recently produced Eugene Lyons's book *The Red Decade.* Rand's chapters were sent to Archibald Ogden, a young, perspicacious editor new to the job. He read the manuscript within a week and phoned to praise it, but opinions on the editorial board were mixed. When the president of Bobbs-Merrill in Indianapolis, D. L. Chambers, wired him to reject the book, Ogden responded: "If this is not the book for you, then I am not the editor for you."[50] It was his enthusiasm that decided the book's fate. The contract that Rand signed on December 10, 1941, compelled her to complete the novel within twelve months. By then two-thirds still remained unwritten, and, to make matters worse, the small advance of one thousand dollars did not allow her to give up her day job as a reader at Paramount.

Rand's capacity for work never failed her, so she carried on with her usual determination. Her detailed outline for the novel allowed her to write at great speed. Staying long hours at her desk, she worked doggedly to meet her deadline, realizing there would be no further extensions. She typed the last pages on New Year's Eve 1942. The book was scheduled to be released in the spring, but the enormous manuscript still had to be edited. In the remaining months Rand had to cut its length and incorporate other changes her editor proposed. Tired and pressed for time, she accepted editorial revisions, the only such instance in her career. On Isabel Paterson's advice she purged references in Roark's speech to Lenin, Stalin, Hitler, and Robespierre. Historical names, Paterson told her, tied the book to a specific time and place. Ogden proposed changing the novel's working title, "Second-Hand Lives." Rand was not good at inventing appealing titles: *We the Living* was initially "Airtight." *Atlas Shrugged*, a clever title proposed by Frank, was previously "The Strike."

By the end of her writing marathon, Rand was exhausted and suffering from chronic fatigue. She had trouble concentrating and keeping up with a tight editing schedule. When she consulted a doctor, he prescribed Benzedrine. The first brand of amphetamine, it hit the American market in the 1930s. During the following decade half a million Americans used it daily; side effects were little known. Soldiers used it during the war to stay awake. Rand was pleased by the result: now she could go almost without sleep and remain focused. On one occasion, she boasted, she stayed at her desk for thirty hours. But the drug was addictive; its prolonged use (and Rand would take amphetamines for years) is known to cause mood and mental disorders. Rand was burning her candle at both ends.[51]

The Fountainhead was officially released on May 10, 1943. Rand, who had been awaiting publication for seven years, did not celebrate. Bobbs-Merrill was promoting her novel merely as a story on architecture. It must be promoted, she argued, "as an important, challenging, intellectual novel."[52] In a letter to her editor she called the publisher's advertisement "horrible crap" that "wouldn't sell a book to a half-wit." The success of the novel—and she expected to sell at least 100,000 copies—was a matter of life and death to her. She ended the letter to her editor with a plea: "My life is at stake. Also yours."[53] Ogden, nonetheless, would remain the one editor Rand revered.

For those unfamiliar with Rand's ideas, her flow of thought was not easy to follow. She perceived "a direct connection between architecture and freedom," apparently inspired by the status of architecture during the New Deal directives on large housing projects. But she made this point on May 8, 1945, when the world celebrated victory over fascism and, incidentally, when Rand was invited to address the South California Chapter of the American Institute of Architects. Elucidating the connection between freedom and architecture, she said that an architect is ("or should be," she corrected herself) an original creator. She argued that architecture was "the most individualistic of all professions," attainable "only to free individuals in a free society." Individualism was "the only sacred cause on earth," and by making an architect the champion of that cause, she showed her reverence for the profession. She quoted Roark's remark, referring to him almost as a real person, "that the curse of the world is not selfishness, but precisely the absence of self."[54] It was an inspirational talk that dismissed the idea that architects consider their clients' needs. She argued the opposite. And she did not mention the end of the global war, the bloodiest in history.

7

Success

Rand was thirty-eight when *The Fountainhead* came out. By late fall 1943 the book had sold 18,000 copies, far below her expectations, and appeared at the bottom of the *Herald Tribune* best-seller list. She blamed slow summer sales on poor advertising. During the war only twenty reviews of *The Fountainhead* came out, one-sixth the number that *We the Living* had fetched. These articles, however, were more substantial. Typically, critical response had dissatisfied Rand. But when on May 16, 1943, Lorine Pruette's piece, "Battle against Evil," appeared in the *New York Times*, Rand's editor, Ogden, phoned to break the news. A psychologist and former Smith College professor, Pruette proclaimed Rand "a writer of great power" who possessed "a subtle and ingenious mind and the capacity of writing brilliantly, beautifully, bitterly." *The Fountainhead* stood out in her memory as "the only novel of ideas by an American woman." Pruette applauded Rand's stance against collectivism and called Ellsworth Toohey "a brilliant representation of a modern devil," the one with "a fascist mind"; he used "the ideal of altruism to destroy personal integrity" and the ideal "of sacrifice to enslave." The book, she wrote, inspires rethinking "some of the basic concepts of our times." Pruette had no complaints about Rand's characters, describing them as "romanticized, larger than life . . . representations of good and evil." This was the best review of Rand's writing career. She wrote immediately to thank Pruette for her courage in stating her novel's theme uncompromisingly as the battle of "the Individual against the Collective." Rand added, dramatically, that the review "saved me from the horror of believing . . . that there is no intellectual decency left anywhere."[1]

Another review by an intellectual, Albert Guerard, appeared on May 30 in the *New York Herald Tribune.* A novelist, essayist, and professor of English (he taught at Harvard, where John Updike was his student), Guerard was twenty-nine and serving in the army's psychological warfare branch. His piece, "Novel on Architectural Genius," described the book as "marvellously clever" and "frankly intellectual," for it "fearlessly discusses life, liberty and the pursuit of happiness." The characters embody "one central idea, one single truth" and must remain abstractions, for "a man of flesh and blood is no argument . . . he is complex and unique." The theme of *The Fountainhead* is not architecture, but "the Genius, or Superman, vs. the Rubble of 'Second-handers.'" The main problem with the novel, as he saw it, was in arguing two dissimilar issues—that of the individual and that of the genius. Roark is a genius whose single-minded pursuit of one truth can extinguish freedom: "If he had his way, he would completely destroy individuality and liberty." Referring to Roark's courtroom speech, Guerard wrote that America became great "not because of the tyranny of a few supermen," but through the Jeffersonian conception of equal opportunity "and the willing cooperation of all men." This review at once predicted the novel's popular success and explained its lack of appeal to highbrows. It recognized Nietzsche's influence. (But the reader of that time would also be reminded about the success of the Superman comic book. Interestingly, this superhero was a Jewish creation, devised in 1938 by two young American Jews, Jerry Siegel and Joe Schuster. As Neal Gabler suggests, the perceived Jewish physical inferiority had been the inspiration behind their Superman hero.[2] Rand had her sources of inspiration, but her attraction to a superhero stemmed from the same psychological craving as Siegel and Schuster's.)

Rand dismissed Guerard's point that individualism is incompatible with preaching one truth. She wanted to spread her message and correctly believed that her book's moral certainty would draw an enthusiastic readership. The novel had a life-changing quality due to the singularity of its vision and persuasive power. Her most devoted readers soon launched word-of-mouth campaigns promoting *The Fountainhead* to everyone they met. Army servicemen, whose letters Rand particularly liked, prized Roark as a strong role model. *The Fountainhead* fan mail flowed steadily for several decades. Rand received thousands of letters from across America and beyond. Like the geography, the age, professions, and ethnicity varied. Her readers were college students, businesspeople, single people, and married couples; some were religious, others had no religion. Some of her fans unquestioningly accepted the book's morality and quoted back passages in their letters to Rand as though quoting from the Bible.

Rand's business acumen can be judged from her clever schemes to promote the novel. In 1943, seeking private sponsors, she approached DeWitt Emery, a company owner and president of both the National Small Business Men's Association and the Small Business Economic Foundation. Rand wrote to Emery, her political ally, that a well-funded campaign led by the anti–New Deal side would give her "a name on a national scale," spreading their message across America.[3] Business owners, however, did not see an immediate benefit in supporting a novelist. Rand, undeterred by this, later tried another approach. In a letter to Ross Baker, sales director at Bobbs-Merrill, she explained how her novel should be publicized. A New York book expert had told her that "the biggest fiction sellers of all times . . . have always been religious novels with a good story . . . and that *The Fountainhead* is a *religious novel.* So it is," she continued; "It gives the modern reader the same thing which simpler people get from a Biblical story—a sense of faith, courage and moral uplift."[4] Rand soon attained the renown she wanted. In 1945 Bobbs-Merrill sublicensed the novel to Blakiston, a small publisher that advertised it more aggressively. That year alone the novel sold almost 100,000 copies and became a national best seller.[5] In December Rand approved a syndicated comic book version of the novel, a mark of genuine popularity. *The Fountainhead* held more surprises: in 1949, after the release of the film version, it again appeared on the national best-seller list.

Because many readers requested information about the author, her publisher proposed that Rand respond in a general letter, which could be distributed as a pamphlet. Rand's 1945 letter "To the Readers of *The Fountainhead*" did not give anything away: "Don't ask me about my family, my childhood, my friends or my feelings," she wrote. "Ask me about the things I think." Rand continued by saying that she didn't write about people "as they are" because of "a blinding picture" in her mind of people "as they could be."[6] An idealist, she lived in the abstract sphere, and her characters were more real to her than people. As she later explained to a fan, "What I am interested in is the great and the exceptional." Her example of a "perfect human being" was Roark.[7]

The novel and the film would establish her standing in American popular culture. In September 1943, when sales of the book began to rise, Warner Bros. phoned to buy movie rights. Rand's asking price was a whopping $50,000. Her agent advised her to accept half, the amount the best-selling mystery writer Dashiell Hammett had recently fetched for *The Glass Key*.[8] But Rand had better instincts than her agent and wouldn't budge, also remembering that in the 1930s Universal traded *Red Pawn* to MGM for another property and profited. A few weeks later, on October 13, Warner Bros. met her demand. The *Hollywood Reporter* carried a notice about the major sale on its front page. The studio wanted Rand to relocate immediately to Hollywood to write a preliminary script. Her agent negotiated a luxury contract: she would be paid progressively from $500 to $1,000 a week. Rand reported to a friend that she became "a capitalist overnight, which is a wonderful feeling."[9] The idea took time to sink in. The day Rand earned fifty thousand dollars she and Frank went out to the same cafeteria where they used to order an occasional dinner from the forty-five-cent menu. But when the deal was finalized in November, Rand bought herself a mink coat for $2,400, and the couple celebrated with Champagne cocktails at the Roosevelt Hotel. "The only advantage to poverty," Rand commented later, "is that if you can get out of it, the contrast is wonderful."[10]

In December the O'Connors set out for Hollywood, departing from Grand Central Terminal aboard the famed express train, the *20th Century Limited*, which took upper-class and business travelers to Chicago. The modernized cars were designed in 1938 by Henry Dreyfuss, a Brooklynite and industrial design pioneer, the type of creative man Rand wrote about. In a way, the train ride to Hollywood marked the beginning of her new book, *Atlas Shrugged*, with its focus on railroads. En route she pondered the benefits of private enterprise. Upon arriving in Hollywood, she wrote to Ogden, whose "editorial genius" became partly responsible for her success, that "travelling in a private compartment will teach anyone the pleasure of capitalism."[11] That train ride was her final departure from poverty.

The couple expected to stay in Hollywood for a few months,

but they would remain for nearly eight years, until October 1951. The story in Hollywood was that Barbara Stanwyck, upon discovering *The Fountainhead*, had persuaded the producer Henry Blanke to have Warner Bros. buy the movie rights. She wanted the role of Dominique, but in the end did not get the role and quit the studio. Rand struck a chord with Blanke, who had worked for her favorite directors, Ernst Lubitsch and Fritz Lang. In her new celebrity status, she was assigned a huge office and a secretary to answer the phone and run errands. After seven years writing the novel, the sense of novelty wore off; adapting the book for the screen felt boring. Nonetheless, she handled the task well, producing the thirty-page synopsis in a few weeks. In the new year, having written a longer treatment and a draft of the screenplay, she discussed with Blanke the prospects of engaging Frank Lloyd Wright as a consultant for the film. Wright read *The Fountainhead* and wrote to praise Rand's architectural research. The theme of individualism was "as old as civilization," he wrote, but now it's lying buried under rubble. "You are digging in that rubble for our salvation as a people. . . . Your novel is Novel."[12] But he was skeptical about Hollywood's ability to bring ideas to the screen. Rand reassured him, vowing to "prove to the world that an honest picture with the great message *can* come out of Hollywood."[13] Because of shortages of building materials after the war, the studio postponed shooting the film until 1948, at which time Rand was asked to complete her adaptation. Although she had no legal rights over production, she controlled it by the power of her personality. Her adaptation was shot "verbatim," which in her words happened "for the first time in Hollywood history."[14] That year she wrote to DeWitt Emery that the picture would be "a real 'Manifesto of Individualism' on the American screen."[15] The studio also had big expectations, but the result was mediocre: *The Fountainhead* as a film became neither a popular nor a critical success.[16]

Back in summer 1944, upon drafting the screenplay for

Warner Bros., Rand signed a five-year contract with Hal Wallis. Born Aaron Wolowicz in Chicago, to a family of eastern European Jewish immigrants, Wallis joined Warner Bros. in 1923 and worked his way up to become the studio's production head. (*Casablanca*, which he had produced, became a wartime classic.) He had recently launched his independent company, which would release pictures through Paramount. Wallis was "the big man of Hollywood," Rand wrote to Ogden, and his new company was "the talk of the town."[17] Rand's contract allowed her to write for pictures six months each year, with a starting salary of $750 a week. The remaining time she would invest in her own work.

Wallis sought talent, and Rand became his first employee; the second, to her chagrin, was the playwright Lillian Hellman, a left-wing intellectual who had recently returned from a trip to Moscow. During the McCarthy era Hellman and her lover Dashiell Hammett, a committed communist, would be blacklisted by Hollywood. Like Rand, Hellman was a political radical and a leading writer in midcentury America who was also a pioneer among women playwrights. While their contrasting political beliefs made them despise each other, their paths occasionally crossed. Patricia Neal, who starred as Dominique in *The Fountainhead*, received the role because of her successful performance in Hellmann's 1946 Broadway play *Another Part of the Forest.*

Rand, now living on a ranch, rarely met Hellman. Because she never learned to drive, Wallis allowed her to work mostly from home. In July 1944 Frank began to look for a property in the San Fernando Valley. He found a house in a modernistic style designed by Richard Neutra and befitting the author of *The Fountainhead.* Located in Chatsworth at 10000 Tampa Avenue, it came with thirteen acres; the asking price was $24,000. At the time the area was sparsely settled; Tampa Avenue was unpaved, just a dirt road running through acres of orange trees. Rand was shocked by the price, but Frank persuaded her that, given the annual inflation rate of 5–7 percent, it was a good investment for her capital. (In 1963 the couple sold their Chatsworth property for $175,000.)[18] Unlike Frank Lloyd Wright, Neutra built for clients, accommodating their tastes and whims. The Chatsworth house was designed for the film director Josef von Sternberg. The avant-garde structure of steel, glass, and concrete was elemental in form and surrounded by two faux moats and an eight-foot exterior steel wall for complete privacy. A distinctive feature of the house was its entrance door, made of copper: a bullet-proof glass inset protected a wood carving of the Torah. The front door announced von Sternberg's heritage: he was born to an Orthodox Jewish family in Vienna. The O'Connors would spend more than seven years in this house, behind this door.

In 1949, when one of Rand's literary fans, the future novelist Ruth Beebe Hill, first came to see her, the famous door was intact. When Rand opened it, Ruth quoted from *The Fountainhead:* "You are the most profoundly religious person I've ever known."[19] Rand invited her in. The house had a huge living room with a philodendron rising from the center to the second level. With no screens on windows and doors, birds were flying in and out. There were two garages on the property. The breezeway between them had a copper roof holding eight inches of water, which served as a pool for exotic fish. From their second-floor bedroom the O'Connors could watch the fish in the pool. This and other ostentatious features attracted reporters. In 1947 the architectural photographer Julius Shulman shot the house and the grounds and captured the O'Connors on a walk through the birch alley. The thirty birches were Marlene Dietrich's present to Josef von Sternberg. Beyond the birches grew pomegranate shrubs, a combination possible only in Hollywood. Shulman took a picture of Rand in her first-floor study, which opened onto a glass-partitioned deck with a view to the foothills. Rand is sitting at her desk, which Frank had designed for her. In this spacious study she wrote most of her new novel, *Atlas Shrugged.* Shulman would remember Rand as "a brilliant woman" who produced one of the most popular books of all times, but who had "a narrow concept towards society."[20] (The latter impression was reinforced by Rand's remark, reflecting Spencer's laissez-faire philosophy, that small owners had "no right to be in business" if they could not compete with big companies.) In summer 1949, when *The Fountainhead* film was released, *House & Garden* magazine published a story about "an extraordinary house, an extraordinary woman, and an extraordinary novel about architecture." The house looked "peacock blue" from a distance, matching the color of a dozen peacocks walking its grounds.[21]

Frank was raising chickens and peacocks and breeding gladioli. He had started a small business, selling his flowers to hotels in Los Angeles. To Nick Carter, her brother-in-law, Rand reported that Frank had found himself as a farmer and was "permanently happy—and ardently enthusiastic."[22] In her first years at the ranch Rand was content with life. When she occasionally experienced writer's block, she would walk into the field to gather stones. All the rocks she collected were gray. She liked their sensual feel; sorting the rocks by size and depositing them in boxes helped her think. But Rand was a city dweller at heart and continued to miss New York. As Frank fittingly remarked, she loved the New York she had built herself—not the real city.

She was hoping to move closer to New York and have a house built in Connecticut. In 1945 she and Frank went to Taliesin, Frank Lloyd Wright's summer headquarters in Wisconsin, and spent a weekend with the architect. Rand asked him to design a house—ahead of her buying a lot. In 1946 Wright sent a drawing of a four-tiered mansion featuring a fountain, a tribute to the novel. Rand found it "magnificent" and thanked Wright for including the fountain: "That was as if you had autographed both my house and my book."[23] The architect's price, $35,000, discouraged further discussion. Rand paid for the preliminary drawings, but the house in Connecticut was never built. Nor did Warner Bros. engage Wright to design buildings for the film: his fee was too steep.

Hollywood was becoming split between procommunists and anticommunists. In February 1944 the Motion Picture Alliance for the Preservation of American Ideals (MPA) was organized with Robert Taylor as president. Rand joined this group on the condition that they would fight "Communism, not Communists." The battle can be won "*only* in the realm of ideas," she emphasized. She was soon on the executive committee, along with Gary Cooper, James K. McGuinness, Lela Rogers (her close friend in Hollywood), and Morrie Ryskind (George Gershwin's collaborator). Americans were open to communist propaganda because, she argued, they are confused "about the principle of Americanism."[24] Rand saw a crying need to educate Americans about communist ideology not in the least because the House Committee on Un-American Activities, formed in 1938, linked communism with Judaism.[25] As she explained in an article, "Textbook of Americanism," the country's basic principle was individualism. Her other contribution to MPA was the "Screen Guide for Americans," written anonymously in 1947, during the McCarthy era. The guide instructed filmmakers on how to detect communist ideas and prevent them from reaching the screen. In May 1947 Rand resigned from MPA over a conflict with McGuinness, a known anti-Semite.[26] She did not openly explain her decision but later similarly withdrew her support for another organization tainted with anti-Semitism. In the 1960s she resigned as a speaker from WBAI-FM radio station without explaining the reason. It is known, however, from her unsent letter to the station: "The specific reason is that WBAI permitted an obscene anti-Semitic 'poem' calling for the killing of Jews, and an obscene utterance, praising Hitler's atrocities, to be broadcast over its facilities."[27] As is apparent from the agonized drafts of the letter, anti-Semitism concerned her deeply, even as she claimed that her ethnicity did not matter to her.

Aside from the MPA, Rand socialized with a circle of libertarian business conservatives in Hollywood that included Leonard Read, head of the Los Angeles Chamber of Commerce, and William Mullendore, an executive at Southern California Edison. (Read and Mullendore's joint publishing company, Pamphleteers, first issued *Anthem* in America.) In 1944, at a dinner Read gave in her honor, Rand met both men and was impressed with Mullendore's uncompromising stance for free enterprise and against unionization. He would become active in the Foundation for Economic Education, a free-market think-tank founded in 1946 by Read. Around this time Herbert Cornuelle, another libertarian businessman involved in the development of free-market think-tanks, visited Rand at the ranch with his teenage brother Richard. Both were fans of *The Fountainhead.* Richard Cornuelle later described Rand as "most electrifying" and "extraordinary."[28]

Morrie Ryskind, the fashion designer Adrian, and Janet Gaynor, his actress wife, were regular guests, along with Ruth Beebe and Dr. Borroughs (Buzzy) Hill, a cancer researcher at UCLA. Adrian designed Rand's clothes for special occasions, and she frequented his fashion shows. Albert Mannheimer, a screenwriter then working in Hollywood on the adaptation of Garson Kanin's *Born Yesterday*, visited on weekends. A handsome man, eight years Rand's junior, he was a former Marxist. When in 1935 the two had first met in New York, he promised to convert Rand to communism, but the opposite happened. Mannheimer was strongly influenced by Rand's views, and at some point she considered making him her intellectual heir. Mutual attraction between guru and convert was unavoidable. In Hollywood the two would retire to her study, the most private part of the house, and discuss ideas with the door closed.

Reportedly, Frank did not enter his wife's study while Mannheimer was there.[29] Jack Bungay, who frequented the ranch as Rand's secretary, recalled that she "was terribly, terribly fond" of Mannheimer.[30] Bungay remembers Rand as dynamic, sensual, and "high voltage. . . . You could feel this magnetism, this dynamo inside this lady."[31]

During her initial months working for Wallis, Rand produced three screenplays, of which *Love Letters* became best known. Adapted from the novel *Pity My Simplicity* by the British writer Christopher Massie, it was a romantic story and murder mystery about an American soldier falling in love with an amnesiac woman who suffers from multiple personality disorder. Released in 1945, the film was nominated for four Academy Awards and became a box-office success. In the annual Filmdom's Famous Five poll, in the outstanding screenplay category, *Love Letters* tied with Tess Slesinger's adaptation of Betty Smith's novel *A Tree Grows in Brooklyn*, a film directed by Elia Kazan.

In late 1945 Wallis assigned Rand to write an original screenplay for a movie based on the atomic bomb. Rand interviewed General Leslie Groves, who directed the Manhattan Project, and Dr. J. Robert Oppenheimer, the wartime scientific director of the project in Los Alamos. In her note to the studio she explained the need to approach the subject responsibly, acknowledging that "the bomb constitutes a weapon of total destruction." They should not "preach anything" that can push the world to the precipice.[32] The idea for the screenplay was that only free men in a free world were capable of great scientific achievements, such as development of the nuclear bomb. Rand believed, mistakenly, that the bomb could not be produced by physicists in totalitarian states. Her outline does not include Oppenheimer's moral doubts, which he raised during her interview. Nor does it deal with the tragic aftermath of the bombing of Hiroshima and Nagasaki in August 1945. The screenplay remained unfinished. MGM was simultaneously working on a film about the bomb and didn't want competition. Wallis sold them the rights to "Top Secret," informing Rand about this after the fact. Furious that her project was sold without her knowing, she took leave for a year, investing this time in writing her novel. In *Atlas Shrugged* she employed her impressions from interviewing Oppenheimer to create the character of the evil-minded physicist Robert Stadler. The negative portrayal can be attributed to Oppenheimer's support for progressive causes and the communist movement. Most intellectuals of the time, including Einstein, whom Rand was hoping to meet during her work on "Top Secret," had socialist sympathies. Rand's final project as a screenwriter for Wallis was the 1947 adaptation of the novel *The House of Mist* by the Chilean writer María Luisa Bombal. Like "Top Secret," the film was never produced. In the fall Rand did not return to the studio. By then she was fully immersed in planning her new novel.

Rand could now afford to hire a cook, secretaries, and servants. In 1947 she employed a family of Japanese Americans, Ryoji and Haruno Kato, whose business had been confiscated after the Japanese bombed Pearl Harbor. Rand sympathized with the Kato couple and employed Ryoji as a handyman and Haruno as a cook, providing her with Anna Borisovna's recipes for borscht and beef stroganoff. The couple's teenage daughter, June, became the first typist of *Atlas Shrugged.* Although she was unskilled, Rand paid her generously to help her go to college.

Rand did not forget about her birth family. After the war she reconnected with her cousin Vera Guzarchik (now Glarner). She asked whether Vera needed material help and anxiously brought up the subject of her family in Leningrad. "If you know anything about them, *do not write* to me now. I'm afraid to know, and don't want to ask."[33] Vera, her husband, Henri, and daughter, Lizette, were living in France, although they had moved from Paris to Lyon, so it took a while for Rand's letter to find them. Eventually, Vera responded and sent a copy of her sister Tanya's letter from Leningrad. Tanya wrote, in July 1946, that there were few survivors in their large family. Rand's mother, her middle sister, Natasha, her cousin Nina, the Konheims, and the Guzarchiks were among those who had perished. During the siege they all congregated in the Guzarchiks' first-floor apartment, the most accessible for the malnourished people surviving on a tiny bread ration during the freezing winter. Anna Borisovna was the first to die, of cancer. Vera Glarner and her family in Lyon were impoverished by war and grateful for Rand's offer to help; in the coming years they would visit her in New York.

There were also people whom Rand helped immigrate. Her cousin Volodya Konheim, who had lived in Berlin before the war, lost his practice as a venereologist. Beginning in 1934 he was desperately trying to escape from Nazi Germany. Volodya was married and knew no English at the time, so Rand was afraid to sponsor him—until 1939, when, at Vera Glarner's urging, she finally sent him and his wife an affidavit of support. Having made a last-minute escape, Volodya settled in New York.

In 1946 Rand's former English teacher, Maria Strakhova, living as a displaced person in Salzburg, managed to locate her. A letter from the American representative of the Intergovernmental Refugee Committee in Austria arrived at Simon & Schuster. It said that Mrs. Marie von Strachow, a White Russian emigrant, was looking for Mrs. Alice O'Connor, who writes under the pseudonym Ayn Rand. Soon after, Rand received Strakhova's letter, stamped by a censor. From this letter she learned that her father had died of a heart attack in 1939. Strakhova could only imply how she managed to escape from the besieged Leningrad, and why it was necessary for her to alter her name. Apparently, she crossed the front line and, as an ethnic German, eventually made it to Austria. She feared repatriation: it would mean certain death in Stalin's camps. Rand was happy to find her former teacher: "You are now my only link to the past," she wrote.[34] She asked her attorney, John Gall, to help deal with the formalities of immigration. The refugee quota then applied only to former inmates of Nazi camps, so bringing the old woman to America would take two years. Strakhova arrived in New York in late October 1948, on the first boat of displaced persons. Rand arranged for her to reach Chatsworth. But Strakhova was Christian Orthodox and now deeply religious; moreover, she was in the habit of proselytizing. Rand tolerated her at the ranch for several months and then helped her former teacher settle separately.[35]

8

Atlas Shrugged

THE NOVEL'S ORIGINAL TITLE was "The Strike." The idea, so the story goes, first came to Rand in 1943, during a phone conversation with Isabel Paterson. As they discussed the response to *The Fountainhead*, Paterson said that it was the writer's duty to explain ideas clearly, so Rand should elucidate her moral philosophy in a treatise. Rand later recalled, "Then, on a spur of the moment, I told my friend, 'But what if I went on strike, if all thinking people went on strike. . . . That would make a good novel,'" she added. When Rand hung up, Frank, who overheard the conversation, told her that it *would* make a good novel.[1] She left the idea to ripen and on January 1, 1945, made an outline: "I start with *the fantastic premise of the prime movers going on strike*. . . . I set out to show how desperately the world needs prime movers, and how viciously it treats them."[2] Unlike *The Fountainhead*, where the focus was on a single creative individual, the new novel would depict a community of

American businesspeople and industrialists. Rand saw industrialists as "the spark-plugs" of production and innovation: like *artists, they participated in the act of creation.*[3] And since industrialists produce wealth and sustenance for life, they should have the power and freedom to make decisions; instead, they are snowed under by government regulations.

Disturbed by growing statism in America, Rand intended to show the consequences of government meddling in the market economy and warn against following a socialist model. *Atlas Shrugged* opens in a dystopian world on the brink of demise; the government is taking control of the economy, causing industrialists, engineers, and other creative people to disappear. Rand had witnessed similar developments after the Bolshevik takeover, when at least one million people, mostly elites, fled. Industrialists, businessmen, and engineers joined the exodus. It was then believed that Bolshevism would fail if all professionals fled. Rand's idea, essential to the plot, is that evil, left to its own devices, becomes self-defeating.

Since her discussions with Paterson, Rand had done her own research on capitalist economics. *The Road to Serfdom* by the Austrian-British economist and philosopher Friedrich Hayek became highly influential in America when it appeared in 1944. The book described the tyranny of a government-controlled economy and warned about the threat posed by socialism to individual freedom. But Hayek recognized the need for a limited government role in establishing health care and unemployment insurance. For Rand there was no middle ground: she mistrusted people who failed to take radical sides. In a letter to the libertarian writer Rose Wilder Lane, Rand blasted Hayek as a "middle-of-the-roader" and "an example of our most pernicious enemy."[4]

The works by the Austrian Jewish economist Ludwig von Mises came closer to her political and economic ideal. Mises fled Vienna before the Nazi annexation of Austria and arrived in America in 1940, settling in New York: the Volker Fund, a charitable organization established during the Depression, helped him obtain a visiting professorship at New York University. Rand was introduced to Mises in the early 1940s by the business and economics journalist Henry Hazlitt, a proponent of laissez-faire capitalism and the Austrian school of economics. (He was married to Rand's former boss, Frances Hazlitt, Richard Mealand's assistant at Paramount Pictures.) Rand's personal relationship with Mises was turbulent, but they viewed each other as allies: after all, both had fled European dictatorships. Years later, Hazlitt told Rand that upon reading *The Fountainhead*, Mises called her "the most courageous man in America."[5] The remark delighted her as befitting her self-image as a fighter. In his book *Omnipotent Government*, which Rand read as part of her research, Mises criticized the welfare state, along with industrial planning. His defense of capitalism and the free-market economy pleased Rand. But Mises, she wrote, "attempted to divorce economics from morality," a flaw that weakened his argument.[6] Rand believed that Marxist economics had lasting influence because of its moral appeal. She blamed Mises for skirting the moral issues and, as a result, failing "to convert a single collectivist." Rand raised this point in her 1946 letter to Leonard Read, who recently had launched the Foundation for Economic Education, to which Mises gave regular lectures. To "sell capitalist economics," she wrote with verve, one must reject the "collectivist" morality, along with its premise of the "common good." The objective of capitalist economics is not the welfare of the poor, but "the personal, private, individual profit motive. When that motive is declared to be immoral, the whole system becomes immoral, and the motor of the system stops dead."[7] Rand coined a vivid metaphor that would carry her argument in *Atlas Shrugged.*

As a lead-up to the novel Rand undertook a nonfiction project, "The Moral Basis of Individualism." It never appeared as a separate book, but it helped rework her code of ethics. The treatise occupied her for two years, until the summer of 1945, at which time she dropped it because her primary interest was fiction. Her notes reveal that she was establishing a link between the moral and the rational. As she wrote in her journal, "A code of ethics must be . . . completely *practical*—or else it is a means of self-destruction (as altruism is)."[8] Christianity's ideal of altruism, she thought, justified the sacrifice of the individual to the collective and, therefore, had to be renounced. In 1943 she decried altruism as "absolute evil."[9] By placing the self at the heart of moral life, Rand rejected Judeo-Christian ethics, the foundation of Western societies. "My three cornerstones: man is an end in himself; no man exists for the sake of another man; each man exists for his own happiness."[10] These ideas would help provide the moral defense of capitalism in the novel. Decades later, expressing her mature views, Rand spoke of an ethical code that upheld laissez-faire capitalism as "the only system that can be defended and validated by reason."[11] Her additional justification for rejecting Judeo-Christian ethics is apparent from her 1946 letter to a fan: "Until the morality of altruism is blasted out of people's minds, nothing will save us from Communism."[12] Rand was on a mission to change the way people lived and thought, having written on October 6, 1949, "My most important job is the formulation of *a rational morality of and for man, of and for his life, of and for this earth.*"[13] (Having rejected the notion of a supernatural God, Rand viewed herself as an innovator of ethical ideals. Religion had monopolized the sphere of ethics, she wrote elsewhere, "turning morality against man."[14] She believed that it fell to her to do the reversal.)

In 1945–46 a wave of union-organized strikes swept the country. The strikes indicated that labor had acquired too much power, a situation blamed on the Wagner Act of 1935, which gave labor unions exclusive bargaining rights. Rand had expressed her antiunion stance in *The Fountainhead:* Toohey, the novel's villain and head of the Union of Wynand Employees, organizes a strike that destroys the newspaper chain. Now rail strikes threatened to shut down the economy. On May 24, 1946, the *Los Angeles Examiner* came out with the headline: "Rail Strike Paralyzes U.S.; Cities Face Food, Coal Famine." *Life* magazine published a picture of wealthy commuters trapped in New York's Grand Central Terminal, stopped from traveling on the eve of the strike. Americans were angry with labor. *Newsweek* magazine reported that the forty-eight-hour strike left the country "on the threshold of chaos." The federal government "was trapped by powers which it itself had conferred on labor," the magazine wrote, also predicting starvation in postwar Europe that had become "dependent on food to mouth shipments from the United States."[15] *Atlas Shrugged* would absorb the articles' apocalyptic mood and themes. Like other anti–New Dealers, Rand opposed America's aid to Europe. In the novel Ragnar Danneskjöld, a philosopher-turned-pirate, seizes and sinks America's relief ships with cargo destined for the People's States of Europe. He is an anti–Robin Hood, robbing the poor to return money to the productive rich. (Rand's opposition to the Marshall Plan put her out of step with the times. Helping Western Europe rebuild its economy after the war was critical precisely because of Soviet expansionism.)

The railway strike hurt every industry and brought the country to a standstill. Because railroads were vital to the economy, Rand realized they should also play a central role in *Atlas Shrugged.* That year she wrote in her journal that the railroads in her novel act "as the blood vessels of the world—and we see what happens when the heart is no longer pumping."[16] Her novel would also show what happens when the industrialists and other creative people walk out. In *Atlas Shrugged* John Galt, the ingenious engineer who invents a new type of motor, launches the strike of "the men of the mind." The strike originates at the Twentieth Century Motor Company after its new owners decide to run the enterprise on communist and Christian principles. They begin to preach equality and brotherly love, paying the ablest and the worst employees equally. This destroys the incentive to produce. Eventually, John Galt makes a sinister promise at a factory meeting to "stop the motor of the world."[17] When engineers disappear, the Twentieth Century Motor Company becomes bankrupt, leaving hundreds unemployed. Later, faced with more government regulations that restrict free enterprise, Galt and his associates expand the strike, making it nationwide.

In 1947 America and the USSR entered the Cold War, and Rand's battle against communism took a different turn. In the spring the U.S. House Un-American Activities Committee (HUAC) began to investigate communist infiltration of the movie industry. The Jewish heads of the Hollywood studios, despite being Republican and anticommunist, perceived HUAC's scrutiny as a threat. Over the years its anti-Semitic twist had manifested itself in pronouncements by Congressman John Rankin and other Christian Nationalists. They equated Jews with communists and urged HUAC to investigate "the rape of America by Hollywood." Speaking on the floor of the House in 1945, Rankin declared that "the communism of Leon Trotsky" was based "upon hatred for Christianity."[18] Now the congressional inquiry into Hollywood communism, which Rankin among others had encouraged, sought information about the political affiliations of directors, actors, and screenwriters, many of whom were Jewish activists. On the opposite side, the anticommunist Motion Picture Alliance welcomed the scrutiny. The MPA provided most of the friendly witnesses for the high-profile hearing in October 1947. Among them were Clark Gable, Walt Disney (he would denounce labor unions, describing their strikes as "un-American"), Morrie Ryskind, and Ginger Rogers. Rand, no longer part of the MPA, volunteered to testify and was invited ad hoc. For an individualist, participation in the government affair was controversial, but single-mindedness protected her from doubt. On October 16 she and Frank boarded a train for Washington.

Rand was expected to testify about the penetration of communist ideology in film and read from her "Screen Guide for Americans." The guide instructed filmmakers not to take politics lightly. It comprised thirteen sections, each beginning with "Don't." "Don't smear industrialists. . . . Don't smear wealth. . . . Don't smear the profit motive. . . . Don't smear success. . . . Don't glorify the collective."[19] Her "don'ts" were directed against communist principles and also against stereotyping Jews as moneylenders and greedy businessmen. During the McCarthy era, film studios requested copies of her screen guide. When communist propaganda and vilification of businessmen disappeared from Hollywood films, Rand took the credit.[20]

On October 20, when she appeared before the committee, chaired by Republican J. Parnell Thomas, the inquiry sought her expertise only on the film *Song of Russia*. Directed by Gregory Ratoff (born Ratner), the film was produced by Metro-Goldwyn-Mayer in 1944, at the height of the wartime alliance with the Soviet Union. Naive and improbable, it told of an American conductor visiting Moscow on the eve of the 1941 Nazi invasion and falling in love with a peasant girl. The head of MGM, Louis Mayer, who testified ahead of Rand as a friendly witness, denied the film contained communist propaganda. He explained that the American government needed this type of picture "to assist the war effort." Rand said she believed Mayer's testimony, but then appeared to contradict him by arguing that "the mere presentation of that kind of happy existence in a country of slavery and horror is terrible propaganda." She mentioned the 1939 Nazi-Soviet Pact to support her contention that both dictatorships deserve equal treatment in film. When asked whether glossing over facts had anything to do with the wartime alliance, Rand argued that the American people had to be told the truth. *The Song of Russia*, she said, shows Stalin's Soviet Union as a place of "complete freedom and happiness, with everybody smiling." Congressman John R. McDowell attempted to turn her testimony into a joke by asking, "Doesn't anybody smile in Russia anymore?" Rand shot back: "They don't smile in approval of their system." This last part of the exchange became ridiculed by the liberal left and made its way into the opening of Lillian Hellman's 1976 memoir, *Scoundrel Time*. Rand's testimony was reduced to trifles, which made her angry and disappointed. The HUAC investigation further dissatisfied her by failing to address communist ideology.

The Washington hearings wrapped up amid negative newspaper coverage that widely interpreted them as threatening freedom of the screen. Rand, who attended cocktail parties of conservatives allied with Senator Joseph McCarthy, argued in her journal that the issue did not belong to the realm of civil rights. The Communist Party of America owed its allegiance to a foreign power and was financed by it. Therefore, the party and its members were guilty of "treasonable actions" and should be judged under criminal or military law.[21] A foe to moral quandary, Rand sought straightforward answers in complex matters. At this point she no longer doubted HUAC's legitimacy to investigate political affiliations of Americans. When the unfriendly witnesses subpoenaed by Congress became blacklisted or imprisoned, which was punishing noncommunists, Rand remained dismissive. In 1949 she argued it was the friendly witnesses who, as the result of the inquiry, "have taken a terrible beating."[22] In Hollywood her position was not unique. For Louis Mayer, who, like Rand, supported McCarthy, the issue also involved loyalty to America.[23] McCarthy, hero of the anticommunist movement, lost his power after 1954, when his fraudulent tactics were exposed and condemned by the Senate. But Rand's deep-seated fear that communism would spread in America was substantiated by world events, such as the postwar Soviet domination of Eastern Europe, the Chinese revolution of 1949, and the Korean War of 1950–53.

Rand initially thought it would take her two years to complete *Atlas Shrugged;* instead, she invested thirteen years in research and writing. After her testimony in Washington, she traveled to New York to collect background material about railroads and steel mills. She familiarized herself with the history and operations of American railroads, central to her plot and to her heroine's career. Dagny Taggart is a woman executive, the railroad's vice president in charge of operations. Rand gave her the job of A. H. Wright, head of the New York Central Railroad, whom she interviewed in November. Mr. Wright "was seventy years old and retiring, and I remember thinking how shocked he would be if he knew that he would become a thirty-four-year-old woman in my novel."[24] Rand researched the structure of railroad companies; taxation and government regulations; maps, timetables, and so on. She planned a scene with Dagny testing her new railroad, built with an innovative type of metal supposedly harder than steel. Dagny and her business partner, Hank Rearden, a steel magnate and inventor of Rearden Metal, take a ride in the cab of an engine on its first run over the new steel track. When Rand, overcoming her fear of accidents, decided to experience the ride herself, Paterson arranged it through a railroad executive who was her friend.

Rand had remarked that if she had not become a writer, she would have been an engineer. Hence her delight during the tour, given by a foreman who explained the diesel engine's workings and demonstrated the motors "and every sort of gadget." At some point the crew put her in the engineer's seat and let her drive at eighty miles an hour. "I have now driven the Twentieth Century Limited," she wrote excitedly to Paterson.[25] (Their friendship would end abruptly in May 1948 following Paterson's disastrous visit to Chatsworth. Her rude behavior with Rand's guests and an anti-Semitic remark—"I don't like Jewish intellectuals"—made privately, in reference to the dramatist Ryskind, were not forgiven. "Then why do you like me?" Rand replied wryly. "Of course! I'm not an intellectual."[26] Typically Rand was reluctant to reveal her background as a Russian Jew—until faced with anti-Semitism. At such moments she felt Jewish.)

While planning the novel, Rand wrote in her journal that she ought to "vindicate the industrialist—the author of material production."[27] She was not alone in championing the business community. In November 1948 *Fortune* magazine ran John Chamberlain's article "The Businessman in Fiction." A libertarian journalist, literary critic, and economic historian, Chamberlain found that a phenomenal number of American novels portray businessmen negatively. The crooked businessman had become a literary cliché. In Lester Cohen's *Coming Home*, steel tycoons sell "cracked steel to the government." Theodore Dreiser's *Cowperwood* trilogy, Dos Passos's *U.S.A.* trilogy, and Jack London's *The Iron Heel* all depict American capitalists as "fascist-minded." Businessmen's shady dealings are the focus of Upton Sinclair's *The Jungle* and Sinclair Lewis's *Babbitt*. "Balzac, who had a great influence on Karl Marx," wrote Chamberlain, "may have caricatured the businessman, but his caricatures had great and sweeping vitality. The latter-day novelists who have picked up Marx would have done better if they had emulated their master and gone themselves to Balzac." In conclusion, he mentioned that Rand was working on a business novel: "Maybe her story will mark a new beginning." Grateful for this mention, Rand replied to Chamberlain that she had read his article "with great pleasure and also with furious anger at the sordid parade of pink brains that you presented so expertly." She was glad to become known as "the antidote and the avenger." The concluding passage in his article corresponded to "the basic theme of my new novel—those who are antibusiness are antilife."[28]

Since the 1920s, when *Babbitt* was published, most novelists had expressed disillusionment with material culture. Rand would show that producers of material wealth had built America. *Atlas Shrugged* glorifies the industrialist and defends the laissez-faire capitalism of the Gilded Age. In the good old days in America, around the end of the Civil War, in 1865, businesses ran without government regulations. Dagny's ancestor in the novel, Nathaniel Taggart, was a "penniless adventurer" from New England who built "a railroad across the continent in the days of the first steel rails."[29] A colorful man, he rejected a government loan and pledged his wife as security for a loan from a millionaire who was her admirer. Apparently he repaid the loan on time, without surrendering his pledge. His statue stands in the terminal named after him. Dagny Taggart, who runs the ancestral railroad, walks past his statue on her way to work; this is her "temple" where she says her prayer of dedication. The theme of a temple to man, along with a statue, had previously appeared in *The Fountainhead.* Again, Rand redirects religious language to secular discourse.

Industrialists who succeed on sheer ability are cast in the novel against those who undermine their competitors through the agency of liberal politics. Dagny's determination to run the company efficiently and profitably puts her in conflict with the "parasites" in the government and in her own family. Her brother James is the nominal head of Taggart Transcontinental; weak, corrupt, and incompetent, he takes credit for his sister's achievements. This character is a variation of Keating, who feeds off Roark in *The Fountainhead.* James relies on political backing from his government friends in Washington, the socialist-minded bureaucrats who believe that there are more important things than making money. He echoes their rhetoric that "money is the root of all evil." (The Bible says, "For the love of money is the root of all evil." By truncating the quotation, Rand gives it a different meaning: she satirizes the liberals' disdain for profit, their discourse about "selfish greed.")

James Taggart exemplifies socialist economic practices, inefficient and wasteful. His costly altruistic project, building a railway line through the desert, is designed to help the People's State of Mexico. When the Mexican government nationalizes his San Sebastian line, as Dagny had anticipated, the Taggart company suffers significant losses. James's humanitarian rhetoric conceals his lust for power, which is apparent when his Washington friends appoint him to manage nationalized properties of the People's States of South America.

Henry Ford, Rand reasoned, opened opportunities for economic expansion; unlike him, government-compliant businessmen, such as James Taggart, become responsible for the opposite process that triggers "*the progressive paralysis* of the world."[30] In *Atlas Shrugged* the bad guys in Washington hold conferences on the national crisis they themselves created. The federal government is composed of unthinking figureheads who use compulsion to promote public welfare. Ever suspicious of humanitarians, Rand scrutinizes their language for hidden agendas. In the novel the State Science Institute claims to be "devoted to the welfare of mankind," but in reality it impedes innovation and progress. The government talks about its "duty to the underprivileged" while angling for broader powers. The bureaucrats create a useless Bureau of Economic Planning and National Resources and appoint Wesley Mouch as its head. (He embodies Rand's term "moochers and looters.") Mouch's regulations pressure industrialists to work at a loss, creating a chain of events detrimental to the economy. As the national crisis deepens, the government responds with more regulations, passing an Equalization of Opportunity Bill, a Fair Share Law, and an Anti-Dog-Eat-Dog rule, all meant to prohibit competition and discourage production. (Mouch's directives freeze prices and salaries, developments that actually took place during the war under President Roosevelt, with John Kenneth Galbraith in charge.) Finding it impossible to function, prosperous industrialists and businessmen disappear en masse, and economic "paralysis" spreads.

Tycoons like Hank Rearden, whose plant produces a new type of metal, are the backbone of the economy. Rearden illustrates the rational principle of capitalist economics that Rand described in her letter to Leonard Read as "the personal, private, individual profit motive." An individualist, a hardworking innovator, he makes his company the best and most efficient. As Rearden tells government bureaucrats, "If it's production that you want, then get out of the way, junk all of your damn regulations."[31] Rearden's story is reflected in the novel's title: he is the industrial martyr, an Atlas who holds the world on his shoulders. In a trial scene, ever-present in Rand's fiction, he is accused of breaking government regulations that control the sale of his metal. A panel of three judges delivers decisions peppered with socialist rhetoric and defending "the principle of the public good." Rearden, speaking in self-defense, insists on the right to own his production, distribution, and profit. The court slaps him with a suspended sentence and a fine. The only way to achieve common good, Rand argues, is to allow capitalists like Rearden to function without interference.

Rearden's remark that he is punished for his success and ability introduces an essentially Jewish theme. As is apparent from Rand's 1961 lecture "America's Persecuted Minority: Big Business," she viewed successful industrialists through the prism of Jewish experience. American businessmen, she said in her lecture, are a small and productive minority who hold the economy on their shoulders, but nonetheless who are "always regarded as guilty" and are penalized for their achievements, not faults. Alluding to the Sherman Antitrust Act of 1890, introduced to prevent monopolies, she writes that this "infamous piece of legislation" had criminalized the activity of successful businessmen. Further dramatizing the theme, she goes on to say that American businessmen, like racial and religious minorities, have to function under special restrictive laws. "In Soviet Russia, the scapegoat was the bourgeoisie; in Nazi Germany, it was the Jewish people; in America, it is the businessmen."[32] This rare direct reference to the Jewish people is meant to draw attention to her cause of laissez-faire capitalism.

Rand's insistence on full separation of politics and economics was inspired by her memory of Bolshevik expropriations and Jewish fear that the government could come and take it all away. The worry that America would resort to socialist practices comes through in her lecture when she says that "a businessman has to live under the threat of a sudden, unpredictable disaster, taking the risk of losing everything he owns."[33] The lecture elucidates her defense of the business community in *Atlas Shrugged*, in which successful industrialists are designed to illustrate major principles of market economics.

Back in 1945, in a letter to Henry Blanke, the producer of *The Fountainhead* film, Rand warned against humanizing her characters: "Heroes don't have toothaches, don't act like the folks next door."[34] Because productivity is a cherished value in the novel, Rearden lives to work. Dagny becomes his first major customer, deciding to build a new railway line with Rearden Metal. Her Rio Norte Line will stretch to the country's economic stronghold, Colorado, benefiting the Taggart company and other industries. For Rearden, Dagny's order is a chance to promote his metal. This is a mutually beneficial deal, and though Dagny and Rearden are attracted to each other, they talk only of production and efficiency.

Rand's focus on production invokes an unfortunate parallel with the works of socialist realism. The Soviet industrial novel is populated with cardboard characters who are heroically dedicated to manufacturing steel, cement, and other necessities. In *Atlas Shrugged* morality is similarly fused with politics and economics. Everything that benefits laissez-faire capitalism is a virtue. The traits impeding economic progress are vices. Rand vindicates productive and talented businessmen and dehumanizes their enemies: government bureaucrats are referred to as "parasites" and "subhuman."[35] Mouch and the gang around him are described as "sub-animal creatures who crawl on their bellies."[36] Having witnessed political indoctrination and class war under Lenin and Stalin, Rand employs the violent and divisive language of Soviet politics. This is an angry novel in which a handful of heroic industrialists are fighting against government wreckers. Since this is a war, Rand uses military terms. "I can't desert a battle," says Dagny as she struggles to save her railroad—and the country—from the consequences of bad government decisions.[37]

Dagny's Rio Norte Line, constructed in record time, is the country's best, since it's built of durable Rearden Metal. But the State Science Institute interferes: it issues a statement condemning the new metal in the name of public safety. (Such concepts are used derisively in the novel. As Rand wrote in 1949 to De-Witt Emery, "The guillotine during the French Revolution was being used by the 'Committee of Public Safety.'")[38] Actually, the government-subsidized institute is jealous of Rearden's independent success. Its department of metallurgical research, costing more than $20 million to maintain, produced nothing in over a decade. The State Science Institute will eventually blackmail Rearden and force him to sign a certificate releasing the rights to his metal.

The sabotage by the State Science Institute creates turmoil in the market; the Taggart stock crashes. To resolve the crisis, Dagny launches a new railway company, independent from the Taggart Transcontinental, and names it the John Galt Line. The ingenious engineer John Galt, who disappeared twelve years earlier, has been forgotten. But his threat to stop the motor of the world has become associated with his name. With the economy in shambles, people helplessly repeat, "Who is John Galt?"

The chant carries a sense of frustration and fear. But Dagny's John Galt Line will spell success—at least until government bureaucrats issue a new set of directives restricting the speed of her trains and their number of cars.

Rand's Manichaean view of the world is not new; dividing characters into heroes and villains worked well for her in the past. But now she doesn't stop at drawing a line between good and evil: in *Atlas Shrugged* the villains are being physically annihilated. Government regulations make Dagny's railroad unprofitable and impossible to run safely. A major catastrophe on the Taggart Transcontinental is imminent and will kill every passenger on the *Comet*. Ahead of the crash, the narrator passes judgment on the victims, arguing that the passengers have brought on their own demise by being "guilty or responsible for the thing that happened to them." Running two pages, the list of passengers about to be killed opens with a professor of sociology "who taught that individual ability is of no consequence." A mother of two, whose husband held a government job "enforcing directives," is culpable by association. The guiltiest is a professor of economics "who advocated the abolition of private property."[39] The passengers are paying the price for contributing to economic collapse. The scene of mass destruction of human life was written after the war, but Rand did not appreciate its implications. She focused on a biblical narrative—about the sins of man that caused the world's disrepair.

In her fictional universe, industrialists, like gods, create the material world and essential conditions for life. In monologues they express the author's rational, procapitalist, individualist morality. "We are the soul, of which railroads, copper mines, steel mills and oil wells are the body," says Francisco d'Anconia, the South American heir of copper mines.[40] His monologue on the moral significance of money is the most effective in the novel. It was endorsed by the economist Alan Greenspan, who in 1951, at twenty-six, joined Rand's circle of followers. Francisco proclaims that "money is the root of all good." America, he declares, is "a *country of money*," which also means "a country of reason, justice, freedom, production, achievement."[41] The monologue is a response to Marx, who castigated capitalist industrial society as dehumanizing and money as having the power to turn everything into its opposite. In the second part of his oft-quoted article "On the Jewish Question," Marx writes, "Money degrades all the Gods of man and turns them into commodities."[42] In the novel money is celebrated as a measure of success. Rand argues that wealth is created by human intelligence, not through exploitation of labor.

Rand aspires to overturn the most persistent stereotype of Jews as greedy businessmen and financiers. The novel defines creation of material wealth as a basic American value. Rearden, whom his dependent family persistently blames for being prosperous, learns to abandon guilt and to take pride in his achievements and profit. Then there is a major parable. Midas Mulligan, a prominent banker, "had once been the richest and, consequently, the most denounced man in the country." Like the legendary King Midas, he transforms everything he touches into gold, but in his case by taking intelligent risks. Harassed by "the humanitarian clique" and told he had "a dollar stamped on his heart," he defiantly changes his real name, Michael, to Midas.[43] Eventually, Midas Mulligan disappears, following John Galt and other strikers, and takes his gold to their retreat in the Colorado mountains.

The novel's mystery plot drives its onerous content, helping lighten it. Early on, during a cross-country trip with Rearden, Dagny finds an unfinished motor in the junk pile of an abandoned factory, the very one that was bankrupted by its socialist-minded owners. A guidebook explains that it's a new type of motor that can potentially supply unlimited amounts of energy by drawing static electricity from the atmosphere. Dagny begins her search for the ingenious inventor, not knowing that she is looking for John Galt. The search for Galt, full of adventure and mysterious meetings, binds the narrative. In one of the best action scenes, Dagny flies a private jet over the Colorado Rockies, only to crash-land in a hidden valley where the mystery man, John Galt, and other strikers have retreated. Here she learns that the reason for the strike is to "show to the world who depends on whom, who supports whom, who is the source of wealth, who makes whose livelihood possible."[44] The passage alludes to a Marxian critique of capitalism.

Galt's Gulch, a utopian community of individualists, presents the author's political and economic ideal. This is a patriarchal society of traders whose relationships are based on mutually beneficial transactions. In this land of plenty the businessmen are self-sufficient and need no government. John Galt, the author's ultimate ideal of a human being, is at once an engineer and a philosopher. Notably, this community is settled by "the men of the mind"—businesspeople, bankers, and creative intelligentsia. Reflecting the notion of Jewish intellectual prowess, Rand's values are merit-based.

Rand created her own bible, with new parables, and the oath taken by Galt's Gulch inhabitants served to replace the covenants. Carved in stone on a structure resembling an "ancient temple" are the words "I swear by my life and my love of it that I will never live for the sake of another man, nor ask another man to live for mine."[45] Their emblem is a three-foot-tall dollar sign of solid gold, placed at the community's entrance. A dollar sign is also stamped on their cigarettes. (A chain smoker, Rand came up with this clever gimmick.) "We have no laws in this valley," Galt explains, "no rules, no formal organization of any kind. . . . But we have certain customs, which we all observe."[46] Because they have rejected altruism, the phrase "to give" is prohibited. Members of the Galt's Gulch utopian community have no families because raising children requires sacrifice at the expense of achievement. (Probably for the same reason Rand advised her followers against having children.)

Flown to the Colorado Rockies on private jets (a modern version of Noah's Ark), the strikers are waiting for the altruist world to collapse. Their community of individualists prospers, but the collectivist world outside is perishing without its best and brightest. (Here the archetypal story of Noah and the flood reaches a climax: the socialist world perishes because of corrupt morals and social structure.) The time has come for John Galt to deliver his damning report to the struggling nation. His sixty-page speech, which took Rand two years to write, contains her deepest-held beliefs. Galt jams the airwaves of the country to prevent the Head of the State, Thompson, from making his anticipated report on the global crisis. Galt's "implacable voice" (television audiences cannot see his image) is coming from the Colorado mountains and fills "the airwaves of the country—of the world."[47] Galt begins his broadcast by explaining that the strike of "the men of the mind" is directed against the collectivists' moral code, the precepts of altruism, mercy, and self-sacrifice: "Your code declares that the rational man must sacrifice himself to the irrational, the independent man to parasites."[48] The morality of collectivists requires you "to serve God's purpose or your neighbor's welfare"; this morality has run its course. John Galt's moral code is founded on rational principles, the most important of which is that man exists for his own sake. One's life is considered the highest value; pursuit of happiness is the moral goal. The ethics is survival-based, which is why Galt declares thinking as the "only basic virtue" and the refusal to think as a vice. The purpose of life is creative work, and all work is creative when performed by a thinking mind. Therefore, man's only commandment is, "Thou shalt think."[49]

However rational, Galt's moral code cannot be analyzed or debated; it comes down as a final revelation. Later, in her nonfiction—articles and lectures—Rand would include long quotations from John Galt's speech to demonstrate the essence of her moral philosophy. Galt denounces the ethical code of "the mystics of muscle" (Marxists) and "the mystics of spirit" (the precepts of Judeo-Christian morality), the concern for the good and the welfare of others. He proceeds to defend laissez-faire capitalism and its underlying principles of "rationality, independence, integrity, honesty, justice, productiveness, pride." (These values are not new, of course; rather, Rand regarded them as the moral coordinates for success in America.) Galt augurs the collapse of the welfare state, governed by the morality of altruism. When "the looters' state" disintegrates, it will be the time for the strikers to return and rebuild the world on rational principles.

In *Anthem* Rand expressed her vision with absolute clarity: Prometheus vows to "raze the cities of the enslaved" and make his home the capital of the new world, "where each man will be free to exist for his own sake."[50] The denouement in *Atlas Shrugged* suggests that the old world must perish to allow Galt to realize his idealistic goals. In the novel's finale, laissez-faire capitalism receives an additional, legal defense. On page 1168 Judge Narragansett, one of the strikers, revises the American Constitution to incorporate a clause about freedom of enterprise: "'Congress shall make no law abridging the freedom of production and trade.'" But to accommodate the belief in laissez-faire individualism, much of the Constitution would have to be revised, for its opening phrase is "We, the people." It speaks of the nation's collective responsibility for its common destiny. As the late Jonathan Sacks, chief rabbi of England, points out in his book *Morality*, survival of freedom depends on cooperation and mutual responsibility for the world: "The free market and liberal democratic state together will not save liberty, because liberty can never be built by self-interest alone."[51]

As the collectivist world in *Atlas Shrugged* moves toward the apocalypse, Galt and the strikers watch it gradually submerge into darkness. Finally Galt proclaims, "'The road is cleared. . . . We are going back to the world.' He raised his hand and over the desolate earth he traced in space the sign of the dollar."[52] Leaving nothing to chance, Rand replaced the cross, the symbol of sacrifice, with a dollar sign, which she associated with freedom of the mind and of trade.

Galt's speech, with its focus on rational morality, later became responsible for utmost controversy. It contains a number of paradoxical pronouncements—for example, that "happiness is possible only to a rational man, the man who desires nothing but rational goals."[53] Rand had associated happiness with success and achievement. But, of course, there is more than one way to understand what it represents: the idea has been argued from the dawn of time. When discussing *Atlas Shrugged* in 2018, the philosopher Jordan Peterson observed, "You cannot make an exhaustive list of rules that enable ethical movement forward." But you can "tell stories that lay out broad principles," and all major stories have a religious core.[54] Rand knew the value of biblical stories, having used the flood narrative from the book of Genesis to re-create her fictional world on capitalist principles.

Rand's absolute rejection of altruism is the most debated part of her ethics. According to evolutionary psychologists, altruism is ingrained in human nature. Historically, individuals and groups have depended on each other to survive. As Elie Wiesel puts it succinctly, "Hadn't our people survived persecution and exile throughout the centuries because of its spirit of solidarity?"[55] Early American settlers also would not have made it without cooperation and the altruistic acts of individuals within communities.

Rand had created a perfect world she could control and fully believe in. In July 1948, when *The Fountainhead* went into film production, she reported to Ogden that the crew would be shooting the scene in the local quarry. "I do feel somewhat in the position of a god, since something which I made out of spirit is now going to be translated into matter."[56] By the time she wrote *Atlas Shrugged* she thought her ideas were infallible, but whether the larger world would accept them remained to be seen.

Rand was finishing *Atlas Shrugged* in New York, where she and Frank had relocated in 1951. As a best-selling writer whose previous book had been made into a film, she was in a position to choose a publisher. By 1956 *The Fountainhead* had sold 700,000 copies, so major New York publishers approached her and her agent inquiring about the new novel. Rand compiled "A List of Qualifications of Ideal Publisher," which included understanding her book's nature, ability to sell it aggressively, and enthusiasm for the publishing job and "for me specifically."[57] In late 1955 she and her new agent, Alan Collins of Curtis Brown, were ready to meet potential publishers. To simplify the search, Rand drew up a list of four: Viking Press (because Archibald Ogden, her trusted editor, was a consultant there), Knopf, McGraw-Hill, and Random House. Hiram Haydn, an editor who had replaced Ogden at Bobbs-Merrill and with whom Rand was on friendly terms, now worked at Random House. Rand phoned Haydn to ask whether its president, Bennett Cerf, a New York–born Jew, and his business partner, Donald Klopfer, were communists. Haydn reassured her and Rand agreed to join them for lunch. During the meeting she explained the book's theme as an uncompromising defense of capitalism. Klopfer perceptively remarked that this theme would conflict with Judeo-Christian ethics. Rand was impressed: she wanted her editors to understand what they were producing. She also liked Cerf's straightforwardness: he admitted that he found her philosophy of rational self-interest "abhorrent"; nonetheless, they were willing to publish anything she wrote. Cerf had read parts of the book, but not John Galt's speech, which remained uncompleted. Haydn, also present during this meeting, later wrote in his memoir, *Words*

& Faces, that he believed a publisher should produce books "with all sorts of political and social coloration."[58] The luncheon meeting with the Random House directors made a strong impression on Rand and, after checking out other publishers on her list, she returned to discuss the terms. Rand requested an advance of $50,000, a guaranteed first printing of 75,000 to 100,000 copies, and a promotion budget of $25,000. Cerf accepted her conditions.

Having become fully confident as a writer, Rand refused to accept editorial changes, which Haydn offered. When eventually she submitted the entire manuscript, along with John Galt's speech, the agreed-on length of 600,000 words was exceeded. Even so, she refused to make cuts. This is when Cerf had to step in and reason with the stubborn author. As he recounts in his memoir *At Random*, he told Rand that nobody would read the entire speech: "You've said it all three or four times before. . . . You've got to cut it." Looking at him with "those piercing eyes," Rand calmly asked, "Would you cut the Bible?" Rand was "a remarkable woman" and they had become friends, but arguing with her was "like running your head against a stone wall."[59] So it was agreed that she would cover the expenses for exceeding the contract size by 45,000 words.

The manuscript was passed on to Bertha Krantz, chief copy editor at Random House. It would normally take her a couple of weeks to show the proposed revisions in style and grammar. But Rand questioned her judgment with each word and punctuation mark, so the meetings stretched for an unprecedented several months. "Everything had to be explained to her in painstaking detail and, according to her philosophy, had to be *rational*." For a while they met in Haydn's office, and Rand would turn to him for a second opinion: "Hiram, is Bert right?"[60] When later they worked at the author's New York apartment, Krantz realized that Rand's stony facade concealed fear and insecurity. Learning that Krantz lived in the Bronx, Rand commented it was a "risky" area; she was also appalled to know that the copy editor took the subway. Living in her safe neighborhood, in a building with a doorman, Rand still bolted her door with steel locks, a habit of many Russian immigrants. Krantz, whose Jewish family immigrated from the same part of Europe, was amused that Rand was silent about her ethnicity. She had "built herself" and wouldn't let people know what she was really like.[61] Although Rand had created herself in the image of her heroic characters, she harbored a typically Jewish—and immigrant—dichotomy between self-confidence and insecurity. Like other eastern European Jews who had witnessed lawlessness, war, and privation, she viewed America as a safe haven. For decades she was afraid of venturing abroad and of taking a plane, thinking it might be hijacked by Stalin's agents.

Atlas Shrugged was published on October 10, 1957, with a first press run of 100,000 copies. Rand's fame as the author of *The Fountainhead*, the publisher's aggressive advertising, and her new novel's controversy contributed to its success. Within days the book appeared as number six on the *New York Times* best-seller list; it then peaked at number four, where it stayed for six weeks. Before the year's end the novel had sold 70,000 copies, becoming Rand's first true best seller. *Atlas Shrugged* was reviewed by every newspaper and attacked on all sides. A decade before her novel's publication, she had foretold it would become "the most controversial book of this century," and she thought that the political left would not be her biggest opponents.[62] In fact, liberal publications treated her book more respectfully: conservatives were insulted by Rand's mockery of Christianity. On October 13 the *New York Times* published a sympathetic profile, "Talk with Ayn Rand." The drama critic Lewis Nichols was amused that Rand, like her characters, spoke in monologues. His comments were mild: "Miss Rand makes no secret of her thoughts on morality, government, justice, business, do-gooders or the doctrine of original sin." Rand believed that her rational morality was "the greatest guarantee of a better world." She spoke of her work on the novel: above her desk she had a railroad map with the Taggart lines marked on it.

Simultaneously, the *New York Times Book Review* ran a negative piece by Granville Hicks, a novelist and reformed Marxist. Hicks compared the author's force in delivering her message with "a battering ram demolish[ing] the walls of a hostile city." Like most reviewers, he dismissed the novel's literary value, his charge being the characters' lack of sophistication (good guys versus bad guys); still, he thought that *Atlas Shrugged* was an earnest book, "and unremitting in its earnesty." His most damaging comment was at the end: despite the author's proclaimed love of life, "it seems clear that the book is written out of hate."[63] (Rand kept this review in a folder marked "BS articles.")

John Hutchens's piece in the *New York Herald Tribune* on October 10 was more critical. According to Hutchens, *Atlas Shrugged* was "a novelizing tract" and "a puppet show in which the figures are . . . speaking in the puppet master's voice." Rand possessed "undoubted narrative power," but her characters were either "heroes all of stainless steel" or villains and "self-confessed scoundrels," just as in works by "proletarian novelists writing on the other side of the fence." Hutchens, however, acknowledged Rand's courage in challenging tradition: "It is not every novelist who would dare to come right out and give us to understand that the Sermon on the Mount has seen its best days."

Time magazine's review, "The Solid-Gold Dollar Sign," published on October 14, opened with an attack: "Is it a novel? Is it a nightmare? Is it Superman—in the comic strip or the Nietzschean version?" The unsigned piece described the novel as a caricature of capitalism and dubbed John Galt "the Moses of the moneybags." Rand was derided as "a sort of literary Horsewoman of the Apocalypse" who shatters the world "with half a million words in order to rebuild it according to her own philosophy."

The most brutal blow to the novel was delivered by the

National Review, the influential conservative publication. On December 28 it published a long article, "Big Sister Is Watching You." The piece, running to 2,700 words, was written by Whittaker Chambers, a former communist spy who had defected from the Soviet underground and testified in the Alger Hiss espionage case. Since then Chambers had become a devout Christian, so the *National Review* editor, William F. Buckley Jr., who assigned the atheistic book to him, must have expected the outcome.

A generation her junior, Buckley grew up in a traditional Catholic family. His first book, *God and Man at Yale*, defended Christian values. Rand met him in 1947 in a circle around McCarthy during the HUAC hearings. Like Rand, Buckley was a McCarthyite; however, they shared little else. Approaching Buckley at a cocktail party, Rand stunned him by saying, with typical bluntness, that he was far too intelligent to believe in God. Buckley would amuse his friends with the story, retelling it with Rand's thick accent.[64]

In the 1950s American conservatism became firmly connected with Christianity, and Buckley may have felt the need to distance his magazine from Rand's godless defense of capitalism. Some of this rationale appears between the lines of Chambers's review, in which he remarks that *Atlas Shrugged* is "essentially a political book" and the author expects her novel to be interpreted "as a political reality." Conservatives shared Rand's anticommunism and belief in limited government. But her atheism, replacing the sign of the cross with the dollar sign, belonged to another camp. "Randian Man, like Marxian Man," wrote Chambers, stands at the center of a godless world. The materialists from the right and from the left are alike: their views enable them to act "beyond good and evil." The novel calls for remaking the world on behalf of an "aristocracy of talents," a "technocratic elite." Rand's "dictatorial tone" and "overriding arrogance" in presenting her views as "the final revelation" were unprecedented. Chambers reserved his punch line for the end: "From almost any page of *Atlas Shrugged* a voice can be heard . . . commanding 'To a gas chamber—go!'" The article cast Rand both as a fascist and as an enemy of Christianity (the latter being an old accusation to Jews). It forever changed her public image. (In 2005 Edward Sorel, the famous illustrator and son of Jewish immigrants from the Bronx, published a satirical sketch of Rand in the *New Yorker*. It shows her as she was seen by her detractors, with a hooked nose and the trademark dollar sign she wore defiantly on her lapel in advocacy of capitalist free enterprise.)

Rand would never forgive Buckley for orchestrating the attack. She found it incomprehensible that her views could be mistaken for fascism. Yet the use of such terms as *subhuman* made her novel an easy target. Chambers's piece, of course, was not a proper review but a political attack; as such, it inspired protests. Unbeknown to Rand, Isabel Paterson sent a letter to Buckley criticizing him for running the article.[65] In December John Chamberlain praised the novel in the *Freeman*, a libertarian magazine. Mises wrote a personal letter to Rand, saying that "*Atlas Shrugged* is not merely a novel. . . . It is also . . . a cogent analysis of the evils that plague our society. . . . You have the courage to tell the masses what no politician told them: you are inferior and all the improvements in your conditions . . . you owe to the effort of men who are better than you."[66] Rand's young followers, including Greenspan, sent indignant letters to the *National Review*. And there were also countless readers, "the masses," who, notwithstanding the controversy, or because of it, continued to promote her book by word of mouth.

9

The Novelist-Philosopher

Rand was forty-five when she met Nathaniel Branden (born Nathan Blumenthal), who would become her disciple and lover. In 1950 the handsome nineteen-year-old was a psychology freshman at UCLA. He first read *The Fountainhead* at fourteen and later reread it, as he recalls in his memoir, "almost continuously, with the dedication and passion of a student of the Talmud."[1] During his adolescence the book affected him as no other had: it rendered irrelevant the morality of selflessness and self-sacrifice he had been taught. Nathaniel's parents were Russian Jewish immigrants to Canada who never fully assimilated. His father owned a clothing shop in Toronto where Nathaniel replaced him on Saturdays. For a Jewish youth growing up without a clear sense of identity, *The Fountainhead* became a moral beacon. Concerned about his obsession, his mother invited Selena Herman, a teacher of Hebrew studies, for dinner and a discussion of the book. Selena had not read the novel, so

Nathaniel synopsized it for her and let her read Roark's courtroom speech. Her opinion was that the speech represented a known philosophy, that of anarchism.

In 1947 Nathaniel wrote to Rand inquiring about her use of the terms *egoism* and *egotism*. Overwhelmed with fan mail, she dismissed his letter. He persisted with two more dispatches, revealing his genuine interest in her literature and political views. On December 2, 1949, Rand responded in two short paragraphs, stating that she believed "in complete, uncontrolled, unregulated, laissez-faire, private-property, profit-motive, free-enterprise Capitalism."[2] Nathaniel followed up with questions about *We the Living*. He also expressed high regard for Rand's "intelligence and personal integrity." This bit of flattery got her attention: on January 13, 1950, she quoted back his words and replied at length. As their exchange continued, she asked for Nathaniel's phone number and made an appointment for him to visit Chatsworth. On February 19 at 8:00 P.M., date and time marked in Rand's Perfection Desk Calendar, Nathaniel arrived at 10000 Tampa Avenue.[3]

Their first meeting lasted nine hours. Frank, silent and benevolent, napped in an armchair, occasionally getting up to serve coffee and sweets. Nathaniel's questions interested Rand, and she talked with unflagging energy until 5:30 the next morning. That day he told his girlfriend, Barbara Weidman, that Rand was "Mrs. Logic." Her conversation was "brilliant, powerful, overwhelming in its clarity and consistency."[4] In turn, Rand was impressed with the young man. Still attributing great importance to appearance, she decided that Nathaniel's face projected romanticism and dedication. She was captivated by the young man who wanted to know her views and soon called him "a genius."

On March 11, a Saturday night, Nathaniel arrived at Tampa Avenue with his girlfriend. Age twenty and a philosophy major at UCLA, Barbara had also read *The Fountainhead* in her teens. As she told Rand, the book became responsible for her involvement with Nathaniel. Early on, when both lived in Winnipeg, where Nathaniel then worked in his uncle's jewelry shop, friends introduced them because they were in love with the same book. Rand called it "a wonderful literary event."[5] (She soon met another young couple, Evan and Mickey Wright, who married because of her novel. Rand was a witness at their wedding and signed their marriage certificate.) Nathaniel and Barbara were a generation her junior and she called them "the kids." They were not *her* children, she would clarify: they were "the children of *The Fountainhead*."[6]

Rand struck both as a woman of "superior intelligence." Her large, expressive eyes projected a "remarkable combination of perceptiveness and sensuality, of intelligence and passionate intensity."[7] Nathaniel when meeting her gaze felt as though he were standing in the beam of a searchlight. During their Saturday night meetings, Rand spoke of politics, literature, aesthetics, and morality. She used her cigarette holder as a wand, "punctuating her words with sharp, jagged gestures."[8] Unbeknown to her students, her energy was fueled by Dexedrine, a highly addictive stimulant of the brain and central nervous system. In the morning she would part with her guests to catch some sleep before a new workday. Then she would write for long hours, driving herself to exhaustion. As Rand later told Barbara, writing *Atlas Shrugged* was the most difficult thing she had ever done. Rand did not write from inspiration: only in action scenes did she release herself to the free flow of thought. Much of the novel was created by rational calculation.[9] Her creative process did not begin with an image or an incident. Rand would first formulate "the right philosophical principle" and then translate it into "the right story."[10] The laborious work drained her physically and mentally: she complained of tension pains in her neck and shoulders.

At that time Rand still maintained a social life, giving dinner parties and dining out. She looked after herself, kept regular appointments with a dentist and a hairdresser who preserved her 1920s looks: a Dutch bob parted on one side and swept to the other.

In May 1950 Ake Sandler, a Swedish-born journalist and political science professor at UCLA, invited Rand to give a talk to his class. He had been a correspondent for the *New York Times* during the war in Finland and later wrote for Swedish and American publications. His father, Rikard, had been Sweden's prime minister and minister of foreign affairs; he was a Marxist who had translated *Das Kapital.* Rand was taken aback by these facts but agreed to give the talk at UCLA. Sandler, "a liberal-conservative-socialist," as he described himself, wanted his students to be exposed to a variety of political theories.

Rand impressed him as an intense lecturer, sharp and intelligent; she spoke on the virtues of capitalism, *The Communist Manifesto,* and the 1848 revolutions across Europe. She sounded democratic on such issues as free speech but was authoritarian in her belief that "there was only one basic truth and that was individualism." She needed listeners and believers, and "was very anxious for her own philosophy to be accepted." Students were "immensely interested" in her unusual perspective, and she hosted further meetings at her residence. There she talked for hours, while students sat on the floor at her feet. "It was a kind of indoctrination," recalls Sandler; a number of his students became her converts.[11]

Rand's marriage had dissatisfied her for some time. Although she spoke of Frank as her rock, the man who never let her down, he was uninterested in her ideas and never initiated sex. At one time she even considered divorce but decided to postpone it until after finishing *Atlas Shrugged.* Frank accompanied her to business meetings, sat obediently and silently through her conversations with literary fans, and concealed what he felt and thought. In fact, he could not speak his mind: it was impossible to disagree with Rand without losing her friendship.

For young men coming into her orbit there was often a sexual element to the relationship. Jack Bungay, her former secretary in Hollywood, and the screenwriter Albert Mannheimer had experienced her powerful magnetism and sensuality. And so did Evan Wright, an engineering student at UCLA and former marine, who advised Rand on technical matters for *Atlas Shrugged* and did some typing for her. Evan Wright was one of Rand's converts, her influence diminishing only when he married; until then he called himself her "adopted son."[12] Rand's relationship with Mannheimer was also many-faceted. He was her disciple and a fellow writer with whom she discussed her work. He was also a man who wrote her a love letter and with whom she flirted.

In 1950–51 Mannheimer continued to visit on weekends, so Nathaniel and Barbara occasionally met him at dinner. Nathaniel was encouraged to phone daily and to come separately from his regular Saturday visits with Barbara. Rand needed followers to carry forth her work, and Nathaniel struck her as a man committed to her moral philosophy. When inviting Mannheimer and Nathaniel on alternate days, she may have been comparing the two: her novels are replete with love triangles. Like Mannheimer, Nathaniel became dependent on her intellectually, psychologically, and emotionally. Rand was soon holding his hand when they sat on a couch, inspiring a whole spectrum of feelings and thoughts in the young man, from physical attraction to idealism and vanity.[13] For a while Barbara was untroubled by the growing attachment between the two: their Saturday meetings were generating a new family united by ideas. Nathaniel's and Barbara's sense of family also included Rand's literary heroes. They were among the first to read chapters of *Atlas Shrugged*, an experience that made them wildly enthusiastic.

Through the novel Rand familiarized the young couple with her theory of sex, according to which love was the response to values. She rationalized desire and linked it with self-esteem. Sexual desire, she wrote, was "the expression of one's mind's deepest values."[14] A man (and it was male sexuality that primarily interested her) becomes "attracted to the woman" who reflects his vision of himself.[15] Entirely cerebral, this theory dismissed human emotion and the complexity of sexual response. When Barbara admitted that she valued Nathaniel but was not attracted to him passionately, this struck Rand as irrational and she began analyzing the young woman's psychology.

During the writing of *Atlas Shrugged* Rand began to view herself as both a fiction writer and a philosopher. Over the years she worked toward developing her own philosophical system that would embrace the main areas of human knowledge: metaphysics, epistemology, ethics, and politics. Her philosophy emphasized objective reality, reason, self-interest, and laissez-faire capitalism. Philosophical knowledge, she wrote in her journal, was "necessary in order to define human perfection."[16] Fiction allowed her to provide memorable moral examples, embodied by Roark and John Galt. When Rand spoke of Galt, her eyes shone with love. It was not like that with actual people, who fell short of her moral ideal.[17]

In June 1951 "the kids" announced they would be studying in New York. Standing on the driveway beside Frank, Rand cried as she watched them leave: the two had become "enormously important" to her. As happened earlier with Mannheimer, her need for intellectual torch passing went hand in hand with her attraction to a disciple and son substitute. In the following months, despite regular telephone conversations and correspondence with Nathaniel, she found their separation intolerable. Part of their exchange dealt with Barbara's psychological progress to becoming "fully rational." She "still presented a difficulty," Nathaniel reported, referring to their experiment with Barbara.

His letters to Rand were flirtatious. "I miss you terribly and think of you always," he wrote to the woman who was his mother's age. In another letter, Nathaniel told her that he looked at her picture daily and wondered whether this was love. In a postscript to Frank he suggested "to trade the picture for the real thing."[18] The twenty-year-old was being smart, but Rand took his flirtation seriously. On September 19, 1951, the date she marked in her calendar, she firmly decided to return to New York.[19] Rand informed Frank they were moving and phoned Nathaniel with the good news.

The relocation was a blow to Frank, who had to abandon everything he loved and lived for—the ranch, his farming, and his small business selling gladioli. He told Rand that she had become "hopelessly dependent" on Nathaniel.[20] She was implacable, setting a close date for their departure: they were leaving in three weeks. Her lawyer, Pincus Berner, agreed to find an apartment in New York; their neighbors Ruth and Buzzy Hill were persuaded to rent the Chatsworth property at a nominal cost. Packers and movers soon walked through the house. Rand told Frank it would take her five to seven years to complete the novel, at which time they would return to Chatsworth. She would break her promise and tell friends that she always hated California; Frank was expected to say he felt likewise.[21]

Upon arriving in New York, the O'Connors settled in a modest, plain-looking apartment in the Murray Hill area at 36 East Thirty-Sixth Street. From the window of her small study, which soon became crammed with her desk and file cabinets, Rand could see the Empire State Building. The sight thrilled her: the building symbolized the success of capitalism, of human genius in a free world. She would remain in this unimpressive flat, ruled over by her unneutered male cat Frisco, until 1963. The new Cadillac convertible that Frank drove all the way from California was given to Nathaniel: Rand was not planning to travel. Nathaniel and Barbara, who lived near Fifth Avenue, came to see Rand on the day of the O'Connors' arrival. Now they would be visiting up to five evenings a week.

The young couple introduced Rand to their relatives and university friends, all of whom were fans of *The Fountainhead.* "The Class of '43," as Rand called them (for the novel's publication date), gathered at her apartment on Saturday nights. They were absorbed in textual study: Rand elucidated her novel's moral philosophy, and her "class" listened with a traditional Jewish reverence for the written word. Most were related in one way or another. Leonard Peikoff was Barbara's cousin; Elayne Blumenthal was a nurse and Nathaniel's older sister; Alan Blumenthal (Nathaniel's cousin) was a future concert pianist and psychiatrist. Harry Kalberman, an accountant executive, would marry Elayne; Joan Mitchell, a graduate art student and Barbara's friend, married Alan Greenspan in 1952. Joan's second husband was Alan Blumenthal. Barbara's brother Sydney and Nathaniel's sisters Florence and Reva joined the group later with their spouses. With the exception of Mary Ann Sures (née Rukavina), an art historian, all were children or grandchildren of eastern European Jewish immigrants, transitioning from the religion of their fathers to secularism. These young people looked up to Rand as their moral guide. Rand had re-created the narrow world of her adolescence, the circle of Nina Guzarchik's Jewish friends and relatives who gathered on Saturdays and called themselves "Uno Momento." Although Rand had said that her Jewishness did not matter to her, she felt most comfortable with ethnic Jews, provided, of course, that they shared her ideas. "The Collective," as she jokingly called them, represented an intellectual continuum, and, not incidentally, her closest disciples came from this milieu. The Collective was receptive to her creed; she could talk to them all night without leaving the world of *The Fountainhead* and later of *Atlas Shrugged.* Rand expected her students to become high achievers. Her philosophy influenced their personal and professional lives: the majority were childless and career-oriented.

Nathaniel would publish a groundbreaking study, *The Psychology of Self-Esteem*, inspired by Rand's belief in self-reverence. Peikoff, then a philosophy major at NYU, would become her most faithful follower. As a young professor he attained notoriety by replacing a course on Immanuel Kant, whom Rand reviled, with one on Objectivism. Greenspan, the most autonomous and successful member of the Collective, would acknowledge her role in expanding his worldview "beyond the models of economics."[22]

As Barbara writes, they "had entered a new planet fashioned by Ayn Rand."[23] In January 1953 she and Nathaniel married. Frank was best man and Rand matron of honor. Mrs. Blumenthal, observing Rand's hold on Nathaniel, asked her son whether he wanted a second mother. In fact, he may have wanted a second father. When on Father's Day Rand asked him for an autographed copy of his first publication, he signed it, "To my father—Ayn Rand."[24] (The jest implied manliness in Rand's character, her formidable strength. The image of a "hard and ruthless woman" appealed to her.)[25] In spring 1954 Nathaniel legally changed his name to Branden. The new surname captured "Rand" in both English and Hebrew, making him "son of Rand," "ben Rand." Like her other converts, Nathaniel became Rand's spiritual son.

In fall 1954 the two couples and Nathaniel's sister Elayne ventured to see the family in Toronto. For Rand, who feared traveling outside the United States, this was her first trip abroad since she married Frank. Because she was afraid of flying it was decided to go by car. Frank was driving the party back to New York when Barbara and Elayne, from the back seat, saw Rand rest her head on Nathaniel's shoulder; he hugged her, and they proceeded to whisper. Two days later, in New York, Rand summoned Nathaniel to her apartment. She spoke of their new intimacy revealed on the journey and led him to admit that he loved her. Then she made him repeat his words and pressed for commitment. Rand was perfectly selfish: she did not consider Barbara or Frank. She wanted to live a romantic adventure, to be compensated for decades of hard work. Rand was nearing fifty; Nathaniel was twenty-four. Their sexual affair would begin in early 1955 and continue for fourteen years.

But first Rand wanted to obtain Barbara's and Frank's consent for the liaison. She plotted a live drama and staged it in her living room. Rand and Nathaniel sat on a couch, holding hands; an "ashen-faced" Frank sat in an armchair. When Barbara arrived, she alone was unaware of what was to come. Rand said "almost matter-of-factly" that she and Nathaniel were in love; their relationship had evolved from that of a teacher and student to become "the romantic, sexual love of a man and a woman."[26] Speaking with her usual persuasiveness, she explained that, given their values, it was inevitable for them to develop sexual passion. Their mutual desire was "right and rational," but the affair could not last beyond a year or two: she would never be "an old woman pursuing a younger man."[27] Barbara was stunned; when she protested, Frank joined in: both declared they would not be part of the scheme. Speaking calmly, Rand presented another argument: after all, it would not be a fully sexual affair: they simply needed some time alone, two evenings a week. Barbara and Frank were not fighters, and their feeble protests were squelched. Having received their consent, Rand announced that her reputation was vital, so the liaison must remain secret. Barbara and Frank were sworn to lifetime secrecy. In Rand's mind, formal consent, regardless of how it was obtained, made the whole business morally right. Yet she was a spiritual leader whose approval was paramount for Barbara. Frank, who had subordinated his life to her, was in his fifties; he had no career and had nowhere to go. Rand designed the rules and herself amended them. In November 1954 she told Barbara and Frank that since they had consented to the affair, it was only logical that it should become fully sexual.

The liaison would not affect their marriages, Rand told them, and since they were rational human beings, there would be no suffering and no victims. This was consistent with her ideas in *Atlas Shrugged.* "Just as there are no contradictions in my values and no conflicts among my desires," says Galt, "so there are no victims and no conflicts of interest among rational men."[28] But in life Rand's desires created a painful conflict. To avoid gossip, she insisted on receiving Nathaniel in the safety of her own flat. Frank, expected to go for a walk, would instead spend time in a bar, eventually becoming an alcoholic. Barbara struggled morally and emotionally, developing acute anxiety and panic attacks: she had to accept that the liaison was "right and rational" but was unable to.[29] Nathaniel would also become trapped in Rand's theories: one day she told him that since she represented his highest values there was no reason why their romance could not continue forever.[30] Although strong and controlling, she wanted to be reduced to a sex object. According to Nathaniel, he had to play the role of an aggressor, familiar to him from her fiction.

The affair began at a crucial time for *Atlas Shrugged:* Rand was writing the Galt speech, in which she summarized her entire philosophy. Frustrated with a lack of progress, she was tense and weary. Her personal life had become a distraction, she told Nathaniel. Inevitably, she took out her frustration on people close to her, turning their lives (and her own) into "pure hell."[31] It took her two years to produce the sixty-page tract. Upon completing it in October 1955, she regained her energy and magnetism, becoming her former fascinating self. The Collective was reading and praising the speech that expressed their premises and belief system. Rand and her disciples had become mutually dependent. She outlined the moral principles and expected compliance; in turn, they formed a protective wall around her. When, upon the novel's publication, the negative reviews began to pour in, the objectivists saw it as an assault on *their* values. Nathaniel organized others to write letters of protest.

The novel came out with a double dedication, to Frank

O'Connor and Nathaniel Branden. Frank's portrait was used for promotion; the publisher's advertisement read: "This is John Galt—who said he would stop the motor of the world—and did. Meet him in *Atlas Shrugged.*" Frank's role was nominal, but important: Mr. O'Connor was part of Rand's image. In interviews she maintained she was romantically involved with her husband. This was one of Rand's many contradictions: despite rejecting traditional morality, she remained old-fashioned, reluctant to reveal her affair. She also believed, for example, that "it would be improper for a woman to be president," and "proper" for a man "to be worshipped."[32]

In December 1957, while promoting the novel, Rand gave the first of several interviews to Mike Wallace, a popular television host and a liberal. When asked whether her "selfish philosophy" boils down "to a jungle law," she pushed back: "If you assume that every man is entitled to survive *regardless* of his own achievements—then you must sacrifice the achievers to the nonachievers. Then you have the jungle law we have today." Rand was a tough debater, and Wallace was "fascinated" with her assertive take on morality and on life.[33] When asked what contemporary thinker or philosopher she valued, she responded with audacity, "Not one." The answer was unfortunate, for it allowed Wallace to ask whether she regarded herself "the most creative thinker alive." Rand replied with usual directness: "If anyone can pick a rational flaw in my philosophy, I will be delighted to acknowledge him and I will learn something from him. Until then—I am."[34] (In another interview she claimed that she owed her philosophical debt only to Aristotle.) While Rand's toughness and sensationalism appealed to audiences, making her a perfect guest on talk shows, her greater ambition—to have her philosophy of objectivism accepted by academe—was out of reach.

Rand's relentless drive to the top ended in a breakdown. In mid-1958, with her novel firmly on best-seller lists, she suffered severe depression. She had always been emotionally unstable, prone to mood swings. Decades of intense work, her use of amphetamines, and the stress of her love affair had contributed to the nervous collapse. Brutal reviews of *Atlas Shrugged* that compared her philosophy with fascism had tipped the scale. For a while she was able to function. She launched a weekly literary class for the Collective and gave talks at Princeton's Present Day Club and Queen's College in New York. She even attempted a new novel, "To Lorne Dieterling," the story of a woman "totally motivated by love for values—and how one maintains such a state when alone in an enemy world."[35] The novel's theme reflected her state of mind: at the height of popular success, she saw herself alienated, living in hostile settings. She had no energy to continue this novel and left it unfinished. In June she stopped marking appointments in her calendar: her life stopped. As her tension pains and mental anguish returned, she spent days crying. Sitting at her desk, in self-imposed isolation, Rand played endless games of solitaire. The sales of her book did not interest her. She did not read, nor did she even open her fan mail. She told Barbara and Nathaniel that it was not the reviews or "the outpouring of hatred" against her that made her bitter; it was the lack of support on the part of prominent intellectuals who did not defend her publicly.[36] Her insecurities prevailed: she saw herself misrepresented, surrounded by mediocrities, and not given her due. She kept repeating the phrase from *Atlas Shrugged:* "What's wrong with the world?" The affair was put on hold; the lover became her therapist. Rand said she was ashamed of herself: John Galt would have handled this situation differently. Her dark moods returned in July 1959, when she plunged again into prolonged depression. Eventually Nathaniel was able to get through to her, saying that she accomplished her mission by creating the ideal character of John Galt; now she needed a new challenge. "This is the right track, darling," she told him hopefully, "this is the right track!"[37] Rand would write nonfiction and deliver successful lectures.

There was also a new beginning for Nathaniel: in January 1958 he launched a lecture course, "Basic Principles of Objectivism," that popularized Rand's philosophy in *Atlas Shrugged.* Having borrowed stacks of her fan mail, he selected letters written within a hundred-mile radius of New York and sent invitations. In winter and spring 1958 he had twenty-eight students. As he began advertising in New York's newspapers, enrollment grew.[38] In 1961 the Nathaniel Branden Institute was established with Rand's approval. It offered additional courses and programs with an average enrollment of 160. The NBI existed for nearly a decade, until its dramatic demise.

In late 1959 Rand received a letter from John Hospers, a professor of philosophy at Brooklyn College. A rising scholar in his early forties, Hospers was an expert in ethics and aesthetics. He held a doctorate from Columbia, where he had studied under Meyer Schapiro, the distinguished Lithuanian-born art historian whose ancestors were Talmudic scholars. Schapiro advocated an interdisciplinary approach to the study of artistic works. He was "the greatest teacher I ever had in my life," wrote Hospers to Rand.[39] Hospers's first published work, *Meaning and Truth in the Arts,* became an acclaimed reference in aesthetics. In *Human Conduct,* which would come out in 1960, he popularized ethical theories and used examples from literature to illustrate moral problems. Quotations from Rand's novels would be included, and in his first letter he asked her to clarify her views on happiness and egoism. Although she had been seeking the attention of serious scholars, Rand reacted irritably. Hospers responded on January 4, 1960, "I dislike exchanges of angry letters because they are so *untruthful.*"[40] But Rand's approach to ethical problems interested him, and he continued to probe her views, hoping to compare and contrast them and to place them in historical context. He began by discussing Roark's pursuit of happiness in *The Fountainhead.* Happiness is a value; however, "if a person deliberately *pursues* happiness all his life, he is not likely to achieve it. Roark was not pursuing happiness, he was pursuing perfection in his chosen work. Happiness comes from this . . . but only as an incidental consequence."[41] (This point comes close to Victor Frankl's idea in *Man's Search for Meaning*, where he writes that "success, like happiness, cannot be pursued; it must ensue, and it only does so as an unintended side-effect of one's personal dedication to a cause greater than oneself.")[42]

But Rand had single-mindedly pursued her goals and created a philosophy that prized ambition and personal achievement. So she replied that she did not understand the point Hospers was making. "I would say: Roark was happy because he spent his life achieving the things (the values) that would make him happy. . . . And—I would add—he succeeded, because his values were rational."[43] Hospers doubted her assertions by saying that whether happiness always "proceeds from the achievement of one's values" is *an open question.*[44] He also thought that the link between being rational and being happy was problematic. "Do you wish to say that (1) all rational human beings are happy . . . and also that (2) *only* rational human beings are happy? And how would you defend this view? . . . Would you admit the possibility of rational human beings who are unhappy?" (Rand apparently did not see this possibility, reacting with question and exclamation marks.)[45] To understand her views on egoism, Hospers gave an example from life: a medical researcher investigates tropical diseases while working in disease-ridden conditions. If his prime motivation is alleviating the sufferings of others, would Rand condemn his activity on this account?[46] Rand responded that if a medical researcher must work in difficult conditions, she would consider his activity as "virtuous and heroic." But if his prime motivation was not his career, "I would certainly condemn it as irrational and evil."[47] (This logic would create impossible contradictions in life, but Rand believed that acting in the interests of others makes one an altruist. For this reason she denounced the profession of social workers as "morally evil.")[48]

Hospers was following Rand's lecturing career, launched at Yale Law School Forum on February 17, 1960, with her lecture "Faith and Force: The Destroyers of the Modern World." As *Time* magazine commented, Rand addressed an audience of six hundred, outcompeting all other events at Yale. That night there was a hockey game with Brown University, a concert by the New Haven Symphony Orchestra, and three other talks on campus, including one by the Roman Catholic bishop at Yale Divinity School.[49]

If civilization was to survive, Rand stated in her lecture, "it is the morality of altruism that men have to reject." She lashed out at contemporary intellectuals, philosophers, writers, and artists who focused on human misery, rather than heroics, and declared that their age would be remembered as "the age of guilt." Delving into politics, she criticized "those liberals of the thirties who armed Soviet Russia and destroyed the last remnants of American capitalism." She called for "a moral revolution . . . the most radical form of rebellion," in the course of which the established moral code would be overturned and replaced with the rational morality of self-interest, expressed by her philosophy of objectivism. As the *Yale Daily News* wrote, "She held an audience spellbound . . . by the sheer magnetism of her personality, both during the formal talk and the question period."[50] Reflecting her growing popularity, the lecture appeared in the prestigious monthly publication *Vital Speeches of the Day*, the volume that opened with Senator John F. Kennedy's address to the Democratic National Convention.[51]

Rand met Hospers in April 1960 at Brooklyn College, where he had invited her to deliver the same lecture. Afterward the two spent six hours in discussion. Rand decried the beatniks and the entire contemporary culture as morally "bankrupt." Hospers, attempting to challenge her views, took her out to concerts, modern ballet, and exhibitions. They would then spend a night in conversation, occasionally breaking at eight o'clock in the morning, at which time Rand would make breakfast for the philosopher. Rand maintained that her judgments were objective, that beauty and goodness had little to do with the reactions of the observer: all aesthetic qualities were included in the object. Her endorsement of Rachmaninoff and Tchaikovsky and rejection of Beethoven, Mozart, and Bach were all allegedly made for objective reasons. Through such conversations Hospers was able to understand the meaning she invested in the term *objectivism.* Rand's philosophy was based on the premise that reality exists "as an objective absolute," independent of anyone's consciousness, and that objective knowledge can be obtained from perception through reason and logical argument. (This issue alone could generate a long philosophical discussion. Marx maintained that man's perception of objective reality is determined by social conditions. Kant, whose philosophy Rand regularly attacked, insisted that the human mind cannot grasp ultimate reality, that the world of our experience is not the reproduction of the world around us.) Rand apparently believed that it would be difficult to find a contemporary philosopher who would take existence of a physical world as axiomatic. Hospers gave examples of the opposite, but he was unable to move her from her established positions.[52] They discussed Sigmund Freud, whose sex theories she dismissed as false. "You do accept the concept of the unconscious," Hospers wrote to her, "of repression, of evasion, of defenses, etc. Freud did not invent these, but his genius consists in showing IN SPECIFIC DETAIL how they operate in human beings. . . . He was just about the most astute observer of the human scene that I can imagine."[53] Challenging Rand's conservative views, he brought up homosexuality. Hospers was made to resign his position at the University of Minnesota because of an accusation that he was homosexual. In his letter to Rand of September 26, 1961, he revealed his sexual orientation and told her about discrimination of sexual minorities, of students refused admission to graduate schools on mere suspicion of being homosexual.[54] Importantly, this revelation did not affect his personal relationship with Rand. In 1968, during a question period at Ford Hall Forum in Boston, she said that she did not approve of homosexual practices or regard them as moral but believed that government laws prohibiting homosexuality should be repealed.[55]

Hospers was among the first academics to recognize that Rand's novels offered ample opportunity for discussion. When he offered a class on her ethical views in *Atlas Shrugged*, three hundred enrolled—an unprecedented number for Brooklyn College. Rand gave him renewed inspiration for teaching, a profession that she regarded as "the most influential in the world."[56] Their conversations sparked his interest in laissez-faire economics and moved him closer to libertarianism. (In the 1972 election he was the Libertarian Party's first presidential candidate.) During his travels in America and abroad he discussed her views on private enterprise. "When I visited Israel," he wrote to her in September 1960, "I asked people concerning the numerous government projects in industry, land reclamation, etc. why private enterprise couldn't do the same job better. They agreed with me that it could, and said that every encouragement is given to private capital in Israel. But Israel, surrounded by enemies, is not a 'good risk' for foreign capital."[57]

Accustomed to scholarly debates, Hospers was struck by an absence of discussion in Nathaniel's lectures on objectivism. As he wrote to Rand, the NBI audience never questioned the premises but only asked about applications of the doctrine. "I felt as if I were in a strange church where I did not belong, where all the other people were singing the chants they were expected to and only I did not conform, and where to deny even a single thing was considered heresy."[58] In November 1960 he criticized the NBI lectures as dogmatic and overly simplistic; the attitude of "'I'm right and everyone else is wrong' . . . tends to MAKE slavish dogmatists out of the audience. They will agree without knowing why."[59] Rand replied that moral uncertainty would not help this audience and that the purpose of the course was to deliver the ideas "we know to be true." The lectures were offered "*only* to those who have understood enough of *Atlas Shrugged* to agree with its essentials."[60]

Aware that Hospers was a talented popularizer, Rand wanted him to present her philosophy to academe. He arranged a discussion with her that included Martin Lean, his department head at Brooklyn College. Lean was impressed with Rand's "intellectual vigor and native logical acuity." He disagreed with some of her political and economic views but found them thought-provoking. Because Rand did not use accepted philosophical terminology, certain "communication difficulties" were created.[61]

But she failed to find common ground with Sidney Hook, chair of the Department of Philosophy at NYU. A prominent scholar of Austrian Jewish heritage, Hook was a proponent of John Dewey's pragmatic naturalism and was Barbara and Peikoff's professor of philosophy. He first met Rand at the University of Wisconsin, where they were co-panelists at an ethics symposium. In 1961 he published a scathing review of Rand's first nonfiction book, *For the New Intellectual.* The book contained a long introductory essay and philosophical excerpts from her novels, including Roark's courtroom speech and John Galt's broadcast on the philosophy of objectivism. Hook's piece, "Each Man for Himself," appeared in the *New York Times.* "The book is written with passionate fervor," he wrote, "more in the style of prophetess of a cult than in the analytic vein of a philosopher." He mocked Rand's contention that "the world suffers from excessive altruism." The idea that all the evils commonly ascribed to capitalism were caused by government interference in the economy disregarded historical facts, such as child labor during the industrial revolution. Rand's abuse of opponents violated the civility of intellectual debate: "The language of reason does not justify references to economists with whom one disagrees as 'frantic cowards,' or to philosophers as 'intellectual hoodlums who pose as professors.' This is the way philosophy is written in the Soviet Union."[62] (Hook's style was not an example of civility, either: he became known as a "scrappy polemist.")[63] Rand was insulted and reacted angrily, requesting that her followers denounce Hook as unprincipled and corrupt. Nathaniel sent a long, reproving letter to the *New York Times* that exceeded the size limit and was rejected. He then raised money to run the rebuttal as a full-page advertisement in the *New York Times Book Review.* Rand was pleased to see it appear on May 28.[64]

The incident gave further substance to her dislike of contemporary philosophers. One of her charges against them was that they failed to read *Atlas Shrugged.* Hospers tried to defend his colleagues: could a professor of philosophy be excused for failing to read a lengthy novel during a busy year? "Must he be damned to perdition for making this mistake?" he asked. In the margin of his letter, Rand replied, in red pencil: "Yes!!"[65]

In October 1962 Hospers invited Rand to present at a Harvard meeting of the American Aesthetics Association. Rand's topic was "Art as Sense of Life." Afterward he had to comment on the strengths and weaknesses of her argument. When Hospers challenged her views in an academic setting, Rand perceived it as a betrayal and, after a heated response, stormed out of the room. Despite Hospers's attempts to reconcile, she never saw him again. He continued to acknowledge Rand in his books and made *Atlas Shrugged* required reading at the University of Southern California, where he taught philosophy in literature and later chaired the Philosophy Department. In 1977 the *Libertarian Review* published his tribute for the twentieth anniversary of the novel's publication. In it Hospers told the story of a high school girl from a Jewish Orthodox family. When her parents forbade her to read *Atlas Shrugged,* she read it secretly at night, by the light of a street lamp. By then Rand's novels had become a part of popular culture and dismissing them was counterproductive.

10

Fame and Influence

On June 13, 1957, Winnipeg's *Jewish Post*, the oldest Anglo-Jewish newspaper in western Canada, reported a troubling development: "Ayn Rand's *The Fountainhead* (no Jewish characters, no Jewish issues) seems to have captivated a thinking segment of the university intellectuals." At the University of Manitoba the novel had become a "bible of conservatism" to formerly left-wing Jewish students. (The newspaper failed to recognize the obvious irony: if Jewish students were captivated by the novel, studying it like a bible, it must have contained Jewish issues.) Sidney Hook, the article continued, visited the university in winter; he reported that things were also changing on American campuses where socialist-minded professors found themselves "constantly heckled and challenged by right-wing Jewish students." He may have been describing the behavior of Rand's disciples, such as Barbara Branden and Leonard Peikoff, both natives of Winnipeg, whom he taught in New York.

After Rand's 1960 debut lecture at Yale Law School, when she ignited a huge audience, she became widely sought as a speaker. The decade marked the height of her influence on American campuses: she received numerous invitations from colleges and universities and had to turn down many. Her dramatic and controversial style, fiery presentations, and moral certainty were winning student audiences. Adding to the magic was Rand's theatrical appearance in a black cape with a dollar sign on the lapel. For a Jew to endorse wealth in defiance of the stereotype of "selfish greed" manifested chutzpah.

In 1962 Columbia's King Crown Radio (WKCR) launched a syndicated series of programs for educational stations. Rand was invited to participate along with the musicians Leonard Bernstein and Leon Fleisher; the journalists Max Lerner (author of *America as Civilization*) and Quentin Reynolds, and CIA Director Allen Dulles. Announcing her program, *Ayn Rand on Campus*, WKCR described her as "America's foremost Objectivist philosopher": her quest "is for a moral revolution and total rationality is her goal." In 1962–64 her weekly recorded broadcasts covered a variety of topics, from "Introduction to Objectivism" and "The Romantic School of Writing" to "The Role of Law" and "America's Foreign Policy." Occasionally she went on air with Nathaniel Branden to discuss, for example, "Masculinity and Femininity in Today's World." In 1965–66 she added talks on ethical, legal, and social issues, such as "The Student Rebellion," "The Morality of Contract," and "The Ethical Aspects of Medicine." Rand's controversial and intense broadcasts captured student audiences. She would begin by attacking their contemporary values and politics, then turn to her orderly philosophical system that explained every aspect of life from an objectivist perspective. In the early 1960s Ayn Rand discussion clubs sprang up on campuses.

The effect of her radio broadcasts on students can be understood from a 1962–63 poll conducted by the *National Review* at twelve major liberal arts colleges and universities. The survey covered sophomores, juniors, and seniors studying at Boston University, Brandeis, Davidson, Howard, Indiana, Reed, Sarah Lawrence, Marquette, South Carolina, Stanford, Williams, and Yale. Questions concerned students' political and religious affiliations. "Ayn Rand on Campus," a separate section, identified the largest group of objectivists at Stanford and Boston universities: it represented 7 and 9 percent, respectively. In all, just over 3 percent (or about one in every thirty college students) definitely favored the objectivist position on political and economic issues. This indicated that "a small but appreciative headway is being made by the Objectivists." Their hard-core membership covered less than one-tenth of the student right.[1]

Rand also interested liberal audiences, which is why Mike Wallace repeatedly invited her on his shows. (He had interviewed Salvador Dalí, Aldous Huxley, Eleanor Roosevelt, Gloria Swanson, and Frank Lloyd Wright, among other celebrities.) When in 1959 she appeared on his popular TV show, *The Mike Wallace Interview*, the host began his introduction with her "revolutionary creed": "Throughout the United States small pockets of intellectuals have become involved in a new and unusual philosophy, which would seem to strike at the very roots of our society." The camera showed an intense, middle-aged woman, her eyes darting as she spoke with energy and defiance. Meeting Wallace's questions head-on, she maintained a sense of drama throughout the three-part interview. When the host mentioned her rejection of Judeo-Christian morality, she declared, "To say I don't like [altruism] is too weak a word. I consider it evil that man has to serve others to justify his existence."[2] Speaking with full confidence, she turned controversy into her major strength, never allowing Wallace to put her on the defensive. Al Ramrus, a writer and television journalist working for Wallace, recalls that when he heard her challenge "most of the sacred beliefs of

Western civilization," he was won over by her courage. "Here was a woman who dared to stand virtually alone against ideas, political systems and cultures that were dominating the planet and had been hallowed by intellectuals."[3] The show was swamped with letters. Wallace thought Rand was "a perfect guest" who got a lot of viewers interested and thinking.[4] Although a pariah among the liberal left, she was seen by others as "a bold voice in a mealy-mouthed age."[5]

When in 1960 Gore Vidal ran for the House of Representatives as a Democrat from New York, he found that Rand was the only writer politicians knew and talked about. Her name became ubiquitous in the press. That year the *National Review*, the publication Rand never forgave for attacking *Atlas Shrugged*, ran a positive article about her. The poet and scholar Merrill Root, troubled by the disavowal of Rand by conservatives, wrote that her works must be given "respectful and sympathetic attention." Root analyzed Roark's pronouncements in *The Fountainhead* and concluded that Rand's position was closer to theism than to atheism.[6]

Rand was not softened by this: to separate herself from conservatives she called herself "a radical for capitalism." Always on the offensive, she was burying her enemies. On December 7, 1960, a month after the presidential election, she delivered the lecture "Conservatism: An Obituary" at Princeton. She disparaged candidates of both parties. The "conservatives" had no courage to admit that the American way of life is about capitalism. The "liberals" were covering up their socialist agenda with such "euphemisms" as "The New Frontier."[7] This was her first attack on Kennedy and his July acceptance speech at the Democratic National Convention. Rand understood "The New Frontier" as a menacing extension of Roosevelt's New Deal.

The politics of the Kennedy era pushed Rand to the far right. During an interview with Wallace she defended Barry Goldwater, a conservative businessman and senator from Arizona. She saw Goldwater, a militant anticommunist, "as the only hope of the anti-collectivist side," and the hope drew her back to politics, which she had abandoned after Willkie's defeat. In 1960 Goldwater wrote to thank Rand for publicly supporting him. He praised *Atlas Shrugged* and sent her his book *The Conscience of a Conservative.* Rand responded with a critique of conservative philosophy, while persuading the senator to defend it on strictly economic grounds. If the term *conservative* "stands for *Capitalism*," she argued, its philosophy must be based on rational principles.[8] Rand was unsuccessfully trying to influence Goldwater and, through him, other conservatives to abandon religion in their political platform. (Yet she did indirectly influence his rhetoric. In 1964, as the Republican nominee for president, Goldwater gave an acceptance speech written by Karl Hess, who had studied objectivism at NBI and was a believer in laissez-faire capitalism.) Shortly before Goldwater lost to Lyndon Johnson, Rand sent her candidate an unsolicited speech in which she linked America's economic achievements to its founding principle of man's individual rights.

Earlier, in 1961, she had met with Robert Welch, a major financial supporter of Goldwater's campaign. Welch, a retired businessman who had made a fortune as a confectioner, funded extreme-right causes. In 1958 he established the John Birch Society (JBS), a secretive organization, described by the *New York Times* as "potentially disruptive and dangerous."[9] Members of the JBS were militant anticommunists who subscribed to conspiracy theories; the organization was thus a spiritual predecessor of QAnon. Rand occasionally read Welch's *American Opinion* magazine, which claimed in 1960 that much of the United States was under communist control. During her nonfiction writing course in 1969 she mentioned the JBS positively, not least because the liberal left described it as fascist.[10] According to Jennifer Burns, "Rand was not bothered by the charges against the

JBS. . . . She didn't understand the extent to which the society had become synonymous in the popular mind with incipient fascism and totalitarian mob rule."[11] Rand had mistrusted middle-of-the-roaders and was drawn to extremes, but her endorsement of JBS, whose members were anti-Semitic, tarnished her politics. In her desire to fight communism she chose some of the strangest bedfellows.

Rand, however, perceived fascism in Jack Kennedy's political platform. His 1961 inaugural address, made in the spirit of the Founding Fathers, became memorable to many for the call to public service: "My fellow Americans: ask not what your country can do for you—ask what you can do for your country." To Rand the Democrats were anathema, and the word *sacrifice* used in this speech represented the communist principle she had been fighting. The call for individual sacrifices to the state prompted her extreme response. In December 1962, during her second annual presentation at the Ford Hall Forum, she delivered an inflammatory talk, "The Fascist New Frontier." She began by quoting proposals of an unnamed political party: "We ask that the government undertake the obligation . . . of providing citizens with adequate opportunity of employment and earning a living. . . . The government must undertake the improvement of public health," and so on. Then came her dramatic announcement: these "fine, progressive, liberal" proposals, which could be taken for Kennedy's, were excerpted from the program of the Nazi Party of Germany, adopted in Munich on February 24, 1920. (She referred to the twenty-five-point program of the German Workers' Party, NSDAP.) The NSDAP program had also stated, "The Party . . . combats the Jewish-materialistic spirit within and around us." Rand read this quote without the crucial word *Jewish*, which would reveal the program's racism. In contrast, Kennedy's New Frontier speech advocated putting "an end to racial discrimination in all parts of our community life."

In the course of her talk Rand cast excerpts from Göring's and Hitler's speeches of the 1930s against Kennedy's to prove that both the National Socialist and "liberal" programs were leading to welfare statism and totalitarian control.[12]

In 1963 she included "The Fascist New Frontier" in a compendium of articles to be issued by Random House. The editorial staff rose up against its publication. As Bennett Cerf recalls in *At Random*, "I read the piece and absolutely hit the roof. I called her and said we were not going to publish any book that claimed Hitler and Jack Kennedy were alike. Ayn charged in and reminded me that I had said . . . that we would publish anything she wrote." Cerf still believed she could say anything in a novel. He proposed issuing the collection without the essay, but she argued that her entire book presents "*an ideological critique of the Kennedy administration*." If Cerf were to suppress it, he would be "acceding to a totalitarian viewpoint."[13] (Rand was accusing the publisher who had won a historic court case against government censorship: in 1933 he became the first in the United States to publish James Joyce's *Ulysses* unabridged. Having socialized with Cerf, Rand must have known this, but she focused on her goal to the detriment of everything else.) Rand gave her ultimatum to Random House: either they publish "every word" or she would withdraw the book. Cerf replied, "Get yourself another publisher."[14] The exchange took place shortly before Kennedy's assassination on November 22. In the aftermath the publisher asked Rand whether she could see she was wrong. Rand remained unmoved, insisting that "the assassination had nothing to do" with the point she had made in her essay. ("The Fascist New Frontier" was issued by NBI and reprinted by the Colorado newspaper *The New Conservative*.) Cerf wanted to part with Rand on good terms and sent her several letters, to which she did not reply. In April 1965 she relented and wrote a few lines to give him "credit for the many good actions you have taken in regard to me."[15]

Rand's nonfiction now appeared in the *Objectivist Newsletter*, which she and Nathaniel launched in 1962. (The newsletter eventually grew into a monthly journal, the *Objectivist*, with a circulation of 21,000.) Her new publisher, New American Library (NAL), reproduced her nonfiction collections. Thematically organized, her articles and lectures appeared as compendiums. All titles with Rand's name on the cover sold hundreds of thousands of copies. *The Virtue of Selfishness* (1964) became the most popular of her collections, eventually selling 1.5 million copies. In *Capitalism: The Unknown Ideal* (1966) her essays were included alongside those of Alan Greenspan, Nathaniel Branden, and another objectivist, Robert Hessen, an economic and business historian.

During 1962 Rand contributed a Sunday opinion column to the *Los Angeles Times*. She viewed contemporary America through the prism of objectivism, and her columns were inevitably moralistic. She railed against Kennedy's welfare state, condemning his domestic and foreign policies; decried altruism and statism; defended capitalism; and promoted her morality of rational self-interest. Predictably, she attacked contemporary culture and education for underestimating the moral value of Romantic literature. At the end of the year Rand's columns were discontinued by mutual consent.

In May 1963 Lewis and Clark College in Portland, Oregon, awarded her an honorary doctorate in humane letters. John Howard, the college's president and Rand's admirer, invited her for the convocation and two days of intense discussion of her novels in October; he promised that all 1,200 students and staff would read *The Fountainhead* and *Atlas Shrugged*. Rand accepted and for the first time agreed to travel by plane. Frank and the Brandens accompanied her on what became a cross-country tour. At the height of Rand's popularity, Nathaniel arranged speaking engagements for both of them before and after the convocation. First they flew to Chicago, where he appeared on the

CBS-TV show *At Random* to promote his book *Who Is Ayn Rand?* The adulatory publication, to which Barbara contributed a biographical essay, comprised his articles on *Atlas Shrugged*, objectivist ethics, and Rand's literary method. On September 28 Rand and Nathaniel held a discussion on ABC-TV's *Irv Kupcinet Show* in Chicago. The following day, at McCormick Place, America's largest convention center, 2,500 assembled to hear her lecture "America's Persecuted Minority: Big Business." (Nash Productions, associated with NBI, organized the talk and its promotion.) Rand's Chicago family that had brought her to America was in the audience. Fern Brown, Sam and Minna Goldberg, and others went backstage to congratulate Rand. "She was like a queen on a throne," Fern Brown recalled.[16] According to Rand's biographer Anne Heller, the Chicago family was not invited to a small reception hosted by Ed Nash of Nash Productions and NBI after the lecture. Rand would never see them again.[17]

On October 1 she received the honorary doctorate at Lewis and Clark and gave a talk, "The Goal of My Writing." Her ultimate goal was "the portrayal of a moral ideal," and she advocated "a free, productive, rational system," laissez-faire capitalism, that made it possible for "ideal men to exist and to function." She spoke of her own "desperate longing for the sight of human achievement" and of following the Romantic tradition that emphasizes the heroic in man.[18] Rand wore a doctoral gown, lent to her by Freeda Hartzfeld, the president's assistant and dean of women. Interviewed by *The Oregonian*, Rand predictably attacked antitrust laws, called to abolish public schools because government infuses the curriculum with its own ideas, and argued that "there was no moral justification for taxes." She justly described her political views as "far right." The newspaper wrote that during the question period, Rand "displayed a sharp wit as well as a remarkable knowledge of a wide range of affairs."[19] Sold on her philosophy, Dr. Howard included the study of objectivism in the curriculum at Lewis and Clark.

The influence of objectivism spread geographically: at Barbara's suggestion, the NBI lectures were audiotaped and sent across America. Their lectures were now advertised in newspapers nationwide, and requests were pouring in. NBI, Nathaniel's successful venture, had branched out to many cities, and on this tour he was showing Rand a part of his empire. The fall series, "Basic Principles of Objectivism," was launched in California, where Rand and her retinue headed for the opening. Nathaniel gave introductory lectures and Rand joined in during question sessions. The rest of the course had to be listened to on tapes, which students would purchase from local NBI representatives.

The courses were also offered in New York, where the objectivists now formed something of a colony, settling close to each other. That year the Brandens moved to an apartment in a newly built high-rise in the East Thirties of Manhattan. NBI's headquarters and the editorial office of the *Objectivist Newsletter* were transferred to the second floor of the building. Barbara was managing editor and Nathaniel's sister Elayne Kalberman, now a dedicated objectivist, became circulation manager. Within months the O'Connors leased an apartment on the sixth floor, three stories below the Brandens'. On the fourth floor Frank had a studio where he painted. Leonard Peikoff moved to the same building, and other objectivists rented apartments in the vicinity. Rand was keeping her spiritual children at close quarters.

The press had been watching Rand's following for a while. On March 27, 1961, in a *Newsweek* article, "Born Eccentric," Leslie Hanscom reported on Nathaniel's weekly lectures at New York's Hotel Roosevelt. A hundred or so "new intellectuals," he wrote, all sprucely dressed and "non-beatnik in aspect," packed the hall for Nathaniel's three-hour "droning delivery" before receiving their reward: Ayn Rand came onstage to answer questions. Submitting a question was a privilege only for attendees who paid seventy dollars for a course of twenty lectures (today around seven hundred dollars). Rand did not have a financial stake in NBI, but when a listener who attended cost-free asked a question, she put him down as a "cheap fraud." (Her brusqueness during NBI's question-and-answer sessions was legendary.) Hanscom described Rand as "a welcome streak of color in the world of authorship" and "a she-messiah." Around this time John Kobler, associate editor of the *Saturday Evening Post*, interviewed Nathaniel and Rand for an article that appeared on November 11, 1961, under the title "The Curious Cult of Ayn Rand." Kobler described the objectivist movement as "a little cult" with a scripture, based on *Atlas Shrugged*, and with its own prophets and converts. Rand attempted to stop publication of the piece, which she considered disrespectful and inaccurate.

According to Nathaniel, there was definitely "a cultish aspect" to the objectivist world. The movement was built on the premises that "Ayn Rand is the greatest human being that has ever lived," that *Atlas Shrugged* was "the greatest human achievement," and that Rand's ideas were infallible. Composed by Nathaniel himself, these and other such axioms established Rand as the possessor of Truth. Rand's tremendous moral authority in the movement ensured that no objectivist could disagree with her on fundamental issues. "Ayn did not create this atmosphere on her own," he writes. "Our entire group fed Ayn's exalted image of herself, and no one did so more fervently than I."[20] Initially, Rand did not want to be the leader of a movement, and it would have been wise of her to abstain. Her following had similarities with Leo Tolstoy's, formed around the famous man during his religious-philosophical phase. In both cases a chief disciple, who was also an intimate friend, ran a vast movement with an iron hand. Rising on Tolstoy's glory, the unknown Vladimir Chertkov dogmatized the creed and became its chief enforcer. Among the Tolstoyans there sprang up a mental coercion that affected the guru and his disciples simultaneously, making it impossible to argue ideas without being accused of moral backsliding. Rand's following was influenced by similar dynamics.

After the publication of *Atlas Shrugged*, a number of young intellectuals, many of them Jewish, were drawn to the objectivist movement. Among them was the journalist Edith Efron, who had interviewed Rand for the *New York Post*, where Mike Wallace had a question-and-answer feature. As Al Ramrus recalls, Edith suddenly "began speaking in a very, very strange way about psychology, art, politics—in a way that I'd never heard before and certainly not from a New York Jewish intellectual."[21] Although Edith became a dedicated objectivist, Rand had purged her, probably for her irreverence.[22]

Murray Rothbard, a future leading theoretician of anarcho-capitalism, was also drawn to the following and later expelled. He became interested in Rand's ideas at twenty-eight. In 1954, when they first met, Rothbard was a libertarian-oriented economist working toward his PhD from Columbia. Influenced by Mises's book *Human Action*, which presented the case for laissez-faire capitalism, Rothbard attended his famous unofficial seminar at New York University. After the lectures Rothbard and his younger friends, including the future economists George Reisman and Robert Hessen, gathered separately to discuss economics, history, politics, and philosophy. They called themselves "the Circle Bastiat," after Claude-Frédéric Bastiat, the nineteenth-century French classical economist of the liberal school.[23] That summer Richard Cornuelle, a young libertarian author studying under Mises, invited Rothbard and his circle to a gathering of Rand's Collective. Afterward, in a letter to Cornuelle, Rothbard complained about the intellectual passivity of Rand's young acolytes, who clung to her "like bees." He attended a few gatherings of the Collective, but Rand's intensity left him depressed.[24] This attitude changed when in 1957 the Circle Bastiat read *Atlas Shrugged*. Impressed with it, Rothbard wrote a fan letter to Rand praising her novel as the greatest work ever written, in effect expressing the axiom that gave the rite of passage to her following. He also mentioned, earnestly, that Rand persuaded him to read Aristotle and to research the field of natural law philosophy. Admitted to the movement, he attended Nathaniel's lectures and joined the objectivists' letter campaign defending *Atlas Shrugged* from its critics. Months later, he was purged in absentia. The expulsion turned him into Rand's bitter enemy and inspired his one-act play, "Mozart Was a Red," a satire on "trials" of dissidents. In an article titled "The Sociology of the Ayn Rand Cult," he compared her explicitly atheist following with Soviet ideological cults and the religious cults proliferating in 1960s America. Rothbard's major charge, which is consistent with other accounts, was the discrepancy between Rand's professed ideals of independence, freedom, and happiness and the practices of her movement that "promoted slavish dependence on the guru." Followers were absorbed in textual study of *Atlas Shrugged;* however, probing questions and debate were discouraged. They lived in fear of moral censure and the threat of expulsion.[25] (Jewish education is question based; Judaism encourages debate and dispute. In contrast, Rand disowned critics by publishing their names in the *Objectivist*, and this forced members to break ties with the outcasts.)

Richard Cornuelle, who first met Rand as a college student, later explained the attractiveness of her rigid philosophical system: "It was a tremendous relief for me to find a point of view that suddenly gave me an answer for everything."[26] Like other isms, objectivism was essentially an ideology, a gateway to interpreting politics, economics, literature, philosophy, and art from a single perspective. It gave young followers a strong sense of certainty about the world. But as Hannah Arendt points out in "Christianity and Revolution," "certainty is not truth, and a system of certainties is the end of philosophy."[27]

When the novelist-philosopher became known as a cultish figure, it only added to her notoriety and fame. Her novels were a publishing legend. By 1964 *Atlas Shrugged* had sold over a million copies. (*The Fountainhead* would sell almost 2 million hardcover and paperback copies by 1967.) In March Rand reached another popularity peak: *Playboy* magazine conducted an in-depth interview. Its publisher, Hugh Hefner, who launched the magazine that became a media giant, was her fan. Rand's political and economic views were close to his *Playboy* philosophy, which stood for a laissez-faire attitude, consumerism, and freedom of expression. Alvin Toffler, a business writer and futurist who had interviewed Vladimir Nabokov, was assigned to interview Rand. His brief introduction to the piece captures her prominence and the divisive nature of her work: "Ayn Rand, an intense, angry woman of 58, is among the most outspoken—and important—intellectual voices in America today." She had criticized all aspects of American society—its culture, religion, politics, and economics. Her books offered radical proposals for changing the way most people think, work, and love. *Atlas Shrugged*, "perhaps the most fiercely damned and admired best seller of the decade," is one of the most discussed books in America. But despite Rand's popular success, she remained an outsider in the literary establishment and among philosophers.[28]

During the interview, which focused on Rand's moral philosophy, she declared that the most depraved type of human being was "the man without a purpose"—and not a dictator, like Hitler and Stalin. Work and achievement, she said, were the highest goals in life. But if a person organizes his life around a single purpose, wondered Toffler, isn't he in danger of becoming narrow? On the contrary, Rand argued, single-mindedness saves him "from pointless inner conflicts." If people seek fulfillment in friendship or family, would she consider them immoral? Yes, she said readily: a man who places others above his creative work is "an emotional parasite." She called sex "one of the most important aspects" in life, but scorned promiscuity—precisely because sex was "too good and too important." Rand "most emphatically" advocated moral absolutes, a black-and-white view of the world. Asked whether objectivism can be called a dogma, she argued it cannot be: a dogma is based on faith, while objectivism is based on reason. But could it harden into a dogma? No, she answered: objectivism requires the use of one's mind and thus is "its own protection against people who might attempt to use it as a dogma." Toffler concluded the interview by asking whether Rand was optimistic about the future. She was: she believed in "man's unlimited potentiality for greatness," which she interpreted as "the capacity to live by three fundamental values of John Galt: reason, purpose, self-esteem."[29] From this interview Rand emerged as an influential outsider, a role Jews have played for generations, living in majority cultures while questioning conventional values and beliefs.

A controller by nature, she was becoming more protective of the creed and wary of any misinterpretations. Only her designated representatives could lecture on objectivism. The Ayn Rand discussion clubs had to indicate that they officially did not represent her philosophy. Jarret Wollstein, a libertarian and student of objectivism whose story Jennifer Burns tells in her book *Goddess of the Market*, offered an independent course on Rand's ideas at the University of Maryland. Although he identified himself as not being sanctioned by Rand, a local NBI representative came to his class to read a statement that he was not an approved teacher. Wollstein faced additional sanctions: he was purged from the movement and prohibited from attending NBI lectures.[30] Rand's suspicion that people tried to cash in on her name was often unjustified. Mimi Gladstein, a professor of literature at the University of Texas at El Paso, wrote to Rand of her plan to issue *The Ayn Rand Companion.* In reply she received a letter threatening a lawsuit if she proceeded. Rand had no legal power to stop her, so the book was published without her permission.[31]

In 1969 Rand drafted a letter of agreement, specifying conditions for her radio and television appearances. Her first requirement was that a program be "a serious discussion of ideas," but the next point began, "There will be no debate." A list of questions and the exact wording of each introduction had to be submitted for her approval. References to critics could not be made.[32] Since Rand was the most criticized writer in America, this last point is understandable—unlike her need to air her views unchallenged. Because she drew large audiences to the shows, all her conditions were accepted.

Her annual presentations at the Ford Hall Forum in Boston became known as "the Objectivist Easter." Arriving from other cities, the objectivists lined up by the building to get seats where Rand would speak; the overflow crowd would fill the next-largest auditorium to hear her over loudspeakers. During question periods her opinion was sought on a variety of issues. Rand was among the first to oppose Jack Kennedy's escalation of American involvement in Vietnam. She believed in noninitiation of force, having made it the basic political principle of objectivism and, like other American isolationists, was against fighting abroad. But in 1967 she argued against the anticipated American withdrawal: "The idea that this country cannot defeat Vietnam is ridiculous, and the whole world knows it. But we are not allowed to use our strength," she added ominously.[33] When, a decade later, she was asked to comment on America's involvement in Vietnam in terms of justice, she said that the injustice was done only to Americans: "We are guilty of colossal, stupid self-sacrifice. We aren't guilty of anything with respect to the Vietnamese."[34] In *Atlas Shrugged* Rand stated that "man's life is the standard of morality"; however, her principles were not designed as universal. At the Ford Hall Forum in 1976 she declared that "anyone who wants to invade a dictatorship or semi-dictatorship is morally justified in doing so."[35] In all cases, American interests and American lives came first. It was also at the Ford Hall Forum that Rand expressed her support for Israel during the Yom Kippur War of

1973. She said she regarded Israel as the only outpost "of modern science and civilization" in the region.[36] Israel became the second international cause to which she donated money.[37]

Rand's personal life was in turmoil. According to Barbara's version of events, Rand's affair with Nathaniel had been put on hold for about six years, but in 1964 she told her lover she was ready to resume it. By then it was too late: Nathaniel had become involved with Patrecia Gullison, a beautiful young model and aspiring actress who attended his lectures at NBI. Patrecia was married, so the affair was kept secret from both her husband and Rand. Nathaniel misled Rand, inventing all sorts of psychological problems to explain his loss of sexual passion. When Rand asked whether their age difference might be responsible, he denied it, believing she simply wanted to be reassured. Trying to unravel the mystery, Rand wrote papers analyzing his psychology and discussed her theories with Nathaniel, who would give her another puzzle to solve. Her theories prevented her from trusting her intuition, so she doggedly pursued false leads. In 1965 Barbara and Nathaniel divorced, and so did Patrecia and her husband, Lawrence. Barbara, as Rand's confidante, had to hear her complaints about Nathaniel. Frank was not spared either. At seventy-one, he was growing forgetful and withdrawn, sliding deeper into drinking and amnesia.

Events began to unravel in July 1968, when Barbara, who had known the truth for a while, prevailed on Nathaniel to stop playing games with Rand. That year Rand filled her private journal with desperate theories, analyzing Nathaniel's every word. He was afraid to disclose the truth, realizing Rand would take away NBI, to which he had given ten years. So he revealed a partial truth in a carefully crafted letter, saying that their age difference had indeed become a barrier to his sexual desire. Barbara thought his letter was as tactful as it could be, but they both knew it would deal a blow to Rand's self-esteem. As expected, she reacted with fury. After a stormy scene, which Barbara had to witness, Rand declared that her relationship with Nathaniel was over.

She moved to dissociate herself from the man she had long promoted as her spokesman and intellectual heir. Nathaniel agreed to the conditions that would curtail his ventures and profits. (According to Rand's biographer Anne Heller, the combined annual income of NBI and its branches was $400,000.) But this was only a prelude to the dramatic end. Having conducted all purges from the movement, Nathaniel knew it was now his turn to be condemned and disgraced. "Judge and be prepared to be judged," was Rand's famous dictum. The judgment day came on August 23. Rand considered changing her will in Barbara's favor. But Barbara had been part of the deception and felt she could not accept this offer. Arriving at Rand's apartment with Alan Blumenthal, Nathaniel's cousin and a psychiatrist, Barbara disclosed facts about Nathaniel's involvement with Patrecia. "Get him down here," Rand demanded. It took minutes for Nathaniel to arrive from another floor. No longer admitted to the living room, he was seated on a straight chair in the entrance. Blumenthal and Barbara watched Rand's vilification—an outpouring of abuse over Nathaniel's head. Frank endured it while sitting in an armchair, his eyes closed. Rand's bizarre charges were producing the opposite effect: instead of destroying her lover, she spiritually liberated him. Among other things, she shouted that if she were "eighty years old and in a wheelchair," he still had to desire her. In the end, she slapped Nathaniel's face three times and bellowed that if he had any decency left in him, he would remain impotent for the next twenty years.

Responsible for Nathaniel's rise, Rand used her influence to destroy him. She ordered his immediate resignation from NBI and issued specific requirements. Nathaniel complied: pale and mortified, he appeared at a staff meeting to confess his immorality (without disclosing the nature of his misdeed). Henry Holzer, Rand's lawyer for the objectivist movement and a follower as well, handled the legal matters of separation. Nathaniel had to transfer his 50 percent interest in the *Objectivist* to Rand, along with the copyright for his articles. Arguing that his articles were influenced by her ideas, she also attempted to stop the publication of his book *The Psychology of Self-Esteem.* But NLA, her publisher and Nathaniel's, refused to give in. The literary agents at Curtis Brown, who represented them both, also told their valuable client that they did not yield to outside pressure. Nathaniel's book did not come out at NLA because he missed the deadline, but it was brought out by another publisher who issued it without the copyright. Nathaniel Branden would produce a series of books on psychology, focusing on self-esteem. (The self-esteem movement, which Rand spearheaded, began to proliferate in the 1960s and 1970s, influencing educational philosophy in Britain and in America.)[38]

Barbara was purged by association, but she refused to appear at her trial. In the statement published in the *Objectivist*, "To Whom It May Concern," Rand informed her readers that she had "permanently broken all personal, professional and business associations" with the Brandens. "I repudiate both of them, totally and permanently, as spokesmen for me or Objectivism." She also alleged that Nathaniel had exploited her intellectually and financially. Unable to reveal the true reason for the split, she accused him of "departure from the principles of Objectivism" and of "ugly actions and irrational behavior in his private life."[39] Barbara was charged with uttering "veiled threats and undefined accusations against me."[40] Rand's letter was signed by four members of the senior Collective—Alan Blumenthal, Alan Greenspan, Leonard Peikoff, and Mary Ann Sures. Even Nathaniel's sisters would sever ties with the outcasts.

Rand was unguarded: Nathaniel had been her spokesman for ten years, and a public quarrel with him could not go unnoticed. She smeared his reputation, and he had to respond. His letter, "In Answer to Ayn Rand," to which Barbara contributed a postscript, was sent to the entire mailing list of the *Objectivist*. It contained sensational lines, suggesting that the cause of the breakup was sexual: "I felt that an age distance between us of twenty-five years constituted an insuperable barrier, for me, to a romantic relationship."[41] Rand's fear that her reputation would suffer became a self-fulfilling prophecy. In December the *National Review* gave further publicity to Rand's schism with her disciple. Commenting on her statement accusing Nathaniel of moral failure, William Buckley wrote gleefully: "Remember, these were the people who were telling the rest of the world how to reach nirvana. By being like them."[42] On December 31, Buckley observed that there was further disintegration of the objectivist movement and quoted the most damaging lines from Nathaniel's defense.

Earlier, on September 2, Rand had decided to liquidate NBI, which had been central to the movement. The institute's demise left true believers grappling for answers. When the dust settled, Rand remained with a handful of followers from the senior Collective, class of '43. As a writer she retained her vast audience: her novels, found at bus stations and popular outlets, continued to make record sales.

With Nathaniel gone, Frank emerged as the man nearest to Rand. For their fortieth wedding anniversary, on April 15, 1969, he ordered her a ring. It had forty rubies, each stone marking a year lived together. Rand wore it during her trip with Frank to Cape Kennedy, Florida, in mid-July. Greenspan, then serving in Nixon's administration, arranged for them to watch the historic launch of Apollo 11, which carried the first humans to the moon. In the article "Apollo and Dionysus" Rand describes the event as "an achievement of man in his capacity as a rational being—an achievement of reason, of logic, of mathematics."[43] Hosted by the Vaught family at Cape Kennedy, Rand and Frank made an impression as a "very devoted" couple. Rand avoided publicity on this trip and looked relaxed; she mentioned her background as a Russian Jew and spoke memorably, but not harshly, of her opposition to welfare.[44]

In April 1972 Albert Ruddy, the thirty-year-old producer of *The Godfather*, decided to film *Atlas Shrugged*. This was Rand's first opportunity in two decades to sell film rights. Ruddy's background would have appealed to her: raised in a Jewish family in Montreal, he studied chemical engineering as well as architecture, and even worked for some time designing homes. He told Rand that he considered *Atlas Shrugged* a greater literary work than *The Godfather*. All this mattered to her, and the contract was quickly drafted at Curtis Brown. Rand's conditions were met, including the most extravagant one: during the shooting she wanted to fly in a private jet to the West Coast. "Darling," she told Ruddy, "if the Russians find out that I'm flying on an airliner, they'll hijack it."[45] The deal fell through when Rand requested an unprecedented final script approval. Ruddy told her that no one could have total control, but she was adamant. The producer left for Europe, and when he returned in August he did not phone Rand.

Life still held some surprises. Rand thought her family in Leningrad had perished. But Nora, her beloved sister, was alive. In March 1973 Lilyan Courtois, an editor of *Amerika* magazine, a Russian-language periodical, received a letter from Nora Drobysheva. At an exhibition in Leningrad, called *Research and Development, USA*, Nora received the December 1971 issue of *Amerika*. It had a photograph and short feature about Rand. Nora recognized her sister and wrote a letter asking the editors to forward it to Ayn Rand, Mrs. Frank O'Connor. *Amerika* was the only nontechnical publication from the free world distributed in the Soviet Union after 1956. The issue Nora received contained brief interviews with ten famous people whose views represented a broad political spectrum. Included along with the singer Peggy Lee, actor Edgar Buchanan, comedians Jerry Lewis and Lily Tomlin, Rand was quoted chiding environmentalists for opposing industrial development. Rand's first reaction to the editor's phone call was mistrust. But when Courtois read Nora's note, she started sobbing. The note could not have been written by anyone else: Nora used their childhood nicknames. "Dear Dact! I love you as before and am proud of you. Don't forget me, and think about me as I think about you every day. Dact II."[46] Rand had not seen her sister for forty-seven years. As she wrote in her first letter to Nora, she "laughed and cried and was very, very happy."[47] It took a year to arrange a trip to New York for Nora and her husband, Fedya. Both were survivors of the Siege of Leningrad, and Fedya, a retired engineer, had also survived two heart attacks. They were secure financially and did not consider emigrating; they requested a visa for three months to see the country. In one of her letters Nora wrote that they dreamed of walking in New York with Rand as their guide.[48] During a telephone call Rand first mentioned her achievements—her novels, plays, and nonfiction. The sisters discussed their shared love of architecture and of Frank Lloyd Wright's designs.[49] *Amerika* magazine wanted to document the reunion, but Rand refused publicity.

Nora and Fedya arrived in New York on April 15, 1974. Rand met them with pomp, having arranged a limousine to take them from the airport to a rental flat. At first she was considerate, arranging a visit to a heart specialist for Fedya and taking the two to Central Park. But soon she began to proselytize, and the sisters got into a heated argument. They clashed over Rand's rejection of altruism. It was unrealistic of Rand to expect that her sister would become converted on the spot: the two had lived strikingly different lives, on different continents, for half a century. Rand's life experience was limited to her work, whereas Nora had lived through the war and the siege, witnessing examples of true altruism when people kept each other alive. Much later, Nora told an interviewer that it was the altruism of their entire family that made it possible for Rand to come to America.[50] Aside from these disagreements, Nora failed to praise her sister's Russian novel, *We the Living*, and kept asking where to get Solzhenitsyn's books, especially *The Gulag Archipelago*, published recently in the West. That year, in February, Solzhenitsyn was deported from the USSR for revealing the truth about Stalinism. But Rand despised him for his nationalist embrace of Christian Orthodoxy. The sisters' bickering may have aggravated Fedya's illness. On May 7 he suffered another heart attack and spent two weeks in a hospital. Rand, by then disillusioned with her sister, no longer wanted her around. Shortly after Fedya's release, she asked Nora whether it was time for them to return to Leningrad. They departed on May 26, and Rand did not go to the airport to see them off. The sisters would never meet or speak again.

Over the years Rand severed many relationships, broke up with the libertarians who had been part of her circle, and would continue to expunge people from her life. Even her original disciples, the Blumenthals and the Kalbermans, were gone by the end. Alan Greenspan, whose rising career Rand followed with pride, was an exception. Her most prominent disciple, he publicly acknowledged her influence. On September 4, 1974, she attended his White House swearing-in as chairman of the Council of Economic Advisers. Rand and Greenspan's mother, Rose Goldsmith, stood by his side during the ceremony. Later they were photographed with the president. One picture with Gerald Ford shows a smiling Rand; Frank, standing next to her, stoops wearily, his eyes closed. (He was in an advanced stage of arteriosclerosis.) *Time* wrote that "Rand is openly pleased over her real-life achiever-hero's rise to the White House."[51] On February 24, 1975, *Newsweek* ran a long article on Greenspan, elucidating his belief that "government interference in the nation's markets, whether it be in the form of antitrust legislation, consumer protection or industry regulation, does far more harm than good." Rand's influence over the major economist was implied in the article's ironic subtitle: "Atlas Jogs." The piece also covered Rand's career and mentioned that she was Greenspan's favorite author. Through Greenspan, who in 1987 became chair of the Federal Reserve, Rand's ideas influenced major Republicans, including the economist Martin Anderson, a top adviser to President Reagan. The economist and investor George Gilder also acknowledged Rand as an important influence. His *Wealth and Poverty* analyzes the roots of economic growth and asserts the moral superiority of capitalism. Described by a *New York Times* reviewer as "a guide to Capitalism," Gilder's best-selling book became the bible of the Reagan administration.

In March 1974, months before being diagnosed with lung cancer, Rand spoke to 1,500 officers and cadets at the West Point Military Academy. Colonel Herman Ivey, who invited Rand and later included her lecture in the academy's curriculum, recalls that she walked slowly through campus, pausing to catch her breath: "It was a terrible thing to see, but she was a game girl. . . . She would not admit defeat."[52] Rand spoke to an overflowing audience about the importance of abstract ideas, principles, and philosophical systems. Her basic talk, "Philosophy: Who Needs It," was spruced up with attacks on Kant: she called his system "the biggest and most intricate booby trap in the history of philosophy."[53] She concluded on a patriotic note, praising American armed forces. Controversy arose during the question session when she was asked to comment on the settlers' extermination campaigns against Native Americans. Rand's response was uninformed and biased: she believed "the most unsympathetic Hollywood portrayal of Indians and what they did to the white man." Europeans had the right to take over the continent because they brought in elements of civilization, while the aboriginals "did not have the concept of property or property rights" and therefore had no rights to the land.[54] (To some extent Rand's reply reflected the position of John Locke, the English Enlightenment philosopher and major inspiration for the U.S. Constitution, who believed that unused property was wasteful.) But the question was asked by a Native American, which she may not have known. Jack Capps, the brigadier general at West Point, recalls that her answer "cooled off the atmosphere considerably." It suggested that a technologically superior culture was also morally right.[55]

During that eventful year, on October 20, Rand gave a talk on economic issues at Ford Hall Forum. Unconcerned with practical knowledge of the economy and finance, her paper "Egalitarianism and Inflation" viewed the issues in philosophical terms. In *Atlas Shrugged* she emphasized the moral value of money but kept her own capital in a savings account—until Greenspan prevailed on her to invest.[56] On December 20, while seriously ill, she gave an interview to the *Christian Science Monitor*. Six days later, her physician, Dr. Murray Dworetzky, had her repeat an X-ray. She was in his office when he talked to her, as always, about the need to stop smoking. Rand replied, "Give me a rational explanation." Her X-rays were brought in. He put them on his viewing box and pointed to a nodule on her lung: "That's a good reason right there."[57] Although a heavy smoker, Rand put out her cigarette, quitting once and for all. On January 10, 1975, she had surgery for lung cancer at New York Hospital. The recovery was long and trying.

In her declining years Rand pursued her passion of stamp collecting. She attended stamp shows and auctions with fellow collectors, one of whom was her surgeon Dr. Cranston Holman. She shopped at Gimbels, her favorite store, played Scrabble with visitors, read Agatha Christie, watched TV cops and robbers, and in her mid-seventies, studied algebra. Rand was now diagnosed with arteriosclerosis, like Frank, whose condition had deteriorated: he began to show symptoms similar to those of Alzheimer's. In 1976 Rand's new attorney, Paul Gitlin, sent his firm's representative, Evva Pryor, to persuade Rand to apply for Medicare. Over a game of Scrabble Evva spoke to Rand about the realities of old age: she could be wiped out by medical bills.

Rand despised government interference but gave power of attorney to Evva, who handled the rest.

Harry Binswanger, a descendant of a prominent Jewish family that had founded Binswanger Glass Company in Richmond, Virginia, first met Rand as a freshman at a lecture at MIT. Later he worked with her on *The Ayn Rand Lexicon*, a concise encyclopedia of objectivism, and also edited her final nonfiction book, *Introduction to Objectivist Epistemology*. There was an incident, he recalls, involving a mutual female acquaintance, Jewish by birth, who failed to respond to anti-Semitic vitriol at a gathering. "Ayn held that it was morally obligatory to say you were Jewish, and that she had done so herself, even though she was an avowed atheist." Binswanger remembers Rand's illuminating remark: "The only time I'm Jewish is when I hear anti-Semitism."[58]

In the late 1970s Rand signed a contract with Jaffe Productions and NBC for developing *Atlas Shrugged* into a television miniseries. She was the first in the history of network television to receive full control of a script. Stirling Silliphant, who collaborated on the nine-hour adaptation, had no authority to change a single word in the dialogue. The project was canceled in 1978 when Fred Silverman became president of NBC. Nonetheless, Rand continued to work on the script almost until the end. During her final public appearance, in 1981, she told a business audience that she was writing a teleplay for *Atlas Shrugged* and intending to produce it herself with private financing.

Frank died in November 1979, at eighty-two, and was buried at Kensico Cemetery in Valhalla, New York. The site had appealed to Rand because Rachmaninoff's grave was there; she chose this final resting place for Frank and herself. During her marriage of fifty years she seemed not to notice Frank, but his absence created a painful void. She knew little about the real man whose photograph hung over her desk to inspire her heroic characters. But in 1980, on *The Phil Donahue Show*, her first public appearance after Frank's death, she said that her position in the world has changed: "I lost my top value." Although frail and depressed, Rand preserved her fighting spirit. During a question session, she clashed with the audience, refusing to accept less than full agreement with her views. This was not her first public confrontation with readers. With age she became more categorical and isolated, demanding that the outside world live by the moral values she outlined. An idealist, she defended her vision for a successful America.

On November 21, 1981, Rand gave her final talk at a business conference in New Orleans. James Blanchard, founder of the National Committee for Monetary Reform (NCMR), persuaded her to appear at their annual investment conference. (Over the years NCMR speakers included the economists Milton Friedman, F. A. Hayek, Robert Bleiberg, and Walter Williams.) Rand's novels had inspired Blanchard, left paraplegic after a car accident, to believe in unlimited human potential. Despite his disability, he became a major expert on precious-metal investing and successfully campaigned for legalizing private ownership of gold. Blanchard arranged for Rand to travel to New Orleans in a private rail car with a gourmet chef, and she set out with Peikoff, her new heir, and a few others. Her talk, "The Sanction of the Victim," shared the central theme with *Atlas Shrugged:* the producers, who carry the capitalist economy on their shoulders, should function without government interference. She concluded with lines from the novel: "The world you desired can be won, it exists, it is real, it is possible. But to win requires total dedication and a total break with the world of your past."[59] There was much in this eloquent passage aside from the intended meaning. It told the story of Rand's fight for achievement and the price she paid for it; it also drew a line over her life.

After the conference Rand developed pneumonia, from which she never recovered. She died on March 6, 1982. The *New York Times* ran an obituary and covered the funeral, attended by eight hundred admirers. In the funeral home Rand's body lay next to a six-foot dollar sign. Believing in the power of a legend, she continued to advocate free-market capitalism from beyond the grave.

ACKNOWLEDGMENTS

I RESEARCHED THIS BOOK at the Ayn Rand Archives, where, during the pandemic, I received permission to work remotely. I'm grateful to the archivist Jeff Britting, who responded to my inquiries with knowledge and courtesy and whose help in this project was essential.

The Ayn Rand Institute has given me the following disclaimer: "Permission to quote from Ayn Rand's published and unpublished works courtesy of Leonard Peikoff. The Ayn Rand Archives at the Ayn Rand Institute is a reference source. Use of its information and services by this author does not constitute endorsement or recommendation of this work by the Ayn Rand Institute or Leonard Peikoff."

I am grateful to Stan Oliver, the executor of John Hospers's estate, for permission to quote from Hospers's letters to Rand, and to Professor Barbara Henry, who helped translate phrases in Yiddish from the Rosenbaums' letters. My thanks go to Ileene Smith, who commissioned me to write this biography; to my editor, Heather Gold; to my copyeditor, Ann Twombly, and to my agent, Don Fehr. I'm also grateful to my husband, Wilfred, for his help in editing this book.

NOTES

Preface

1. Arthur Hertzberg and Aron Hirt-Manheimer, *Jews: The Essence and Character of a People* (San Francisco: HarperSanFrancisco, 1998), 31.

Chapter 1. Born Jewish

1. The dates are given by the Gregorian calendar currently in use. Rand's date of birth by the Julian calendar Russia used until 1917 is January 20.
2. Mikhail Beizer, *The Jews of St. Petersburg*, trans. Michael Sherbourne (Philadelphia: Jewish Publication Society, 1989), 6.
3. Benjamin Nathans, *Beyond the Pale: The Jewish Encounter with Late Imperial Russia* (Berkeley: University of California Press, 2002), 215.
4. Ibid., 126.
5. E. L. Shvarts, "Telefonnaya knizhka," https://www.rulit.me

/books/telefonnaya-knizhka-read-287941-98.html; "Kaplan Mikhail Borisovich," *Biographica*, Istoriya Sankt-Peterburgskogo universiteta, https://bioslovhist.spbu.ru/hist-pg-ld/2365-kaplan-mihail-borisovic.html.

6. Benjamin Nathans, "Saint Petersburg," *The YIVO Encyclopedia of Jews in Eastern Europe*, https://yivoencyclopedia.org/article.aspx/Saint_Petersburg.

7. Anna Borisovna (AB) to Ayn Rand (AR), May 12, 1933, Ayn Rand Papers (ARP), Ayn Rand Archives, 067–293a.

8. Yohanan Petrovsky-Shtern, *Jews in the Russian Army, 1827–1917* (Cambridge: Cambridge University Press, 2009), 134, 202–3.

9. Anne Heller, *Ayn Rand and the World She Made* (New York: Doubleday, 2009), 9.

10. Zinovy Rosenbaum (ZZ) to AR, February 7, 1934, ARP, 068–347.

11. Nathans, *Beyond the Pale*, 314.

12. Ayn Rand, *We the Living* (1936; repr., New York: Dutton, 1995), 217–18.

13. Yuri Slezkine, *The Jewish Century* (Princeton: Princeton University Press, 2004), 115.

14. Quoted in Hans Rogger, *Jewish Policies and Right-Wing Politics in Imperial Russia* (London: Macmillan, 1986), 48.

15. Barbara Branden, *The Passion of Ayn Rand* (Garden City, N.Y.: Doubleday, 1986), 23.

16. Irving Howe, *World of Our Fathers: The Journey of the East European Jews to America and the Life They Found and Made* (New York: Harcourt Brace Jovanovich, 1976).

17. Scott McConnell, *100 Voices: An Oral History of Ayn Rand* (New York: New American Library, 2010), 13.

18. AB to AR, February 2, 1934, ARP, 068–346.

19. AB to AR, April 28–29, 1926, ARP, 062–035.

20. Ayn Rand, "Victor Hugo Allows Peak at Grandeur," *Los Angeles Times*, September 16, 1962.

21. Ayn Rand, *The Romantic Manifesto: A Philosophy of Literature* (1969; repr., New York: Signet, 1975), 161.

22. Shoshana Milgram, "Three Inspirations for the Ideal Man,"

in *Essays on Ayn Rand's "The Fountainhead,"* ed. Robert Mayhew (Lanham, Md.: Lexington Books, 2007), 183–84.

23. AB to AR, June 8, 1926, ARP, 062–053a.

24. Stefan Zweig, *The World of Yesterday* (1942), trans. Anthea Bell (Lincoln: University of Nebraska Press, 2013), 436.

25. AB to AR, November 10–11, 1933, ARP, 068–333.

26. Zweig, *The World of Yesterday*, 235, 244.

27. Yitzhak Arad, *The Holocaust in the Soviet Union* (Lincoln: University of Nebraska Press, 2009), 11.

28. Beizer, *The Jews of St. Petersburg*, 108.

29. Jeff Britting, *Ayn Rand* (Woodstock, N.Y.: Overlook, 2004), 11.

30. Ibid., 14.

31. Ibid.

32. Nina Berberova, *Kursiv moi* (Moscow: Soglasie, 1996), 112.

33. Lyudmila Nikiforova and Mikhail Kizilov, *Ayn Rand* (Moscow: Molodaya gvardiya, 2020), 53.

34. Britting, *Ayn Rand*, 14.

35. Branden, *The Passion of Ayn Rand*, 21.

36. Laura Engelstein, *Russia in Flames: War, Revolution, Civil War, 1914–1921* (New York: Oxford University Press, 2018), 514, 517.

37. Branden, *The Passion of Ayn Rand*, 30.

38. Nikiforova and Kizilov, *Ayn Rand*, 86.

39. AB to AR, February 5, 1933, ARP, 067–279.

40. Nikiforova and Kizilov, *Ayn Rand*, 94–95.

41. Ayn Rand, "TV's 'Cyrano' Shows Decline," *Los Angeles Times*, December 16, 1962.

42. Rand, *We the Living*, 6.

43. Ayn Rand, "The Lessons of Vietnam," in *The Voice of Reason: Essays in Objectivist Thought*, ed. Leonard Peikoff (New York: Meridian, 1989), 137, 139; emphasis in original.

44. Nathaniel Branden and Barbara Branden, *Who Is Ayn Rand? An Analysis of the Novels of Ayn Rand* (1962; repr., New York: Paperback Library, 1964), 129.

45. AB to AR, January 30, 1933, ARP, 067–277.

46. Rand, *We the Living*, 98.
47. Ibid., 3–4.
48. Ibid., 14.

Chapter 2. A Second Columbus

1. AB to AR, July 2–3, 1930, ARP, 066–222.
2. E. L. Shvarts, "Telefonnaya knizhka," https://www.rulit.me/books/telefonnaya-knizhka-read-287941-98.html.
3. AB to AR, November 16, 1933, ARP, 068–334.
4. Chris Matthew Sciabarra and Pavel Solovyev, "The Rand Transcript Revealed," *Journal of Ayn Rand Studies* 21, no. 2 (2021): 199.
5. Barbara Branden, *The Passion of Ayn Rand* (Garden City, N.Y.: Doubleday, 1986), 42.
6. Sciabarra and Solovyev, "The Rand Transcript Revealed," 174–75.
7. Ibid., 159.
8. Dmitry Likhachev, *Vospominaniya* (Saint Petersburg: Logos, 1995), 111.
9. Jeff Britting, *Ayn Rand* (Woodstock, N.Y.: Overlook, 2004), 22.
10. Steven E. Aschheim, *The Nietzsche Legacy in Germany* (Berkeley: University of California Press, 1992), 102–3.
11. Ibid., 103n71.
12. Ibid., 106.
13. Natasha to AR, February 26, 1928, ARP, 065–169.
14. Martha Weitzel Hickey, *The Writer in Petrograd and the House of Arts* (Evanston, Ill.: Northwestern University Press, 2009), 187–88.
15. Irina Odoevtseva, *Izbrannoe* (Moscow, 1998), 201.
16. Leon Trotsky, *Literature and Revolution*, chap. 5, https://www.marxists.org/archive/trotsky/1924/lit_revo/ch05.htm.
17. Evgeny Zamyatin, "Tomorrow," in *A Soviet Heretic: Essays by Yevgeny Zamyatin*, trans. Mirra Ginsburg (Chicago: University of Chicago Press, 1970), 51–52.
18. Ibid., 51–52, 105–6.

19. Zamyatin, "The New Russian Prose," in *A Soviet Heretic*, 106.

20. AB to AR, January 15–22, 1928, ARP, 065–164, and October 2, 1930, ARP, 066–228.

21. Seymour Becker, *Nobility and Privilege in Late Imperial Russia* (DeKalb, Ill.: Northern Illinois University Press, 1985), 106–7.

22. *Journals of Ayn Rand*, ed. David Harriman (1997; repr., New York: Plume, 1999), 53; hereafter cited as Rand, *Journals*.

23. For more on Lev Bekkerman, see https://www.poslednyadres.ru/news/news899.htm.

24. For more on Pal'men, see https://code.ascon.ru/palmen/.

25. Scott McConnell, "Parallel Lives," in *Essays on Ayn Rand's "We the Living,"* ed. Robert Mayhew (Lanham, Md.: Lexington Books, 2012), 50–52.

26. Nina Guzarchik to AR, February 9, 1934, ARP, 068–349.

27. Ayn Rand, *We the Living* (1936; repr., New York: Dutton, 1995), 122, 152.

28. AB to AR, January 21, 1926, ARP, 062–009.

29. AB to AR, January 22–23, 1926, ARP, 062–009.

30. Ayn Rand, "Pola Negri," in *Russian Writings on Hollywood*, ed. Michael Berliner (Marina del Rey, Calif.: Ayn Rand Institute Press, 1999), 2–9.

31. Rand, "American Movie Directors," in *Russian Writings*, 18.

32. AB to AR, May 21, 1926, ARP, 062–048. The Yiddish text in the letters appears in Cyrillic; I used the standard YIVO transliteration.

33. AB to AR with a note from ZZ, January 18, 1926, ARP, 062–005a.

34. Hand-written, unsigned note without an envelope, January 20, 1926, ARP, 062–006. This was the day of Rand's twenty-first birthday by the Julian calendar (O.S.). The note is in Russian, but "Alice" is spelled in English.

35. AB to AR, February 21, 1926, ARP, 062–015.

36. Nora to AR, January 21–22, 1926, ARP, 062–008.

37. Vera Guzarchik to AR, June 25–27, 1926, ARP, 063–059.

38. AB to AR, February 1–2, 1926, ARP, 062–012.

39. AB and ZZ to AR, January 22–23, 1936, ARP, 062–009.

40. AB and ZZ to AR, February 21, 1926, ARP, 062–015.

41. AB to AR, March 7, 1926, ARP, 062–018.

Chapter 3. Apprenticeship in Hollywood

1. Scott McConnell, *100 Voices: An Oral History of Ayn Rand* (New York: New American Library, 2010), 22.

2. Nora and AB to AR, June 3–4, 1926, ARP, 062–052. Although Rand's letters were lost during World War II, their content is known from her family's responses.

3. AB to AR, April 4, 8, 1926, ARP, 062–023.

4. Natasha to AR, April 10–11, 1926, ARP, 062–024.

5. Nora to AR, April 10–11, 1926, ARP, 062–024d, and May 19, 1926, ARP, 062–047.

6. AR to Lev Bekkerman, August 28, 1926, in *Letters of Ayn Rand*, ed. Michael S. Berliner (New York: Dutton, 1995), 1–2.

7. Nora to AR, April 10–11, 1926, ARP, 062–024.

8. AB to AR, April 28–29, 1926, ARP, 062–035.

9. AB to AR, April 4, 8, 1926, ARP, 062–023.

10. Scott Eyman, *Empire of Dreams: The Epic Life of Cecil B. DeMille* (New York: Simon and Schuster, 2010), 221. For information about Cecil B. DeMille I am indebted to Scott Eyman.

11. Anne Heller, *Ayn Rand and the World She Made* (New York: Doubleday, 2009), 61.

12. Ayn Rand, *The Fountainhead* (1943; repr., New York: Plume, 2005), xiii.

13. Eyman, *Empire of Dreams*, 9. Quotation from the *Jewish Tribune* (an undated clipping in DeMille's collection) is from ibid., 245.

14. AB to AR, October 14–15, 1926, ARP, 063–094.

15. AR to DeMille, July 3, 1934, in *Letters*, 11.

16. Quoted in Eyman, *Empire of Dreams*, 253.

17. Barbara Branden, *The Passion of Ayn Rand* (Garden City, N.Y.: Doubleday, 1986), 78.

18. AB to AR, January 16–17, 1936, ARP, 070–451.

19. Rand, *Journals*, 6.

20. Ibid., 10.

21. The Rosenbaums to AR, January 3, 1927, ARP, 064–107.

22. AB to AR, January 1, 1928, ARP, 065–161.

23. AB to AR, May 21, 1928, ARP, 065–176.

24. Ayn Rand, *We the Living* (1936; repr., New York: Dutton, 1995), 331, 398.

25. *The Early Ayn Rand: A Selection from Her Unpublished Fiction*, ed. Leonard Peikoff (1984; repr., New York: Signet, 2005), 7.

26. Rand, *Journals*, 27, 29.

27. Heller, *Ayn Rand*, 56.

28. Branden, *The Passion of Ayn Rand*, 93.

29. Heller, *Ayn Rand*, 100.

30. AB to AR, February 28, 1929, ARP, 065–198.

31. The Rosenbaums to AR, March 18, 1929, ARP, 065–199.

32. AB to AR, April 20, 1929, ARP, 066–201.

33. AB to AR, September 11, 1929, ARP, 066–210.

34. ZZ to AR, June 27, 1929, ARP, 066–204.

35. AB to AR, August 18, 1929, ARP, 066–209.

36. Heller, *Ayn Rand*, 72.

37. McConnell, *100 Voices*, 43.

38. Ibid., 44.

39. "Russian Girl Finds End of Rainbow in Hollywood," *Chicago Daily Times*, September 26, 1932.

40. Harrison Carrol, "Ayn O'Connor Has Peddled a Film Story to Universal," *Los Angeles Evening Herald*, September 14, 1932.

41. S. A. Malsagov, *An Island Hell: A Soviet Prison in the Far North*, trans. Francis Hamilton Lyon (London: A. M. Philpot, 1926); Yuri Bezsonov, *My Twenty-Six Prisons and My Escape from Solovetski* (London: J. Cape, 1929).

42. AR to DeMille, July 3, 1934, in *Letters*, 11.

Chapter 4. Red Decade

1. Nina Gouzarchik to AR, January 16, 1927, ARP, 064–113.

2. Rand, *Journals*, 52.

3. Ibid., 53.

4. Ayn Rand, *We the Living* (1936; repr., New York: Dutton, 1995), 430, 433.

5. Ibid., 71.

6. Ibid.; emphasis in original.

7. Ibid., 397.

8. AR to Jean Wick, October 27, 1934, in *Letters of Ayn Rand*, ed. Michael S. Berliner (New York: Dutton, 1995).

9. AR to Jean Wick, March 23, 1934, in *Letters*, 5.

10. Tim Tzouliadis, *The Forsaken: An American Tragedy in Stalin's Russia* (New York: Penguin Press, 2008).

11. Eugene Lyons, *Assignment in Utopia* (London: George G. Harrap, 1937), 428–29.

12. Paul Hollander, *Political Pilgrims: Travels of Western Intellectuals to the Soviet Union, China, and Cuba* (New York: Oxford University Press, 1981), 169.

13. Eugene Lyons, *The Red Decade: The Stalinist Penetration of America* (Indianapolis: Bobbs-Merrill, 1941), 106.

14. Ibid., 15.

15. Ibid., 104.

16. AR to Alan Collins, September 23, 1946, in *Letters*, 327.

17. Lyons, *Red Decade*, 285.

18. "Russian Girl Jeers at U.S. for Depression Complaint," *Oakland Tribune*, October 7, 1932.

19. AB to AR, December 3, 1933, ARP, 068–336.

20. AR to Jean Wick, October 27, 1934, in *Letters*, 19.

21. AR to H. L. Mencken, July 28, 1934, in *Letters*, 13.

22. AR to H. L. Mencken, August 8, 1934, in *Letters*, 14.

23. AR to Jean Wick, June 19, 1934, in *Letters*, 10.

24. AB to AR, February 18, 1935, ARP, 069–408.

25. Barbara Branden, *The Passion of Ayn Rand* (Garden City, N.Y.: Doubleday, 1986), 117.

26. Ayn Rand, *Night of January 16th* (1936; repr., Toronto: Signet, 1971), 3.

27. Branden, *The Passion of Ayn Rand*, 117.

28. Rand, *Night of January 16th*, 2.

29. Rand, *Journals*, 70.
30. Rand, *Night of January 16th*, 88.
31. Ibid., 118.
32. Ibid., 56.
33. Ibid., 119.
34. AB to AR, December 18–20, 1934, ARP, 069–402.
35. AR to Mary Inloes, March 16, 1935, in *Letters*, 22.
36. The Rosenbaums to AR, September 11, 1935, ARP, 070–437.
37. Rand, *Night of January 16th*, 11.
38. AR to Gouverneur Morris, January 23, 1936, in *Letters*, 25.
39. AB to AR, September 21, 1935, ARP, 070–439.
40. The Rosenbaums to AR, October 18–19, 1933, ARP, 068–330.
41. ZZ to AR, September 1, 1934, ARP, 069–381.
42. AB to AR, October 24, 1934, ARP, 069–395.
43. AB to AR, October 18, 1935, ARP, 070–442.
44. AB to AR, October 24, 1934, ARP, 069–395.
45. AR to Gouverneur Morris, November 29, 1935, in *Letters*, 23.
46. AB to AR, December 19, 1935, ARP, 070–446.
47. AB to AR, January 11, 1934, ARP, 068–342.
48. The Rosenbaums to AR, telegram, December 23, 1935, ARP, 070–447.
49. AB to AR, April 3, 1936, ARP, 070–458.
50. Ida Zeitlin, "The Individual in Communist Russia," *New York Herald Tribune*, April 19, 1936.
51. AB to AR, June 3, 1936, ARP, 070–464.
52. AB to AR, June 19, 1936, ARP, 070–465a.
53. AB to AR, January 4, 1937, ARP, 070–471.
54. The Rosenbaums to AR, May 31, 1937, ARP, 070–473.

Chapter 5. I versus We

1. AR to Gladys Unger, July 6, 1937, in *Letters of Ayn Rand*, ed. Michael S. Berliner (New York: Dutton, 1995), 42.

2. Ayn Rand, *For the New Intellectual* (1961; repr., New York: Signet, 1963), 67.

3. "Zamyatin Evgeny Ivanovich," *Russkie pisateli 20 veka: Biograficheskij slovar'* (Moscow, 2000).

4. AR to Jean Wick, March 23, 1934, in *Letters*, 4.

5. Yevgeny Zamyatin, *A Soviet Heretic: Essays by Yevgeny Zamyatin*, trans. Mirra Ginsburg (Chicago: University of Chicago Press, 1970), 57.

6. Ibid., 51–52.

7. Yevgeny Zamyatin, *We*, trans. Gregory Zilboorg (1924; repr., New York: E. P. Dutton, 1952), xi.

8. Alex Shane, *The Life and Works of Evgenij Zamjatin* (Berkeley: University of California Press, 1968), 145.

9. Shoshana Milgram, "*Anthem* in Manuscript," in *Essays on Ayn Rand's "Anthem,"* ed. Robert Mayhew (Lanham, Md.: Lexington Books, 2005), 8.

10. Ayn Rand, *Anthem* (1938; repr., New York: Signet, 1961), 93.

11. Ruth 1:16, King James Version.

12. Rand, *Anthem*, 95.

13. Ibid., 109.

14. Rand, *Journals*, 245.

15. Rand, *Anthem*, 118, 116.

16. Rand, *Journals*, 81.

17. Ayn Rand, *The Fountainhead* (1943; repr., New York: Plume, 2005), xi.

18. Rand, *Anthem*, 110.

19. AR to Newman Flower, January 1, 1938, quoted in Shoshana Milgram, "*Anthem* in the Context of Related Literary Works," in Mayhew, *Essays on Ayn Rand's "Anthem,"* 164.

20. Milgram, "*Anthem* in Manuscript," 22.

21. Young Marlow, "Glamour Off," *Reynolds News*, May 22, 1938.

22. AR to DeMille, September 5, 1946, in *Letters*, 316–17. (DeMille's letter is not published in this volume; it's summarized in an editorial comment.)

Chapter 6. *The Fountainhead*

1. Ayn Rand, *The Fountainhead* (1943; repr., New York: Plume, 2005), 13.

2. Ibid., 39.

3. Shoshana Milgram, "*The Fountainhead* from Notebook to Novel," in *Essays on Ayn Rand's "The Fountainhead,"* ed. Robert Mayhew (Lanham, Md.: Lexington Books, 2007), 15–16.

4. Walter Kaufmann, *Nietzsche: Philosopher, Psychologist, Antichrist* (Princeton: Princeton University Press, 1950), 313.

5. Milgram, "*The Fountainhead* from Notebook to Novel," 24.

6. Rand, *The Fountainhead*, xiii.

7. AR to Kenneth MacGowan, May 18, 1934, in *Letters of Ayn Rand*, ed. Michael S. Berliner (New York: Dutton, 1995), 8.

8. Barbara Branden, *The Passion of Ayn Rand* (Garden City, N.Y.: Doubleday, 1986), 132.

9. Quoted in Shoshana Milgram, "Three Inspirations," in Mayhew, *Essays on Ayn Rand's "The Fountainhead,"* 195.

10. AR to Mrs. Blodgett, August 28, 1943, in *Letters*, 92.

11. Nina Gouzarchik to AR, June 30, 1932, ARP, 067–259.

12. ZZ to AR, September 1, 1934, ARP, 069–381.

13. ZZ to AR, August 18, 1935, ARP, 070–432.

14. AR to F. L. Wright, December 12, 1937, in *Letters*, 109.

15. Kaufmann, *Nietzsche*, 179.

16. Rand, *Journals*, 99.

17. Ibid.

18. Friedrich Nietzsche, *Thus Spoke Zarathustra* (1883), trans. R. J. Hollingdale (Baltimore: Penguin Books, 1961), 225.

19. Frank Lloyd Wright, *An Autobiography* (1943; repr., New York: Duell, Sloan and Pearce, 1957), 152.

20. Rand, *The Fountainhead*, 606.

21. Ibid., 196.

22. Rand, *Journals*, 93.

23. Rand, *The Fountainhead*, 209.

24. Rand, *Journals*, 231.

25. AR to Paul Smith, March 13, 1965, in *Letters*, 631.

26. *Basic Writings of Nietzsche*, trans. Walter Kaufmann (New York: Modern Library, 2000), 357.

27. Rand, *The Fountainhead*, 269.

28. Personal communication from Jeff Britting regarding "Oral History with Ayn Rand, Conducted by Barbara Branden," tape recording, New York, December 1960–May 1961.

29. Wright, *An Autobiography*, 154, 160.

30. Rand, *The Fountainhead*, 351.

31. Rand, *Journals*, 183.

32. Rand, *The Fountainhead*, 633.

33. Friedrich Nietzsche, *Beyond Good and Evil*, in *Basic Writings of Nietzsche*, 318.

34. Rand, *The Fountainhead*, 710–17.

35. Ibid., 716.

36. Jeff Britting, "Adapting *The Fountainhead* to Film," in Mayhew, *Essays on Ayn Rand's "The Fountainhead,"* 105–6.

37. Scott McConnell, *100 Voices: An Oral History of Ayn Rand* (New York: New American Library, 2010), 70.

38. AR to DeWitt Emery, August 14, 1941, in *Letter*, 57.

39. Albert Jay Nock, introduction to Herbert Spencer, *The Man versus the State* (1884) (Caldwell, Idaho: Saxton Printers, 1940), vii.

40. Jennifer Burns, *Goddess of the Market: Ayn Rand and the American Right* (New York: Oxford University Press, 2009), 73–74.

41. Quoted in Jeff Britting, "*Anthem* and 'The Individualist Manifesto,'" in *Essays on Ayn Rand's "Anthem,"* ed. Robert Mayhew (Lanham, Md.: Lexington Books, 2005), 70–80.

42. Quoted in ibid.

43. Isaiah Berlin, *Against the Current: Essays in the History of Ideas* (Princeton: Princeton University Press, 2013), 354.

44. AR to Channing Pollock, April 28 and May 1, 1941, in *Letters*, 45, 46.

45. AR to Tom Girdler, July 12, 1943, in *Letters*, 84.

46. AR to Isabel Paterson, May 17, 1948, in *Letters*, 215.

47. Richard E. Ralston, "Publishing *The Fountainhead*," in Mayhew, *Essays on Ayn Rand's "The Fountainhead,"* 68.

48. Rand, *The Fountainhead*, viii–ix.

49. Anne Heller, *Ayn Rand and the World She Made* (New York: Doubleday, 2009), 146–47.

50. Ralston, "Publishing *The Fountainhead*," 68.

51. W. H. Auden, Graham Greene, Arthur Koestler, and Jean-Paul Sartre also took Benzedrine to sustain inspiration. Only Greene managed to break his dependency.

52. AR to Archibald Ogden, May 6, 1943, in *Letters*, 69.

53. Ibid., 72.

54. Rand, "A Speech to Architects," May 8, 1945, ARP, 106–18x.

Chapter 7. Success

1. Lorine Pruette, "Battle against Evil," *New York Times*, May 16, 1943; AR to Lorine Pruette, May 18, 1943, in *Letters of Ayn Rand*, ed. Michael S. Berliner (New York: Dutton, 1995), 75.

2. Neal Gabler, *Barbra Streisand: Redefining Beauty, Femininity, and Power* (New Haven: Yale University Press, 2016), 134–35.

3. AR to DeWitt Emery, May 17, 1943, in *Letters*, 73.

4. AR to Ross Baker, December 11, 1945, in *Letters*, 251.

5. Richard E. Ralston, "Publishing *The Fountainhead*," in *Essays on Ayn Rand's "The Fountainhead,"* ed. Robert Mayhew (Lanham, Md.: Lexington Books, 2007), 73.

6. Rand, "To the Readers of *The Fountainhead*," in *Letters*, 669.

7. AR to W. M. Curtiss, November 30, 1945, in *Letters*, 237.

8. Anne Heller, *Ayn Rand and the World She Made* (New York: Doubleday, 2009), 157.

9. AR to Ruth Alexander, October 22, 1943, in *Letters*, 99.

10. Barbara Branden, *The Passion of Ayn Rand* (Garden City, N.Y.: Doubleday, 1986), 184.

11. AR to Archibald Ogden, December 18, 1943, in *Letters*, 105.

12. F. L. Wright to AR, April 23, 1944, in *Letters*, 112.

13. AR to F. L. Wright, June 22, 1944, in *Letters*, 114.

14. AR to John Chamberlain, November 27, 1948, in *Letters*, 415.

15. AR to DeWitt Emery, April 17, 1948, in *Letters*, 396.

16. Scott McConnell, *100 Voices: An Oral History of Ayn Rand* (New York: New American Library, 2010), 73.

17. AR to Archibald Ogden, July 19, 1944, in *Letters*, 148.

18. Branden, *The Passion of Ayn Rand*, 186.

19. McConnell, *100 Voices*, 116.

20. Ibid., 83–84.

21. "A Steel House with a Suave Finish," *House & Garden*, August 1949.

22. AR to Nick Carter, October 5, 1944, in *Letters*, 165–66.

23. AR to F. L. Wright, October 10, 1946, in *Letters*, 117.

24. MPA, "Inserts for Memorandum," ARP, 103–22B.

25. Neal Gabler, *An Empire of Their Own: How the Jews Invented Hollywood* (New York: Anchor Books, 1988), 351–55.

26. Ibid., 364.

27. AR, unsent, undated letter to WBAI-FM, ARP, 061–18x. In her notes Rand charges the radio station with promoting racist and anti-Semitic views and using free speech to justify racial hatred.

28. McConnell, *100 Voices*, 151.

29. Heller, *Ayn Rand*, 176.

30. McConnell, *100 Voices*, 63.

31. Ibid., 59–60.

32. Rand, *Journals*, 314.

33. AR to Vera Glarner, December 2, 1945, ARP, 126–01A.

34. AR to Maria Strakhova, August 8, 1946, in *Letters*, 302.

35. Heller, *Ayn Rand*, 180.

Chapter 8. *Atlas Shrugged*

1. Sidney Fields, "I Am, Therefore I Will Think," *New York Mirror*, November 3, 1957.

2. Leonard Peikoff, "Introduction to the 35th Anniversary Edition," in Ayn Rand, *Atlas Shrugged* (1957; repr., New York: Plume, 1999), x.

3. Rand, *Journals*, 550.

4. AR to Rose Wilder Lane, August 21, 1946, in *Letters of Ayn Rand*, ed. Michael S. Berliner (New York: Dutton, 1995), 308.

5. Anne Heller, *Ayn Rand and the World She Made* (New York: Doubleday, 2009), 248–49.

6. AR to Rose Wilder Lane, August 21, 1946.

7. AR to Leonard Read, February 28, 1946, in *Letters*, 259.

8. Rand, *Journals*, 272.

9. Ibid., 244.

10. Ibid., 288.

11. Alvin Toffler, "Ayn Rand," interview, *Playboy*, March 1964.

12. AR to Burt MacBride, August 30, 1946, in *Letters*, 312.

13. Rand, *Journals*, 610; emphasis in original.

14. Ayn Rand, *The Fountainhead* (1943; repr., New York: Plume, 2005), xi.

15. "Mr. Truman Cries 'Halt!' to Labor at Zero Hour of Nation's Creeping Paralysis," *Newsweek*, June 3, 1946, 19–22.

16. Rand, *Journals*, 416.

17. Rand, *Atlas Shrugged*, 671.

18. Neal Gabler, *An Empire of Their Own: How the Jews Invented Hollywood* (New York: Anchor Books, 1988), 357–58.

19. Harold Heffernan, "How to Combat Reds Told in List of Don'ts," *Detroit News*, October 4, 1947.

20. Barbara Branden, *The Passion of Ayn Rand* (Garden City, N.Y.: Doubleday, 1986), 203.

21. Rand, *Journals*, 382.

22. AR to Edna Lonigan, March 26, 1949, in *Letters*, 433.

23. Gabler, *Empire of Their Own*, 417.

24. Rand, *Journals*, 573.

25. AR to Isabel Paterson, February 7, 1948, in *Letters*, 189–90.

26. Heller, *Ayn Rand*, 214.

27. Rand, *Journals*, 550.

28. John Chamberlain, "The Businessman in Fiction," *Fortune*, November 1948, 134–48; AR to John Chamberlain, November 27, 1948, in *Letters*, 415.

29. Rand, *Atlas Shrugged*, 59.

30. Rand, *Journals*, 471, 416; emphasis in original.

31. AR to Leonard Read, February 28, 1946; Rand, *Atlas Shrugged*, 982.

32. Ayn Rand, "America's Persecuted Minority: Big Business," in Rand, *Capitalism: The Unknown Ideal* (New York: New American Library, 1966), 44–45.

33. Ibid., 50.

34. AR to Henry Blanke, December 6, 1945, in *Letters*, 244.

35. Rand, *Atlas Shrugged*, 766–67.

36. Ibid., 715.

37. Ibid., 807.

38. AR to DeWitt Emery, May 8, 1949, in *Letters*, 443.

39. Rand, *Atlas Shrugged*, 605–7.

40. Ibid., 620.

41. Ibid., 414–15; emphasis in original.

42. Quoted in Shlomo Avineri, *Karl Marx: Philosophy and Revolution* (New Haven: Yale University Press, 2019), 45.

43. Rand, *Atlas Shrugged*, 315–17.

44. Ibid., 741.

45. Ibid., 731.

46. Ibid., 714.

47. Ibid., 1009.

48. Ibid., 1032.

49. Ibid., 1018.

50. Rand, *Anthem*, 122.

51. Jonathan Sacks, *Morality: Restoring the Common Good in Divided Times* (New York: Basic Books, 2020), x–xi.

52. Rand, *Atlas Shrugged*, 1168.

53. Ibid., 1022.

54. "The Impact of Philosophy on a Person's Life," philosophy discussion at Ayn Rand conference, Ayn Rand Institute, July 9, 2018, https://www.youtube.com/watch?v=lOU7-33BMY4.

55. Elie Wiesel, *All Rivers Run to the Sea* (New York: Alfred A. Knopf, 1995), 63.

56. AR to Archibald Ogden, July 10, 1948, in *Letters*, 402.

57. Richard Ralston, "Publishing *Atlas Shrugged*," in *Essays on Ayn Rand's "Atlas Shrugged*," ed. Robert Mayhew (Lanham, Md.: Lexington Books, 2009), 126.

58. Hiram Collins Haydn, *Words & Faces* (New York: Harcourt Brace Jovanovich, 1974), 261.

59. Bennett Cerf, *At Random: The Reminiscences of Bennett Cerf* (New York: Random House, 1977), 253.

60. Heller, *Ayn Rand*, 280.

61. Ibid., 281.

62. AR to Isabel Paterson, February 7, 1948, and February 28, 1948, in *Letters*, 192, 198.

63. Granville Hicks, "A Parable of Buried," *New York Times*, October 13, 1957.

64. Jennifer Burns, *Goddess of the Market: Ayn Rand and the American Right* (New York: Oxford University Press, 2009), 139–40.

65. Heller, *Ayn Rand*, 285.

66. Quoted ibid., 283.

Chapter 9. The Novelist-Philosopher

1. Nathaniel Branden, *Judgment Day: My Years with Ayn Rand* (Boston: Houghton Mifflin, 1989), 18.

2. AR to Nathaniel Branden (NB), December 2, 1949, in *Letters of Ayn Rand*, ed. Michael S. Berliner (New York: Dutton, 1995), 461.

3. AR's Perfection Desk Calendar, February 19, 1950, ARP, 176–01x.

4. Barbara Branden, *The Passion of Ayn Rand* (Garden City, N.Y.: Doubleday, 1986), 233.

5. Ibid., 235.

6. N. Branden, *Judgment Day*, 64.

7. B. Branden, *The Passion of Ayn Rand*, 234.

8. Ibid., 235.

9. Ibid., 246.

10. Rand, *Journals*, 479.

11. Scott McConnell, *100 Voices: An Oral History of Ayn Rand* (New York: New American Library, 2010), 130–36.

12. Ibid., 145.

13. N. Branden, *Judgment Day*, 155.

14. Ayn Rand, *Atlas Shrugged* (1957; repr., New York: Plume, 1999), 857.

15. Ibid., 490.

16. Rand, *Journals*, 479.

17. N. Branden, *Judgment Day*, 109, 124.

18. Ibid., 105.

19. AR's Defiance Quality Calendar, September 19, 1951, ARP, 176–02x.

20. N. Branden, *Judgment Day*, 105–7.

21. B. Branden, *The Passion of Ayn Rand*, 251.

22. Alan Greenspan, *The Age of Turbulence: Adventures in a New World* (New York: Penguin Press, 2007), 53.

23. B. Branden, *The Passion of Ayn Rand*, 245.

24. N. Branden, *Judgment Day*, 100.

25. AR to DeWitt Emery, August 5, 1941, in *Letters*, 56.

26. B. Branden, *The Passion of Ayn Rand*, 258.

27. Ibid., 260.

28. Rand, *Atlas Shrugged*, 1022.

29. N. Branden, *Judgment Day*, 171.

30. Ibid., 200.

31. B. Branden, *The Passion of Ayn Rand*, 267.

32. *Ayn Rand Answers: The Best of Her Q & A*, ed. Robert Mayhew (New York: New American Library, 2005), 139.

33. McConnell, *100 Voices*, 155.

34. "Mike Wallace Asks Ayn Rand," *New York Post*, December 12, 1957.

35. Rand, *Journals*, 706.

36. N. Branden, *Judgment Day*, 241.

37. Ibid., 248.

38. Ibid., 237.

39. John Hospers to AR, May 25, 1960, ARP, 141–HO1.

40. John Hospers to AR, January 4, 1960, ARP, 141–HO1.

41. Ibid.

42. Victor Frankl, *Man's Search for Meaning* (1959), rev. ed. (New York: Washington Square Press, 1984), 17.

43. AR to John Hospers, March 5, 1961, in *Letters*, 538.

44. John Hospers to AR, May 9, 1961, ARP, 141–HO4.

45. Ibid.

46. John Hospers to AR, January 4, 1960, ARP, 141–HO1.

47. AR to John Hospers, March 5, 1961.

48. AR to John Hospers, April 29, 1961, in *Letters*, 544.

49. "Down with Altruism," *Time*, February 29, 1960.

50. Michael Uhlmann, "The Power of Personality," *Yale Daily News*, February 19, 1960.

51. *Vital Speeches of the Day* 26, no. 20 (August 1, 1960): 630–36.

52. "John Hospers on His Friendship with Ayn Rand," International Society of Individual Liberty, 1996, https://www.youtube.com/watch?v=wLO4yttQet4.

53. John Hospers to AR, November 2, 1960, ARP, 141–HO2; emphasis in original.

54. John Hospers to AR, September 26, 1961, ARP, 141–HO4.

55. *Ayn Rand Answers*, 18.

56. "John Hospers on His Friendship with Ayn Rand."

57. John Hospers to AR, September 3, 1960, ARP, 141–HO2.

58. John Hospers to AR, May 25, 1960, ARP, 141–HO1.

59. John Hospers to AR, November 12, 1960, ARP, 141–HO2.

60. AR to John Hospers, January 3, 1961, in *Letters*, 532–33; emphasis in original.

61. Jennifer Burns, *Goddess of the Market: Ayn Rand and the American Right* (New York: Oxford University Press, 2009), 187.

62. Sidney Hook, "Each Man for Himself," *New York Times*, April 9, 1961.

63. David Sidorsky, "Sidney Hook," *Stanford Encyclopedia of Philosophy*, https://plato.stanford.edu/entries/sidney-hook/.

64. Anne Heller, *Ayn Rand and the World She Made* (New York: Doubleday, 2009), 327.

65. John Hospers to AR, May 23, 1961, ARP, 141–HO4.

Chapter 10. Fame and Influence

1. *National Review*, Educational Supplement, October 8, 1963.

2. Mike Wallace interview of Ayn Rand, *The Mike Wallace In-*

terview, February 25, 1959, https://www.youtube.com/watch?v=7ukJiBZ8_4k.

3. Scott McConnell, *100 Voices: An Oral History of Ayn Rand* (New York: New American Library, 2010), 159.

4. Ibid., 156.

5. Rex Reed, "Ayn Rand: A Bold Voice in a Mealy-Mouthed Age," *New York Sunday News*, February 25, 1973.

6. Merrill Root, "What about Ayn Rand?" *National Review*, January 30, 1960.

7. Ayn Rand, "Conservatism: An Obituary," in Rand, *Capitalism: The Unknown Ideal* (New York: New American Library, 1966).

8. AR to Barry Goldwater, June 4, 1960, in *Letters of Ayn Rand*, ed. Michael S. Berliner (New York: Dutton, 1995), 566.

9. "John Birch, Policeman," *New York Times*, November 19, 1964.

10. *Ayn Rand Answers: The Best of Her Q & A*, ed. Robert Mayhew (New York: New American Library, 2005), 76–77.

11. Jennifer Burns, *Goddess of the Market: Ayn Rand and the American Right* (New York: Oxford University Press, 2009), 207.

12. Ayn Rand, "The Fascist New Frontier," *New Conservative*, May 1, 1963.

13. AR to Bennett Cerf, October 30, 1963, in *Letters*, 618.

14. Bennett Cerf, *At Random: The Reminiscences of Bennett Cerf* (New York: Random House, 1977), 252–53.

15. AR to Cerf, April 3, 1965, in *Letters*, 635.

16. McConnell, *100 Voices*, 27.

17. Anne Heller, *Ayn Rand and the World She Made* (New York: Doubleday, 2009), 332–33.

18. Ayn Rand, *The Romantic Manifesto: A Philosophy of Literature* (1969; repr., New York: Signet, 1975), 162–72.

19. "New Frontier Tagged with Fascism Label," *Oregonian*, October 3, 1963.

20. Nathaniel Branden, *Judgment Day: My Years with Ayn Rand* (Boston: Houghton Mifflin, 1989), 256.

21. McConnell, *100 Voices*, 163.

22. N. Branden, *Judgment Day*, 309.

23. David Gordon, "The Circle Bastiat," https://mises.org/wire/circle-bastiat.

24. Burns, *Goddess of the Market*, 144, 152.

25. Murray N. Rothbard, "The Sociology of the Ayn Rand Cult," http://rothbard.altervista.org/essays/the-sociology-of-the-ayn-rand-cult.pdf.

26. McConnell, *100 Voices*, 152.

27. Hanna Arendt, *Essays in Understanding: 1930–1954*, ed. Jerome Kohn (New York: Harcourt Brace, 1994), 155.

28. Alvin Toffler, "Ayn Rand," interview, *Playboy*, March 1964.

29. Ibid.

30. Burns, *Goddess of the Market*, 221.

31. Barbara Branden, *The Passion of Ayn Rand* (Garden City, N.Y.: Doubleday, 1986), 391.

32. AR to Carol Hinchen (agreement between AR and *Night Call* radio show), February 27, 1969, ARP, 041–01a.

33. Ayn Rand, "The Wreckage of the Consensus," Ford Hall Forum, 1967. *Ayn Rand Answers*, 86.

34. *Ayn Rand Answers*, 92.

35. Ibid.

36. Ibid., 96.

37. In 1940 Rand had contributed to Fighting Funds for Finland. This became her first international cause.

38. Jonathan Sacks, *Morality: Restoring the Common Good in Divided Times* (New York: Basic Books, 2020), 38.

39. Heller, *Ayn Rand*, 378–79.

40. B. Branden, *The Passion of Ayn Rand*, 354.

41. Ibid., 355.

42. William F. Buckley's reply to letter to the editor, *National Review*, December 17, 1968.

43. Ayn Rand, "Apollo and Dionysus," in Rand, *The New Left: The Anti-Industrial Revolution* (New York: Signet, 1971), 59.

44. McConnell, *100 Voices*, 420–21.

45. Ibid., 510.

46. Nora Drobysheva to AR, undated, ARP, 012–52a.

47. AR to Nora Drobysheva, May 5, 1973, in *Letters*, 657.

48. Nora Drobysheva to AR, December 26, 1973, ARP, 013–52b.

49. AR's notes ahead of her call to Nora Drobysheva, ARP, 012–52a.

50. McConnell, *100 Voices*, 9.

51. "The Chairman's Favorite Author," *Time*, September 30, 1974.

52. McConnell, *100 Voices*, 488–89.

53. Ayn Rand, *Philosophy: Who Needs It* (1962; repr., New York: Signet, 1984), 11.

54. *Ayn Rand Answers*, 103–4.

55. McConnell, *100 Voices*, 497.

56. Ibid., 590.

57. Ibid., 500.

58. Dr. Harry Binswanger, recollection sent to author.

59. Ayn Rand, "The Sanction of the Victim," paper presented to the National Conference on Monetary Reform, New Orleans, November 21, 1981, ARP, 031–03x.

INDEX

Jewish Lives is a prizewinning series of interpretative biography designed to explore the many facets of Jewish identity. Individual volumes illuminate the imprint of Jewish figures upon literature, religion, philosophy, politics, cultural and economic life, and the arts and sciences. Subjects are paired with authors to elicit lively, deeply informed books that explore the range and depth of the Jewish experience from antiquity to the present.

Jewish Lives is a partnership of Yale University Press and the Leon D. Black Foundation. Ileene Smith is editorial director. Anita Shapira and Steven J. Zipperstein are series editors.

PUBLISHED TITLES INCLUDE:

Rabbi Akiva: Sage of the Talmud, by Barry W. Holtz
Ben-Gurion: Father of Modern Israel, by Anita Shapira
Judah Benjamin: Counselor to the Confederacy, by James Traub
Bernard Berenson: A Life in the Picture Trade, by Rachel Cohen
Irving Berlin: New York Genius, by James Kaplan
Sarah: The Life of Sarah Bernhardt, by Robert Gottlieb
Leonard Bernstein: An American Musician, by Allen Shawn
Hayim Nahman Bialik: Poet of Hebrew, by Avner Holtzman
Léon Blum: Prime Minister, Socialist, Zionist, by Pierre Birnbaum
Louis D. Brandeis: American Prophet, by Jeffrey Rosen
Mel Brooks: Disobedient Jew, by Jeremy Dauber
Martin Buber: A Life of Faith and Dissent, by Paul Mendes-Flohr
David: The Divided Heart, by David Wolpe
Moshe Dayan: Israel's Controversial Hero, by Mordechai Bar-On
Disraeli: The Novel Politician, by David Cesarani
Alfred Dreyfus: The Man at the Center of the Affair,
by Maurice Samuels
Einstein: His Space and Times, by Steven Gimbel
Becoming Elijah: Prophet of Transformation, by Daniel Matt
Becoming Freud: The Making of a Psychoanalyst, by Adam Phillips
Betty Friedan: Magnificent Disrupter, by Rachel Shteir
Emma Goldman: Revolution as a Way of Life, by Vivian Gornick
Hank Greenberg: The Hero Who Didn't Want to Be One,
by Mark Kurlansky

Peggy Guggenheim: The Shock of the Modern, by Francine Prose
Ben Hecht: Fighting Words, Moving Pictures, by Adina Hoffman
Heinrich Heine: Writing the Revolution, by George Prochnik
Lillian Hellman: An Imperious Life, by Dorothy Gallagher
Herod the Great: Jewish King in a Roman World, by Martin Goodman
Theodor Herzl: The Charismatic Leader, by Derek Penslar
Abraham Joshua Heschel: A Life of Radical Amazement, by Julian Zelizer
Houdini: The Elusive American, by Adam Begley
Jabotinsky: A Life, by Hillel Halkin
Jacob: Unexpected Patriarch, by Yair Zakovitch
Franz Kafka: The Poet of Shame and Guilt, by Saul Friedländer
Rav Kook: Mystic in a Time of Revolution, by Yehudah Mirsky
Stanley Kubrick: American Filmmaker, by David Mikics
Stan Lee: A Life in Comics, by Liel Leibovitz
Primo Levi: The Matter of a Life, by Berel Lang
Maimonides: Faith in Reason, by Alberto Manguel
Groucho Marx: The Comedy of Existence, by Lee Siegel
Karl Marx: Philosophy and Revolution, by Shlomo Avineri
Golda Meir: Israel's Matriarch, by Deborah E. Lipstadt
Menasseh ben Israel: Rabbi of Amsterdam, by Steven Nadler
Moses Mendelssohn: Sage of Modernity, by Shmuel Feiner
Harvey Milk: His Lives and Death, by Lillian Faderman
Arthur Miller: American Witness, by John Lahr
Moses: A Human Life, by Avivah Gottlieb Zornberg
Amos Oz: Writer, Activist, Icon, by Robert Alter
Proust: The Search, by Benjamin Taylor
Yitzhak Rabin: Soldier, Leader, Statesman, by Itamar Rabinovich
Ayn Rand: Writing a Gospel of Success, by Alexandra Popoff
Walther Rathenau: Weimar's Fallen Statesman, by Shulamit Volkov

Man Ray: The Artist and His Shadows, by Arthur Lubow
Sidney Reilly: Master Spy, by Benny Morris
Admiral Hyman Rickover: Engineer of Power, by Marc Wortman
Jerome Robbins: A Life in Dance, by Wendy Lesser
Julius Rosenwald: Repairing the World, by Hasia R. Diner
Mark Rothko: Toward the Light in the Chapel, by Annie Cohen-Solal
Ruth: A Migrant's Tale, by Ilana Pardes
Gershom Scholem: Master of the Kabbalah, by David Biale
Bugsy Siegel: The Dark Side of the American Dream, by Michael Shnayerson
Solomon: The Lure of Wisdom, by Steven Weitzman
Steven Spielberg: A Life in Films, by Molly Haskell
Spinoza: Freedom's Messiah, by Ian Buruma
Alfred Stieglitz: Taking Pictures, Making Painters, by Phyllis Rose
Barbra Streisand: Redefining Beauty, Femininity, and Power, by Neal Gabler
Henrietta Szold: Hadassah and the Zionist Dream, by Francine Klagsbrun
Leon Trotsky: A Revolutionary's Life, by Joshua Rubenstein
Warner Bros: The Making of an American Movie Studio, by David Thomson
Elie Wiesel: Confronting the Silence, by Joseph Berger

FORTHCOMING TITLES INCLUDE:

Abraham, by Anthony Julius
Hannah Arendt, by Masha Gessen
The Ba'al Shem Tov, by Ariel Mayse
Walter Benjamin, by Peter Gordon
Franz Boas, by Noga Arikha
Bob Dylan, by Sasha Frere-Jones
Anne Frank, by Ruth Franklin

George Gershwin, by Gary Giddins
Ruth Bader Ginsburg, by Jeffrey Rosen
Jesus, by Jack Miles
Josephus, by Daniel Boyarin
Louis Kahn, by Gini Alhadeff
Mordecai Kaplan, by Jenna Weissman Joselit
Carole King, by Jane Eisner
Fiorello La Guardia, by Brenda Wineapple
Mahler, by Leon Botstein
Norman Mailer, by David Bromwich
Louis B. Mayer and Irving Thalberg, by Kenneth Turan
Robert Oppenheimer, by David Rieff
Rebecca, by Judith Shulevitz
Philip Roth, by Steven J. Zipperstein
Edmond de Rothschild, by James McAuley
Jonas Salk, by David Margolick
Rebbe Schneerson, by Ezra Glinter
Stephen Sondheim, by Daniel Okrent
Susan Sontag, by Benjamin Taylor
Gertrude Stein, by Lauren Elkin
Billy Wilder, by Noah Isenberg
Ludwig Wittgenstein, by Anthony Gottlieb